ODDS AND SODS

My Sundays were usually taken up with phone calls which might generate publicity for Ladbrokes. Yet on a particular one in July 1988 all was quiet. When the telephone did ring, I was more than happy to let my wife Pat answer it! "It's for you," she called out. "The White House wants you."

Believing that she was simply winding me up I said: "Oh, yes, the White House in Regent's Park I suppose." Yet when I picked up the handset, an American voice drawled: "Is that Mr Ron Pollard? This is President Reagan's office from the White House here." Reagan's aide then explained that David Frost had been in the day before and had mentioned to the President that I was betting on the American election. The President wished to know what the odds were on George Bush winning. I told him, was thanked profusely and then asked, "Do you mind if we ring again? The President really is keen to keep in touch with what you people are thinking and doing over there." I told him that it would be a pleasure and that they should call at any time.

About the author

From William Hill's office boy in 1943, Ron Pollard became PR director of Ladbrokes and helped it to become one of the biggest leisure companies in the world.

In 1963, in the wake of the Profumo scandal, Ron decided to expand betting beyond the realms of the turf: by quoting odds on the Conservative leadership contest he opened the floodgates for punters to bet on anything from politics to the Miss World contest and even the likelihood of snow at Christmas. He became renowned for opening a book on almost any event – as his favourite saying goes, 'If it moves, you can bet on it'.

He spent a career at the top of the betting industry and when he retired in 1989 he had become a legend. He still works as a consultant for Ladbrokes and is a director of the company. Now the bookmaker has turned bookwriter with one of the most illuminating autobiographies of the year.

He and his wife Patricia live in Middlesex.

ODDS AND SODS

Ron Pollard

CORONET BOOKS
Hodder and Stoughton

First published in Great Britain in
1991 by Hodder and Stoughton Ltd.

Coronet edition 1992

*With thanks to Karen Earl and her
ladies of Bloomsbury Square.*

British Library CIP

Pollard, Ron
 Odds and Sods: A memoir.
 I. Title
 920

 ISBN 0-340-56241-2

Printed and bound in Great Britain
for Coronet Books, a division of Hod-
der and Stoughton Ltd, Mill Road,
Dunton Green, Sevenoaks, Kent
TN13 2YA. (Editorial Office: 47
Bedford Square, London WC1B 3DP)
by Clays Ltd, St Ives plc. Photoset by
Rowland Phototypesetting Ltd, Bury
St Edmunds, Suffolk.

To Patricia
whom I love dearly

ACKNOWLEDGMENT

When I sat down to tell the story of my life I realised that I would not be able to write it without some help, and I turned to one of my oldest friends, Ken Lawrence, formerly Sports Editor of the *Daily Express*. We had a lot of fun working together and I would like to thank him for all his assistance, without which this book could not have been written.

CONTENTS

Here beginneth a book . . .

AND it came to pass that a firm known as Ladbrokes, merchants of chance, heard strange murmurings among the populace, who spake as if with one voice : 'Who shallst be Archbishop of Canterbury when Dr Michael Ramsey goeth forth in November ?

And a spokesman came amongst them, saying 'Verily I' (or something) 'We must open a book.'

'Actually,' the spokesman added yesterday, 'We have never involved ourselves in religion. But we have been inundated with inquiries about the state of the betting, the favourites, the outsiders and the non-runners in this contest.

'Because of the demand, we will be opening a book in the very near future, with all the relevant runners and complete with starting prices.'

Here endeth the text for today. Go forth and place your bets.

Daily Mail, Friday, March 22, 1974

AUTHOR'S NOTE

There will be many people reading this book who do not know the intricacies of betting, and for them, there is one simple way of understanding odds that I always use.

When you see odds written down, you are betting the amount on the right, to win the amount on the left. So, if you wager £1 at odds of 6-1, and win, you will receive £6 from the bookmaker, plus your original stake of £1. If you lose, you lose your £1.

If the figure on the right is greater than the figure on the left, you are betting 'odds on' rather than 'odds against'. Thus, at 1-6, you are wagering £6 to make a profit of £1.

The examples above do not, of course, take into account betting duty.

FOREWORD

It must be a unique honour to be invited to contribute the Foreword to the autobiography of a man who has spent twenty-five years trying to pick your pocket. When he has been reasonably successful at it and at the same time sustained unwavering allegiance to the Socialist movement the chances of writing even a lying platitude of goodwill about him might seem distinctly remote.

Wrong. Ron Pollard is a warm and loyal friend, a vivid raconteur, a wonderful late-night drinking companion and, beyond argument, the greatest odds-maker in the world.

It is in this capacity – calculating the shrewdest of betting odds for Ladbrokes – that down the years he has caused so many of us to keep writing out cheques in that company's favour. But what set Ron apart and saw him overtake even the legendary American, Jimmy the Greek, in celebrity was his enjoyment in expanding wagering way beyond the conventional boundaries of the turf, boxing and football. Ron's field extended from the profound to the bizarre.

His staggering defeat of the most experienced psephologists in a French parliamentary election was probably the greatest if least-publicised coup of his life. But he would quote you odds on anything: from the name of the first Anglican Archbishop of the twenty-first century to the chances of a Martian candidate in the Booker Literary Awards before the end of the twentieth.

The most engaging thing about him was that no one ever saw him do a stroke of work. It was a dangerous misconception, of course. The truth was that he never stopped work. When you ran across him lunching in the

Commons or dining some Cabinet Minister in clubland he was actually working flat out. Banned one year from attending any of the Miss World rehearsals, he calmly pulled on overalls and cap, borrowed a tool kit and spent the morning as a spurious fitter quietly assessing the physical attributes of the lovelies on whom he was shortly to make a profitable book.

He has a vast circle of friends for two reasons. In a risky business he has always respected the strict line that separates resource from deceit. And, whatever the weather or the state of the book, he has laughed a lot.

They reckon that the biggest fibs are told on gravestones or in the Forewords to books. That is not so in this case.

Ian Wooldridge, OBE

1

IT'S ALL THANKS TO YOU, MISS KEELER

I stood, trying to look anonymous, in the dining-room of the Dorchester Hotel. Even my old Mum would not have recognised me in a false grey moustache and a waiter's uniform. The dining-rooms, the bars and the reception areas of our great hotels are like huge windows on the world: pull aside the curtains and there is always someone or something to be seen. But on this dull November day, the last thing I wanted was to be seen; the more invisible I was, the better.

Around the room were seventy or so of the world's loveliest ladies, the Miss World finalists. It was the annual lunch of the Variety Club of Great Britain and, as every year, the girls were guests of honour. One to each table and all dressed in their national costumes, they would stand on their chairs to be introduced to the cheering club members as the lunch progressed. But I needed a longer, closer look at them all, for this was the day each year, six days before the final, when I held a press conference to give my opinion on who would win and to set the prices which would go all around the world.

For some years I had been instrumental in Ladbrokes taking bets on many varied events, including the Miss World competition. It was always essential to know the 'form' in order to assess whether a honey-blonde from Australia would grab the judges' attention or whether this year's eye-catcher would be the willowy Miss Jamaica.

Being a cautious man by nature, I would never bet on a big horse race, or on a world heavyweight title fight if I didn't know the form and I was most certainly not intending to lay odds on who was to be Miss World without a sighting of the runners.

That did not always prove to be easy, however. Despite the publicity I generated each year for them on television and radio and in newspapers and magazines, Eric and Julia Morley, the organisers of the competition, did all they could to stop me from seeing the contestants. Eric and I had always been friends, and they were not opposed to publicity, but they simply did not like my being around. While I had never humiliated a contestant, however much of a no-hoper she may have been, by making her 1,000-1 when others were at 250-1, the organisers still found my presence embarrassing at times. If, say, Miss Ghana was listed at 100-1 and Miss Nigeria at 200-1 there was likely to be conflict between the two countries' officials. So the Morleys tried to show their disapproval of me and our betting by keeping the girls out of my sight.

Each year, therefore, I was forced to resort to subterfuge and bizarre disguises. Once I dressed up as a carpenter, complete with my trusty moustache and a big bag of tools and was able to wander around a TV studio as the girls prepared for the show. Before that, in November 1974, I slipped into the press line-up helped by a *Sunday Express* reporter, Peter Vane, kitted out with pencil, notebook and dark glasses. Now here I was, determined as ever not to be foiled by the Morleys, an inconspicuous waiter. While the Head Waiter at the Dorchester was a willing accomplice to my deception, the last thing I wanted was for someone to beckon or call me over actually to wait upon them!

Lunch finally over, and my mind fairly settled, I slipped away to change into my clothes and head back to the office and my press conference. As I stood on the hotel steps awaiting a taxi, I found myself recalling, for no accountable reason, a much earlier visit to the Dorchester; my first one, in fact. During the intervening years, I would pay many a

2

visit to this imposing palace in Park Lane, but my first, in 1949, would always remain an intense and influential memory.

I was about twenty-three, a wide-eyed innocent in the jungle of the bookmaking business. I had worked with William Hill, the biggest of the country's odds-makers, before I went into the Army and returned to the firm when the war was over. I was a junior ledger clerk, learning the game from the bottom and, if need be, running the odd errand. On this particular occasion I was to take £2,500 in cash – and that was an awful lot of 'readies' in the late forties, worth more than £100,000 today, I suppose – to Mr Fred Harkus at the Dorchester.

Never before had I carried so much money. I was only earning about a fiver a week and as I made the short journey from Hill's offices up Park Lane, I was extremely worried about what was in my pocket. Add to this the fact that I was ill at ease in the Dorchester, feeling properly out of place, and you will realise that this was one of those times when I would be very glad to get rid of a large amount of money!

Fred Harkus was a personal friend of William Hill; he was also agent to many top jockeys of his era. In the years immediately after the Second World War it was not uncommon for all the big bookies (Hill, Percy Thompson, Willie Preston and Max Parker) to have one of the top jockeys on their payroll. Most often, a jockey would be riding to trainer's orders; sometimes, however, he would be riding to a bookmaker's orders. His fee for doing so, which they called 'the usual', would be £100 on the winner of the race involved at whatever price it was returned.

This particular jockey had ridden a hot favourite at the Glorious Goodwood meeting. It finished second – not a good result for all those punters out there on the favourite. The big winners were, of course, the bookmakers and on this occasion the jockey. He collected 'the usual' which, as the horse which beat him was at 25-1, this time meant a

£2,500 pay-off. Relieved of my awesome burden, I caught a No. 36 bus home to Peckham!

In the years between those two visits to the Dorchester a tremendous amount happened in my life. I lost that innocence and would learn not to be surprised at anything, except perhaps the happenings of 1963.

Without a doubt, that was the most momentous year of my life, one of immense change for me personally, for Great Britain generally and, I can now see, for the betting business. It was the year which was to see me launched on to the nation's TV screens as a 'personality', the year I started the political betting which was to change the face of gambling but was also to make me contemplate suicide.

Yet none of it would have come about but for a certain Miss Christine Keeler. She was not a Miss World contestant, though such was her magnetic beauty that she might well have been; she was a nineteen-year-old good-time girl who was to destroy a Government Minister and, ultimately, a Prime Minister. But for her, and that foible so often the downfall of men – a weakness for the opposite sex – I very much doubt whether anyone outside the rather insular world of bookmaking and racetracks would ever have heard of Ron Pollard.

I would never have become the 'star' of an ITV World in Action programme from the Conservative Party Conference; would never have had my advice sought by so many politicians on who would win this election or that; and most certainly would never have had the shock of picking up the telephone at my London home to discover President Reagan's office calling from the White House in Washington.

The Keeler Affair had its beginnings in 1962. By the following year, rumours were rife throughout Westminster and Fleet Street that a Government Minister was implicated in a sex scandal. A Russian diplomat based in Britain was said to be involved and the nation's security was in jeopardy; it was the stuff of which the biggest and blackest headlines are made.

Jack Profumo was the Minister in question. He was in charge of Defence. When it was alleged that he had been dallying with the extremely photogenic Miss Keeler who was at one and the same time being friendly with the Russian, Profumo was, to use a modern idiom, economical with the truth.

When pretty ladies are around, press cameramen tend to abound. Her picture was never out of the newspapers. This, and the persistence of George (later Lord) Wigg, the Shadow Defence Minister who relentlessly hounded Profumo in the House of Commons, ensured that poor Profumo never had a chance. The Minister (who has since repaid his debt with his charity work a thousand times over) finally had to admit that he was involved; that he had lied to MPs.

To a House of Commons that jealously guards its traditions, that was and still is unacceptable. Profumo was forced to resign; and so eventually was his boss, the Prime Minister, Harold Macmillan. A fierce struggle for the Conservative leadership was to ensue.

I have always been a political animal, so attracted by the cut and thrust at the Palace of Westminster that my greatest regret in life will always be that I was never a Member of Parliament, and for a long while I had been pondering whether we dared bet on politics; the Keeler affair was to prove the catalyst.

Back in 1959, when I was a clerk at William Hill, a colleague, Cecil Appleton, and I worked on a system of forecasting election results. That year we decided that the Tories would win by 100 seats: we had it absolutely right. There were not, in 1959, the sophisticated, computerised polls that predict elections in this electronic age, but you may remember the BBC's Bob Mackenzie and his 'Swingometer' – a splendid election gimmick which did show what the swing was in a given seat. Well, 'Appy' and I had already devised our own 'swingometer'. Using the mathematical methods that are applied every day in racing, together with my judgement as to what the swing would be one way or another, our 1959 'swingometer' told us which seats, nationwide, would be won and lost. Please do not ask me how I reach my personal judgement, for although I use it still today, I cannot properly explain it. It may help you to understand better, however, when you have read the next chapter. Anyway, when we came up with the correct result, 'Appy' and I knew we were on to something, yet we did nothing with it, locking it away in our minds until the Keeler Affair brought it all back.

I had no idea of what was to come; I cannot claim any vision of the immense PR and financial success it was to be. Somehow it just seemed the ideal time to discover whether the public would bet on politics. So I spoke with Cyril Stein, my employer and the Managing Director of Ladbrokes, suggesting that 'here was the chance for us to get on the front pages rather than the back'. He did not hesitate. "Well, don't just stand there, Ron," he said. "Get on and do it."

Thus in 1963 I inaugurated the Tory Leadership Stakes, quite the most momentous move of my life. Nothing would be quite the same ever again. It was like a fever; for two weeks I did not know whether I was a bookmaker or a film star. The telephone did not stop ringing. I was constantly on television and radio. Everyone wanted a quote (and got one, of course!). Television crews piled in from all over the world: Russians, Swedes, Germans, Italians. It seemed they would never stop. Then the Japanese came (insisting upon giving me a pair of onyx cufflinks as a gift before they left), and the French and Canadians, Americans and Aussies. For two weeks it was bedlam, with all of them wanting to know who was backing whom – and why.

Rab Butler was my 5-4 favourite; Lord Hailsham stood at 7-4; Reggie Maudling was 6-1. It was, as they say in my business, 'Ten to one or more the rest of them'. We certainly hit the front pages. '10-1 bar three for No. 10' screamed one headline, immediately turning a Tory scrap into a General Election issue. How the newspapers hyped it up – and I swear it was none of my doing.

Sir Alec Douglas-Home, who originally intimated he was to be a non-runner, but had none the less been installed at 16-1, suddenly joined the fray. And, as a compromise candidate, he duly won. Ladbrokes took £14,000 on the exercise, winning just 10 per cent, £1,400. But that £1,400 was peanuts; the major gain was that the Ladbrokes name was now known all around the world. We had a million pounds' worth of publicity. And it opened the door to something enormous: for what can never be denied is that while Ladbrokes is today a major company worth something like £2.6 *billion*, political betting was the catalyst. Without it, Ladbrokes would never have achieved such status.

During this campaign, many people who until then had been only names in newspapers to me were ringing up like old chums. Tony Crosland, a fine Labour Minister over the years, wanted me to disclose what I knew. Both Randolph Churchill, lightweight son of the heavyweight Winston and a Hailsham supporter, and Lord Lambton, who was behind Maudling, wanted to 'push' their men. Before all this, no one had ever heard of me. Now they were all saying, "Ring Ron." It was ludicrous; but it was very good business.

One of the many callers was Bernard (later Sir Bernard) Docker. "Are you now intending," he wished to know, "to bet on the next General Election!" "Yes," was the answer, "when the time came we would." "Well," said the multi-millionaire, "I want the first bet. I must have the first bet."

When it came to self-publicity, Bernard and his wife Nora were graduates in the art; their names were for ever cropping up in the diary columns of the newspapers with extravagant tales of their huge yacht, *Shemara*, their golden Rolls-Royce and their obtrusive and self-indulgent parties. I knew that this would only guarantee him yet another mention in the gossip columns, but I assured him that I would ring him, and when we opened our book in 1963 I did so. He duly had his bet (£500 if I remember aright, on Labour at 4-5) and I suppose he was the first winner on that Election.

7

The biggest winner though was the man who laid the (at that time) world's record single bet – hotelier Maxwell Joseph. He laid £50,000 (the equivalent of about a million today, I suppose) on a Socialist victory and collected £32,272. He had decided on this huge bet as a form of insurance – a way of protecting his property against inflation which he feared might soar if Labour won – and simply rang to inquire what odds we were offering. Cyril Stein dealt with him personally and didn't even blink when he inquired how much Joseph wished to invest; he simply quoted him £30,000 at 11-8 on and the other £20,000 at 7-4 on. "Thank you. That is a bet," said Joseph, the business done in moments.

While this was going on, I was in Birmingham to do a television show, Midland Montage for Lionel Hampden; I remember being on the programme, talking politics, with Lady Isobel Barnett. Cyril rang to tell me of the bet with Joseph and, only half-joking, said, "I'm afraid I have knocked your figures sideways, Ron. You will need a nice bit of Conservative money now." I certainly would if my books were going to balance – and I worried all the way back to London how I might get it. But I need not have worried at all. I didn't even have to look for a client; he came and knocked on my office door quite literally. I was hardly at my desk the following morning when a gentleman asked to see me. He was ushered in and told me that he wished to have a large bet on the Conservatives: would I accommodate him? I could hardly believe my ears. Yes, I told him, I thought I might be able to do that, and I whisked him off to the boardroom and gave him a drink. There he placed £20,000 on the Tories to win. We shook hands and I could hardly wait for him to leave so that I could dash into Cyril's office with my good news. "This white fellow from Jamaica has just called in and he wants £20,000 on the Tories" I told him triumphantly.

"Have you laid him?" Cyril asked. "Have I laid him? Of course I have bloody well laid him," I replied with a real chuckle. Cyril came out with one of his more favoured retorts: "You always were lucky, Ron." So I might have been – but at least my books balanced again!

These were stirring times. The telephone seemed to be going non-stop; journalist after journalist was trying to find out who the mystery man was who had laid the £50,000 bet. I was as keen as anyone for the publicity, but had to abide by our own code of ethics – a bet struck in private remains private unless the man wishes to reveal his name himself. "You know the rules. You will just have to do your homework or leave it that it was 'a leading British industrialist'," I told them all. However much I would have wished to help, it simply wasn't possible. But the boys did their homework – or Maxwell Joseph's PR men helped them out; I have never known which. Certainly the newspapers the following day were full of the story and they all had Joseph by name.

With bets like these and an enormous number of small ones we had taken £603,000 by polling day and as the results started to come in it looked like going Labour's way. It is no secret that I am a deeply committed Socialist, but while I dearly wished them to succeed I had made them my favourites not out of sentiment but because I was convinced they would win and backed my judgement. Now I was watching my prediction and my predilection coming true.

Cyril Stein, a fellow Socialist who for years had canvassed for Labour, knocking on mainly Tory doors in the St John's Wood area of North London where he lived, invited a few of us back to his home to celebrate. During thirteen years of Conservative rule, there were times when we thought we might never see a Socialist government again, so you can imagine our joy on this night. Our party was 30-40 seats up; a good lead. So it was 'Have another drink, Jack' time. The headache only came, as it so often does, when we awoke. As the results from the shires came in, so Labour's lead was being whittled away. It was beginning to dawn on me that far from a triumph, Labour might not win. Even if they did not lose, they might have no overall majority. And if that was the case, it would be a calamity for Ladbrokes. We stood to lose £1.5 million, and the fact of the matter was, that was money we did not have.

As the Labour lead grew ever more slender, I could stand it no longer. I went into Cyril's office to remind him of our situation. We had taken risks, so sure were we of a Labour victory; taken bets which we quite frankly should not have done. If Labour did not win, we would not be able to pay – we would be bankrupt.

Perhaps not as aware as I was of the dramatic reversal of the later results and the drift towards a very close result, Cyril laughed. I felt more like crying. I was at desperation's trapdoor and was having still to step towards it. The tension became so intense that I had to go out and walk the streets. If Ladbrokes went bankrupt, there would be only one person to blame, for while Cyril had known what I was doing and hadn't called a halt, it was still my responsibility. I had been at this game all my life; I was supposed to be as good an odds-man as there was. Yet here was my firm in dire jeopardy – and it was all my fault. How could I have been so stupid?

In my solitude and despair, I did not even realise where I was walking; all I knew was that there would be no escape if Labour did not win. If that happened, I decided, there could be only one way out for me: I actually decided I would kill myself.

Eventually I came across a phone-box and rang – who else? – my mother. I prayed that she would be in. When she answered I told her: "Mum, if Labour don't win, the firm will be bust. I am going to have to end it all."

I do not know to this day whether she thought I wasn't serious, or if it was a bluff to calm both me and her; but she just laughed. "Go off and think about what you want for your dinner," she said. Dinner? That was the last thing I wanted. I wanted a few more Labour seats.

I went back to my office to watch the closing results and it was close, oh so close. The one result that I had been impatiently waiting for and was so tantalisingly late was Meriden; I knew that one really mattered – if Labour lost that one, then they had lost the election. When, finally, Labour won Meriden by 363 votes I knew that they would get in with perhaps half a dozen seats. It turned out to be only five in fact . . . but in every way, a life-saver.

We had been in the fixed-odds business for some while, whereby people bet on football matches at individual prices, and on the last Saturday of 1963 things turned sour: we lost £500,000. As was normal at a Christian holiday time, Cyril had 'escaped' to Israel, and I telephoned him there. He was philosophical: "You have had a good run. I wouldn't worry about it, Ron." The following week we lost £1.5 million and now it was time to worry. It was time to get out.

Let me explain how this came about. Quite simply, the odds on anyone nominating three draws from a selected list of soccer matches is 28-1. That is not something to argue about – it is pure mathematics and you do not dispute or fly in the face of that in gambling. But we did. In a bid to snatch our rival's business, we went 33-1. They went 40-1. It was stupid, and basically we knew it. But as we went higher, William Hill topped us until we reached the ludicrous position of three draws being offered at odds of 60-1. It was the fast lane to ruin and we paid the penalty – £2 million in two weeks. Hills must have suffered similarly, but they were in a much stronger position than us. I remember one of our accountants, a Mr Holmes, bursting into my office shouting, "You're insolvent, you're insolvent" and rushing out never to be seen again. But few knew just how close we were to putting up the shutters.

Today, of course, you would not take bets in such a way that you could not pay out. Yet, unbelievably, this was the second time in twelve months that we had looked down the barrel of bankruptcy with me deeply involved.

A few weeks later, Stein called the Racing Manager, John Probert, and myself to his office. It was a stark message he had for us. "The firm is in a bad state. You must not lose. If you do, it is the end." This did not seem terribly reasonable to John and me. Everyone would tell you that bookmakers never lose, but in fact they sometimes do. And now we mustn't. This had to be a tightly kept secret: if word leaked out, losers would not need to pay us, and winners might start to wonder why we were paying out a little late.

We were really only scrambling through, robbing losing Peters to pay winning Pauls. The two main factors in our salvation were the boldness of the National Bank of Ireland and our entry into political betting. The Bank bailed us out with a further £250,000 loan, with a firm proviso that we should not go back for more. And people betting on the 1964 Election brought us, in advance, £191,000 of our £640,000 'take'. This was money in the bank and was in fact used to run the company throughout the year. Somehow, then, we were saved, but they had been hairy days.

Clearly we learned lessons from these traumas, important business lessons. But we also discovered something that would be vital to our future. Until this time we had thought of betting in terms of dogs and horses and very little else. Now we knew different and that we were on to a big, big winner. For it was abundantly clear that the public would gamble on absolutely anything. If it moved, if it was on TV, if it caused an argument in a pub, they wanted to bet on it. Miss World, elections, the Eurovision Song Contest, man on the moon, the next Pope, aliens arriving from outer space and the Loch Ness Monster, we obliged them all.

2

THE CHINAMAN ON MY SHOULDER

You do not have to be a sports lover to know that the America's Cup is a yacht race and Americans have always believed that it belonged to them and them alone. Every four years several upstart countries with ideas bigger than either their yachts or their pockets would challenge and try to win the Cup; but they never did. America had won it way back in 1851 and for 132 years had retained it against twenty-four challenges. Losing it was never contemplated. That huge, ugly piece of silverware was in their eyes quite properly bolted down in its permanent home, the New York Yacht Club. That was just about the limit of my knowledge of ocean yacht racing and the America's Cup. So, when in 1983 I suddenly found myself being asked to quote odds on that year's race, I really had no idea what to offer. I had to say "I am sorry. I cannot decide right now; I wish to sleep on it." And when I had slept on it, my mind was clear. Alan Bond, the Ealing-born no-hoper and his boat *Australia II* would win; the unbeatable Dennis Conner and *Liberty* would lose.

The first person I rang was Ian Wooldridge, an old friend and probably the finest British sportswriter over the past twenty-five years. He was in America covering the race for the *Daily Mail* and when I told him that I was, quite outrageously, making the Aussies favourites he was only slightly surprised. But then, Ian was one of the few people who knew of my secret Chinaman, a long-since-dead

Chinaman, whom I believed to be my spirit guide and who has helped me for more than thirty years.

I have been a fervent Spiritualist for all that time; while I do not suggest that I 'hear' or 'see' things, my Chinaman influences me on a mental level and guides me. Spiritualists will understand what I mean by guidance – I will suddenly do something for no apparent reason that will turn out to be of help to me. For all I know he plays a role in my life all of the time without me being conscious of him but there are times when I am very aware of the Chinaman's help. That is why, sometimes, I seem to know the result of things before they happen. Do not get me wrong: I am not saying that I know the winner of tomorrow's 3.30 race or that I can predict eight draws for the Treble Chance, but Ian accepted my instinctive judgement because I had explained all this to him some years earlier (at the Hickstead Show Jumping Championships, in fact). When I said that I had been 'helped', he understood.

He wrote his story for his newspaper and it quickly filtered back to the West Coast. It caused a mighty storm. The Americans did not know of my Chinaman and they certainly did not accept my verdict. "Who is this mad Limey?" the headlines asked. But history records that Dennis Conner, to the horror of all America, did lose and that Alan Bond, to the untold joy of all Australia, did win. It was one of the greatest upsets in sporting history.

I came to spiritualism by accident, really; certainly I wasn't born into it. I was twenty-nine when the events that were to fashion all the beliefs in my life came about. Merely to keep her company, I went with my mother-in-law to Kennards, a multiple store in Croydon. There she was to see a psychometrist – a Spiritualist medium who, with psychic powers, 'reads' and gets vibrations from a person's personal possessions. I was not at all interested in such mumbo-jumbo, said so, and waited outside for her. While I waited I was drawn into a conversation with a lady sitting next to me. It was a fascinating story she had to tell.

Seventeen years earlier, a friend of hers had visited

Marjorie Wheble, the psychometrist my mother-in-law was now talking with. The friend had been told never to travel on a train and for seventeen years had not done so. Recently, however, she had been forced to take a short journey by train along the south coast. The train was involved in an accident; the lady was killed. I found it unbelievable ... and yet I was intrigued. When my mother-in-law came out she said to me, "Go on Ron, you go in." I did not particularly wish to but the story I had just been told was so compelling that I couldn't resist. What happened next was to influence the rest of my life.

Marjorie Wheble's room was about as big as one of those booths on railway platforms where you can take your own passport photograph. She was sitting beside a tiny card-table and we just looked at each other for a few pregnant moments. I was a sceptic and she understood that. Then she asked for one of my possessions. I handed her my comb which she held for only a short while before saying: "Goodness gracious. I wish I was going to have your life. You are going to be in all the papers, everyone wants to know what you are saying, and you are going to Buckingham Palace and meet members of the Royal family."

Now, this was 1955 and I was a clerk working for William Hill. I was enjoying what I was doing, but had no great ambitions. The nearest I had been to Buckingham Palace was on the top of a bus. I simply could not accept what I was hearing. It was just a load of tosh. I suspect you must have been able to cut my scepticism with a knife by now, but Marjorie Wheble ignored it and went on: "You haven't been married long but some time you will be moving." Well, my wife and I were newly wed and were living in my sister's basement flat. We did not have a great deal of money but we were saving for a place of our own. All fairly obvious sort of stuff; nothing very startling about that as a revelation, you might suspect. But Mrs Wheble continued: "You will not buy a house; you will buy a white bungalow and a black Labrador dog is involved. And that bungalow is where your destiny lies."

As I will explain, she was absolutely right about everything, but the most important thing I learned from her that day was that I had been blessed with this guide, this Chinaman who had died in the fifteenth century. She told me how lucky I was and how crucial a role he would play as the years went by "if only I would listen". I still do not know whether I 'listen' because I never hear anything. But I always have this distinct awareness of not being alone and for thirty-five years this has been a great comfort to me.

When I look back to 1983 and the rather emotional evening when I was honoured as 'Spiritualist of the Year' and I told all those mediums gathered in a London hotel about "this great woman, Marjorie Wheble, who had fashioned my life" I did not tell them that when I left her Croydon cubby-hole all those years before I had said to my mother-in-law, "That woman is bloody mad!" Yet everything she told me was to come true and I never fail to heed the 'help' that is always on offer. Since that first meeting with Marjorie, spiritualism has been a constant thread throughout my life even though I never know when it is going to play an important role; it could be today, it could be next week, but it will certainly be some time. It is like an unseen prop and I have come to trust it and rely upon it.

I do not need to defend my faith and my beliefs, nor do I wish to push my religion down people's throats, but let me give you one more illustration of what I mean. Four years after my meeting with Marjorie I went, as I regularly did on my Wednesday afternoons off, to see an estate agent at Elm Park in Essex. Although my wife and I had saved some money, we were not exactly flush with it. Essex was the cheapest area around London and I was seeking a house in the Dagenham, Hornchurch, Upminster area. It had been an unrewarding task; there had been little for us to consider in months and now it seemed I was out of luck again. "Sorry, Mr Pollard, we haven't much for you again this week. Tell you what we do have, though. A very nice little bungalow with a lovely garden."

Would I like to see it? Well, having travelled all that way I decided that I might just as well and the agent took me in his car to see this bungalow; it seemed more like a doll's house. No sooner had the door been opened to our knock than a large, black Labrador had pinned me against the fence.

I had long since forgotten the message from Marjorie Wheble and it was not until I went home to tell my mother-in-law about the bungalow I had seen that she reminded me: "Don't you remember what you were told?" Then it all came flooding back. A white bungalow. A black dog. And her words: "That bungalow is where your destiny lies." So I paid £2,250 for the bungalow and that is where I lived when I stood for Hornchurch Council and Nye Bevan and Hugh Gaitskell came down to speak (all right, I need no reminding that I did not win the seat even with that support!). It was also from that bungalow that I was to write the letter of application for a job with Ladbrokes that was to change my life. So if I am ever asked about destiny and whether the future is predetermined, I have to say most emphatically: 'Yes. It most certainly is." People may not like the word 'manipulated' but I have always insisted that we are manipulated to go along certain routes, even if we do not see their value at the time. The morning I rang Ian Wooldridge to tell him I had been 'helped' in my decision to make the Australians favourites, he totally understood.

I am not sure whether my Chinaman was helping me from the day I was born, or whether it was the brandy and port I was receiving! My mother was three months pregnant with me when, because of the poverty that ravaged the working class in the twenties, my eighteen-month-old sister Marjorie died of double pneumonia. My mother was so distressed and became so poorly that the doctor instructed her to take a brandy and port each day. When

I made my appearance at the Lying-in Hospital just across Westminster Bridge, on June 6, 1926, her condition had passed on to me and I too was prescribed a drop of brandy and port daily. I love it to this day, and at least I can say I was set off correctly!

There was no question of fathers being present at the birth in those days – quite rightly, if I may say so. Dad went out, got drunk as was the time-honoured custom, and when he turned up at the hospital to see Mum and view his new son and heir he was sporting two black eyes. He had managed to get himself into a fight!

Fights in the street, even between man and wife – indeed, particularly between man and wife – were common in South London at that time, though not, I hasten to say, between my parents. If ever we saw a fight while out shopping, Mum would shepherd us across the street, making sure that we were not involved.

I suspect that while I was born into a Tory family, my sister's death must deep-down have had a profound effect upon me, leading to my strong Socialist beliefs. Very early in life I used to think my grandfather (James Joseph Pollard, just as my father was James Joseph and I am Ronald James Joseph) was 'a right bastard'. He was what they called the Receiving Officer for Southwark, the DHSS man of today. After doling out the pennies and the shillings to the unemployed, of whom there were a very great number, he would disguise himself as a chimney-sweep and go into the pub to see if any of them were spending their relief money on beer. He also sent many people to Australia for their 'misdemeanours'. Later I was to know him better and to become friends despite my feelings about his work, and to this day I keep a photograph of him in my study. It has a particular meaning for me for, at a seance some years ago, I received a message through the medium that my grandfather was displeased that his picture was not on display. If people think that those who have departed are no longer with us, perhaps this little story will help convince them that is not so and even give them some comfort.

When I asked my mother about Grandfather's photograph she said she had put it away in a drawer and forgotten about it. "Well, you had better get it out again because Grandad is not well pleased about it," I told her. When Mum died in November 1986, I took the photograph and Grandad is no doubt delighted that it is in pride of place between a photograph of Mum and Dad and one of me with Neil Kinnock.

We were a close and happy family and we worked hard for everything that was ever achieved. My father was the accountant to a world-famous mineral water company, Hooper Struve, who used to supply the King and Queen. It was not a major job, but he had a head for figures that I may have inherited.

My mother, Emily Elizabeth – known as 'Cis' because her elder brother always called her 'little Sis' – was wonderful. Poor we may have been, with an outside toilet and a tin bath in the scullery, but we always lived in a nice, clean house. Like Dad, Mum was so industrious. Because she had to look after me and my young sister Joyce, Mum worked at home as an industrial glove machinist. She would make sometimes as many as seventeen dozen pairs of these heavy leather gloves a week and they all needed trimming. I shall never forget how Dad would arrive home from work, sit down with Mum and start to work with those huge scissors to trim the gloves around the fingers and thumbs. It was such hard work; his fingers were always sore and bruised. Young as I was, I would wonder even then at the injustice in a man and his wife, honest and hard-working, having to toil night after night in such a way.

There wasn't much money around in those days but despite this we always had a holiday together every year; Dad insisted on that. We would go to Broadstairs, Margate or Herne Bay – places like that. They were very happy times when the whole family was away together. I remember 1936 particularly because we all went to Bembridge on the Isle of Wight. It was the furthest any of us had ever been and there was great excitement. One night, as a special treat, Joyce and I were allowed to watch the *Queen Mary*, all lit up, sail regally past the island on her way to wherever. It was such a marvellous sight and one which I shall never forget.

By the time I went to school we had moved to Peckham. I did reasonably well but was never top of the class. Joyce was different — and she used to drive me mad. In every subject she was first or second, while I was twelfth or thirteenth. I suppose I was a bit too sports-minded, always playing football or cricket. Dad loved that really, even though he grumbled and demanded that I paid more attention to lessons. But he always came to watch me play, with words of praise or criticism when they were needed, or even a little sympathy, which is so important when you are young. I had a trial for our local football team, Nunhead, when I was about fourteen, but I was too small, just a slip of a lad and I could not compete against the bigger boys. Dad was there, as ever, saying the right thing.

At least I did manage to pass the examination which everyone had to take at eleven to decide the next step of your education — an undoubted relief to my parents! I went to Peckham Central School, which was to supply me with one eternal and ultimately utterly satisfying memory. At school, as indeed I remain today as my wife never fails to keep reminding me, I was quite useless at woodwork. Tools and I were not compatible; I simply could not use them and I am ashamed to say that, fifty years on, I still do not possess a single one! Given a large piece of wood, I could only ever reduce it to a matchstick. Mr Adams, the woodwork master, was tormented by this and would get so very angry with me. One day he could take no more and throwing a piece of wood at me stormed: "You will never get anywhere, young man. You are useless; totally useless. You will always be unemployed — out of work. No one will be able to do anything with you."

To my immense joy some years later, I met the old woodwork master on the street. "I didn't do too badly, did I,

Mr Adams?" I chided and we laughed long and loud at the memory of those distant days.

My education was effectively ended only three months after my thirteenth birthday by the outbreak of war. Dad made the decision that we were to stay together: we children would not be evacuated. "If we are going to die, we will die together," I remember him saying (perhaps there was something of the Spiritualist in him as well!). I spent some time flitting in and out of Alleyn's School at Dulwich at all sorts of odd hours but I left school with no qualifications at all.

In 1940, when he was thirty-nine, Dad was called up and I had to persuade him to let me join one of the fire-watching groups that were being formed. He was not very keen, but the bombs were dropping on London and I wanted to play my small part in the war effort.

The Germans would drop anything up to 500 incendiaries at a time and we had to watch for them and rush with buckets of sand to put out any fires they started. One night, while on leave from his base in Ireland, Dad seemed to get quite excited about the leisurely way I was dealing with matters. Perhaps furious would be a better word. When a German plane came along and dropped a stick of bombs, I was just standing there, finishing my conversation with a neighbour, instead of keeping a proper watch and rushing out immediately with my buckets. He was quite right, of course, to remonstrate with me so fiercely and I have never forgotten the incident. Nor have I forgotten when, in the middle of the night and with the raid over, Dad considered it safe to go back to bed with Mum. He found a big hole in the ceiling of their bedroom where an incendiary had dropped, without exploding. I had not been introduced to my Chinaman at this time of my life, of course, but I have realised since that if someone was helping me even then without my realising it, it must have been him.

By the summer of 1941, although I was barely fifteen, it was time to go out to work. In those days, young men were brought up in London to have a responsibility for the females in the family. As Mum and my sister were at home it was important, therefore, that I did not work too far away. By some good fortune, a neighbour who was company secretary to a firm of builders' merchants in Rye Lane, Peckham, asked if I would like to go there as the office boy and junior clerk. It was close enough for me to get home if there was a raid, so I was pleased to take the job. I ran messages from the ironmongery department to the glaziers, then to the wallpaper department but at the same time I was learning ledger work and book-keeping from a very nice man called Charles Wing. He was also a much-maligned man. Here we were in 1941, in the middle of an awful war and being bombed every night, and he was a member of the Peace Pledge Union.

Those people were then considered by the vast majority of the public much as a left-wing organisation is today: against the national interest. PPU members were totally against war; they would rather give in than fight – a view opposed by around 99.9 per cent of people. At work they 'took the mickey' out of him, but Charles Wing had a great depth of heart and sincerity and while PPU members were despised as conscientious objectors, I was pleased that I knew him and I recall with pride having learned some of the finer traits of life from him. And all that book-keeping and ledger work he taught me was to be of considerable value in my later life. If it is true what they say, that blessed are the meek, then he will have found a place in Heaven. I hope so, anyway.

There was not much fun to be had, working all day and spending most nights in the air-raid shelters under the arches, but on Saturday afternoons a group of us would head for the greyhound racing at Catford. We weren't really punters – we did not have the money – but we went for some fun and afterwards we would go home and play cards for ha'pennies and pennies. Because of these visits to the dog track, we used to buy that old sporting newspaper, the *Greyhound Express*, and in 1943 they carried an advertisement which I spotted for a ledger clerk to join the book-makers, William Hill. There must have been a lull in the bombing and the 'doodlebugs' and rockets that were to follow, because I felt easy enough in my mind to apply for the job knowing that I would have to pick up a No. 36 bus all the way into London and that in an emergency it would take me half an hour or more to get home.

Ever since I had first read the Bible and the David and Goliath story, I had thought I might like to be a book-maker; after all, not many would have backed the winner in that contest, would they? So I wrote off and was invited for an interview. My father, once more home on leave, asked if I would like him to go with me. Yes, I said, he could certainly come up with me to Park Lane, but I did not want him coming in. Dad was quite happy about that, so he came up on the bus with me and waited outside while I went in to meet the legendary William Hill.

Hill was then forty-one, a farmer's boy from the Midlands who made his first book in Birmingham when he was just twenty and ran it single-handed for fifteen years.

It was only around 1937 or 1938 that Hill made himself into a company and quickly became the leader of the pack. And that was the first thing that struck me: here was the bookmaking firm reputed to be the world's biggest, yet there were only about five people working in the offices. Still slightly puzzled, I found myself being ushered into one of those big Park Lane rooms once lived in by the aristocracy, with a huge desk in the middle. On the left-hand side of the desk was a couch and on the couch were two men. One was called Bill Stratton (later to be prosecuted by Bill Hill for fraud, but to be cleared). And beside him was the famous Welsh boxer, Tommy Farr, who some still argue beat Joe Louis back in 1937. These were Hill's 'minders'.

To a young man from my background, this was daunting indeed. Still, the interview went well. I was offered the job at the princely salary of £3.10s. a week, which was a tremendous lift for someone earning only £1.15s. Dad was excited and so pleased that I had done it by myself; he was a great believer in self-reliance. And so, on July 5, 1943, I joined William Hill and my bookmaking education was to begin. So, too, were some other, nasty, lessons of life . . .

I was very happy, but those early days were a monumental shock to me. There was racing on only two days a week, and we were handling cash betting. This was totally illegal. In those days, the only place you could bet with cash was actually on the racecourse. All other transactions were required to be on credit terms. I was from a decent, good, hard-working family that had never had anything to do with the police, criminals or the underworld, and had been taught to respect the law and have nothing to do with anything that wasn't your own – hardly the first principles of William Hill. And here I was, the original innocent abroad, working for the man who was breaking the law every day by handling cash bets. That was only the beginning. To my further astonishment, the police would ring up to say they were coming around to raid us on Thursday and would we please make sure there was some money about. When the police did arrive, the thousands and thousands of pounds that would normally be lying about were not to be seen. I was locked in a cupboard with all that money and a small amount was left on the table for the police to see.

The police would duly arrive, they would pick up the money and then they would charge us. The day *before* the court hearing was due, Hill's lawyer would ring and say he had been advised by the police as to how much we would be fined and would we please write out a cheque for that amount.

This is all very much in the past, of course, but it was a shock to me to discover that the system of justice in this country could work that way and is probably responsible for my deep suspicion of police activity ever since. Over the years the police had taken illegal payments from prostitutes and bookmakers. (That probably accounts for the fact that the Savile Row personnel were changed regularly,

24

in order that everyone got a fair crack of the whip!) When the Street Offences Act and the Betting and Gaming Act (which legalised off-course cash betting) came in in 1961, the police were to lose two major sources of income. I do believe, however, that they have since found alternative sources. Years later this was confirmed to me when I myself saw in a betting shop how it was necessary to pay a fiver, and sometimes a tenner, to the police for the 'right' to keep the door open in very hot weather. The Act stated that doors should not be open, but because of the suffocating heat, we kept it open and fitted strip curtains; this meant that people walking past could not see in (as the Act required) and it did ease the heat problem. Every few weeks a policeman would come in and tell us that we could not keep the door open but he went away with our cash in his pocket leaving the door open as he did so. We called it their 'pension'. Now, in the late sixties and early seventies, there were around 10,000 betting shops and if this practice were applied throughout the land (and I find it hard to believe that, by chance, I was the only one so treated) a lot of money changed hands. God knows what William Hill had paid to be informed of police raids, tip-offs which allowed him to protect very large amounts of money indeed. More than a tenner, I guess.

For all that he was a man with an eye for the main chance, Bill would have nothing to do with betting shops when they were first sanctioned, even though they were to make bookmakers very rich. Ladbrokes opened their first betting shops warily in the Isle of Wight in 1962. They were very conscious that their clients were used to shopping in Harrods and Fortnum and Mason and to phoning their bets in; but Max Parker convinced them to go in. William Hill in contrast was deeply unsure of them; not until 1970 did he open up a betting shop. I think part of his suspicion stemmed from the fact that his only experience of betting shops was in Ireland where they were then, and in some instances still are today, poor and rather run-down establishments. And the reason for his reluctance was that he was a convinced Communist, and while he thought it right and proper to take money from the wealthy, he had no ambition to take it from the poor. Like Robin Hood, he preferred to give it to them as I was to discover when I had been working for him for just five months. I had heard that there was an annual bonus paid to all staff (in fact, I learned much later that Bill put 20 per cent of his profits aside for the staff) but I did not really expect it myself, having been there such a short while. A few days before Christmas, Mr Hill called me into his office and said that he thought I was doing very well and that he was increasing my salary. He added that he saw no reason why I should not get my share of the bonus either, and he handed me an envelope.

All I could stammer as I stumbled out of his office was, "Thank you very much, sir." I did not dare to think about what might be inside the envelope he had handed me and was barely able to contain myself as I rushed for the nearest lavatory and locked myself in. The cheque inside was for £64, an incredible sum for someone whose Post Office Savings Book contained less than £5.

Those savings had been accumulated by hard work. I had a Saturday morning job with a local off-licence, making their deliveries on a bicycle with a big basket on the front loaded with bottles of beer and Guinness. It was heavy and extremely hard work pushing the pedals around to get up even the slightest of slopes. Now here I was with a fortune, shivering and shaking with excitement, rather like a toddler seeing the Christmas tree lights go on for the first time, the baubles glistening, glinting and sparkling. I wouldn't have been surprised if I had started to sparkle myself, such was my excitement; I could hardly wait to get home and share my good news.

When the day's work was done, I put the cheque and its envelope in my inside jacket pocket, put on my overcoat and headed for that trusty old red No. 36 bus. I sat myself right at the back so that I could see everyone in front of me. I had a newspaper but could not read it, so anxious was I that nothing should happen to my money. Looking back, it seems absolutely daft. I was not going to be robbed, for people were not mugged in those days as they are in London today and anyway, who would imagine a slip of a lad like me having anything worth stealing? I could hardly lose it, as I had my hand tightly across my coat so really, apart from it being spirited away by magic, nothing could have happened to my cheque. None the less, I was taking no chances. I kept my hand on that inside pocket all the way home where I was, of course, immediately relieved of it. Mum impounded it, insisting that it was "all going straight in your savings book". I really did feel quite rich!

When the time came for my entry into the conflict against Hitler, it was a dreadful disappointment to me. I had spent thousands of hours training for the Royal Air Force with my two best pals, Ted Johnson and Charlie Atkinson. The three of us have never lost touch, incidentally, and I remain close to Ted to this day.

Ted, Charlie and I had joined the 1235 Air Training Squadron; Ted and I became Flight Sergeants, Charlie a corporal. It never occurred to any of us that we would do anything other than join the Royal Air Force. But when my call-up papers arrived they were for the Army. It appeared that because RAF losses were lower than had been expected, thousands of would-be airmen were being 'transferred' to the Army. I was so upset that my father actually went to the Air Ministry and was seen by an Air Marshal. There was no chance there: even his son, the Air Marshal told Dad, had been put into the Army and that instead of complaining we should be grateful that there were fewer casualties than the RAF had feared.

Thus it was that I became S/14880342 Private Pollard and found myself on the way to Bodmin in Cornwall for my initial six weeks' training. I have to say that I did not take kindly to it but my Chinaman was certainly looking after me when a notice went on the board asking anyone who knew anything about shorthand and typing to make application for a course to be held at Clapham Common – all of five miles from where I was brought up.

Unfortunately, although my sister was good at shorthand and typing, I knew nothing about it. But I could see no reason why such a small matter should prevent me from getting to Clapham for this wonderful fourteen-week course. With a little white lie or three, I applied – and was selected. Now I was going to need every bit of help Joyce could give me; I knew that without her I could not possibly pass the course. Between us, we somehow managed and at the end of fourteen weeks I passed out as a fully fledged shorthand typist. There was, of course, a price to pay for those fourteen idyllic weeks in Clapham; within ten days of passing out and having seven days' leave, I received my embarkation papers. I was ordered to report to a house in Canewdon Road, Westcliff-on-Sea (it is still there in fact) and prepare to embark for an unknown destination. Even though the battle against Germany was coming to a close we quickly realised that we were in the real business of war when we were told that we were now 'on active service'; anyone leaving the area without permission would be severely dealt with under Active Service Regulations. It was just a little bit frightening, I must say.

I was coming up to nineteen and was still at Westcliff when VE Day (Victory in Europe) was announced. It was a time of great jubilation, and we were told that we could go home for a week to join the celebrations. Having always said that when the war was over I would get drunk, I duly did so for the first time in my life, with my grandfather. While I hadn't thought much of him, it turned out that my grandfather had not held too high an opinion of me, either; he thought I was a bit of a wimp, as they would say nowadays. But after this rather special night he said to Dad, who was none too sober himself, "That lad of yours; he's all right, Jim." After that I didn't have much trouble with my grandfather and, as I have said, to this day I keep his photograph in my study.

Almost before my first hangover had gone I was setting

sail. I had only ever been to Herne Bay, the Isle of Wight and places like that and here I was, with all my equipment in a pack, heading for somewhere they wouldn't tell us but was certainly further than Shanklin. And where were we all, masses of young men like myself, fearful of what lay ahead, worried about leaving their families behind? In the bottom of the boat, that is where, having to 'swing' a hammock and hoping against hope that we would not be the first to be sea-sick! I can picture us all now, leaning over the side of the ship as we left port, singing a popular song of that era, 'Don't Fence Me In'.

Our first stop was in Gambia; then we pulled in at Freetown in Sierra Leone which has the largest natural harbour in the world. Our last port of call was Takoradi, on the Gold Coast or what is now known as Ghana. Here we all got off for a thirty-hour train journey to Accra, stopping on the way only to cut down trees to feed the engine's boilers. For the first time in my life I was to see those big, black busty beauties – and they were all bare! It was almost too much for a modest, well-brought-up boy from Peckham, and I can recall to this day the sergeant-major's words of encouragement: "You might not think much of 'em now, lads, but before long they'll all be looking like Betty Grable." And he was quite right.

I first found myself appointed to the West African School of Infantry at Teshi which was seven miles outside of Accra. I was made Orderly Room Sergeant, with that rank, which meant that I had gone from private to sergeant in eight months. It was a very nice number. The Royal Engineers had built a swimming pool at Teshi, the surf on the beach was as good as Bondi and I was still able to play table tennis. I had started playing as a fifteen-year-old when I joined the Air Training Corps and now in the Army I was, if I can say so modestly, playing to a pretty high standard. I won the Unit Championship and the Gold Coast title two years in succession and was a finalist in the Nigerian Championships. All of them gained me little trophies, but the big reward came when the Commanding

Officer asked if I would be prepared to join a special table tennis unit that was touring the West Coast entertaining the troops. On the basis that the morale of the troops – and I was one of them – and their entertainment was paramount, I agreed with what probably appeared indecent haste.

It was to be a most wonderful three months. I joined this élite group of players which included two world champions who still rank as the finest players I have ever seen – Victor Barna and Richard Bergmann. It would be nice to say that I saw them off, but I didn't! I was never to beat either of them, although I did get 17 points once off Victor, who always attacked and therefore gave you a chance, and 12 points off Richard, who would give you nothing. And that was it; the rest of the while I was the fodder. The troops loved it, watching someone who would regularly beat them being hammered by these two brilliant players.

They were really great times and I enjoyed them to the full. Being inside American flying bases so often only made life more enjoyable. The difference between the way our troops and American servicemen were treated was enormous. The Yanks were looked after in every possible way; when it came to comfort and consideration the British were inferior in every aspect (and in 1990 when our Desert Rats were in Saudi poised for the Gulf War, nothing seemed to have changed). All the big American stars were flown in to entertain their airmen and I would meet them all – entertainers like Bob Hope and Bing Crosby, and the comedienne and singer, Carole Landis. Back in Peckham I had queued at the local cinema to watch them on the screen and now I was standing talking with them, working alongside them. It was all quite overwhelming and little did I realise then that Bing would, in years to come, be our guest at Ladbrokes.

For health reasons, Caucasian servicemen were supposed to serve only eighteen months in West Africa and this led me into what seemed at the time a terrible dilemma. When my three-month stint on the table tennis circuit was over I went back to the West African School of Infantry as a shorthand typist once more. This entailed flying occasionally to and from the Burma front with a Brigadier Jefferies who was in charge of the various battalions of the Royal West African Frontier Force that were being sent to the zone and doing all his notes to the War Office back home and to his officers at the front line. I was naturally surprised one day when my Commanding Officer, Lt-Col. Thorn, offered me an immediate field commission. It was very tempting, but he was adamant that if I accepted, I could not return to the UK. So I declined his offer and no doubt altered the whole structure of my life – not that I have any regrets about that.

Therefore, in 1947, I returned home from the blistering heat of West Africa to one of the coldest winters Britain had endured in forty years. We sailed home on the *Empire Ken*, a ship with a fascinating history. It had been one of Hitler's 'strength through joy' vessels. These were the ships on which the Third Reich, in its endeavour to create a 'Super Race', put the pure, Aryan-blooded young men and women to propagate the new generation of blond-haired Germans who would be the master class of the world. Well, that was the German thinking.

Our crew for the journey home was thinking only of Hogmanay. They were mainly Scottish, and to them it was most important that we berthed before December 31. Unfortunately, although we set sail on December 18, 1946, we ran into terrible weather in the dreaded Bay of Biscay and there were a lot of broken-hearted seamen who set foot on British soil again at Liverpool, on January 2, 1947.

When I reached London, Dad was waiting at the station to greet me and seemed surprised at how much weight his 'slip of a lad' had lost in the heat of Africa. It was wonderful to see him again, and I cannot really find the words to describe how I felt when we reached Peckham. 'Marvellous' is simply a mammoth understatement.

There were huge banners across the street: 'Welcome home, Ron' they read, making me feel a real hero. And there were parties that were quite overwhelming. They had all, my family and the lovely neighbours, saved their rations and when I wore my bush hat to the pub they simply would not let me buy a drink.

But, as all good things come to an end, so I was posted to Thetford in Norfolk; flat, desolate, isolated Thetford where it seemed the icy winds howled straight in from Siberia and the thermometer appeared ten degrees lower than anywhere I had been before. It was a very bad winter for Britain and particularly bad for three of my colleagues at the Thetford camp, like me just back from the tropics. They died, such were the conditions. Once again my father intervened when he heard of the tragedies; he complained to the authorities about young men being brought back from intense heat to such intense cold. I do not know what happened to everyone else, but within a very short space of time I was transferred to the War Office in Horse Guards Parade. London was certainly warmer than Thetford and I also had a sleeping-out pass which meant I could go home each night.

I worked there for a Lt-Col. Paul Crook and we were responsible to Field-Marshal Montgomery. I retain this vivid memory of Monty instructing us to be in his office at nine-thirty one morning. I was there on time; the colonel, however, was not. He turned up ten minutes late and I have never heard anyone given such a dressing-down. He told us to return the next morning at nine; a hard task-master was Monty.

Early in 1948 demob number 64 came up. Mine! And so I returned to civvy street and to William Hill. It was only then that I learned how Bill had shown his generosity to me once again. Throughout the whole period I was in the Army, he had sent my mother £1 each week which she had saved, religiously putting it into my Post Office Savings Book.

3

BIG BILL, A GIANT IN EVERY SENSE

Cheltenham is the Mecca of National Hunt racing. I love the place. It has an atmosphere all of its own, tucked as it is under Cleeve Hill in the very heart of the Cotswolds. Every March the place comes alive as thousands of Irishmen make the pilgrimage to the Festival with the single intention of having a good time. That means meeting up with old friends, staying up drinking and playing cards all night for nearly a week, at which they are past masters, and taking English bookmakers to the cleaners, at which they like to think they are masters but frequently come to glorious grief!

Nothing was very different in 1962 except that I was no longer working with William Hill, but had joined Ladbrokes. This was my first major meeting for my new employers and I was, naturally, hoping to get off to a flying start. But, as every year, Catholic priests in their droves, the *Sporting Life* tucked under their arms, were there with the usual full representation of their flock to ensure that I did not. As they streamed on to the course, little could any of them have dreamed of the three dramatic days that were ahead and the soul-destroying hours that were about to change the lives of two particular Irishmen.

There are eighteen races at the Festival, six on each of the three days, and in 1962 Ladbrokes were there as usual. There is, of course, no legal enforcement of gambling debts: it is strictly a matter of honour between the two parties. A man says he wishes to put an amount of money on an animal, a bookmaker accepts, and that is the contract. It is amazing, therefore, how few bad debts there are. Rarely indeed does either party break that bond and dishonour the debt. You may well be surprised to know that some big losers actually end up paying off their debts *for the rest of their lives*.

Two Irishmen – both doctors – were regular clients of Ladbrokes, with credit accounts. Gambling was in their blood (show me an Irishman and I will show you a gambler!). They would no more think of missing Cheltenham than they would consider breaking their Hippocratic oath. When they reached Cheltenham on the Tuesday, the first day of the meeting, they placed similar bets with us for the three days. In simple terms they bet on favourites to win themselves a specified sum. As soon as a favourite won, the bet was over; they had won their money. Although no longer so, at that time this was a popular bet.

To maintain the privacy of their betting let us for the sake of explanation assume that it was £10 they wished to win. Therefore, if the first-race favourite was at even money, their bet would begin with £10 on it, the amount required to win £10. If it did so, fine; they would collect their winnings and head off to the Guinness tent or think about striking a new bet. If it lost, however, the stake on the second race was increased; now they not only needed to win the £10 but the loss from the first race had to be covered. And thus the bet goes on . . . and on . . . until a favourite does win. I suspect that this wager, a little like the doubling-up system (£5 on the first race, £10 on the second, £20 on the third and so on until you get a winner) lost favour because losses can grow so alarmingly – see the Appendix at the end of this chapter! In the case of our two doctors, they always knew the most they could win, but never what they could lose, and that is a very slippery slope indeed if the favourites keep going down.

Additionally, while most punters would only bother about Day One, these two laid the bet for the whole meeting. It seems scarcely conceivable that it should be so hard to win just £10.

On Day One, they began with £4.44 on the first favourite of the meeting – Trelawny at 9-4. Next they would have had to stake £28.88 to get back their £4.44 and win a tenner as Scottish Memories was at 2-1 on. Flying Wild (11-4) required £15.75 on it, Big Diamond (9-2) £13.13, Python, a 9-4 chance, has £32.09 staked and when it comes to the last race of the Tuesday, Brittas is 9-2 and carries £23.18. In seeking to win only £10, the loss so far is £117.47. These losses are carried forward to Day Two, so when Rupununi is made favourite at 6-4 it requires an outlay of £84.98 to regain them and win a tenner. It is duly beaten and Chaos is an aptly named favourite for the next, at 3-1; when that goes down, burdened by a further £70.82, the Irishmen's bank accounts are beginning – only beginning, mind you – to look just a little depleted.

Another Flash was a firm favourite for the Champion Hurdle at 11-10 and our two, seeking a humble tenner, have £257.52 on it. Another Flash was third. In the last three races the stakes climbed – £332.79 on Willow King (13-8), £262.07 on Sandy Abbot (100-30) and £567.83 on High Tempo (2-1). By this time our doctors must have felt they had a headache coming on. On the assumption that they were seeking to win just £10, their losses over two days have totalled £1,693.48 and when Gold Cup day opened with Mariner's Dance an even-money favourite for the first, the starting bet has to be £1,703.48. When Pas Seul opened at 8-11 for the Gold Cup and then drifted out to be returned at 9-4, the doctors were saved a bigger stake than the £1,514.20 they actually did have to outlay – but with Pas Seul only fifth, they still lost. Stenquill (5-2) went down carrying £1,968.47; Irish Imp at a long-priced 11-2 meant they 'only' had to stake £1,252.66 on the fourth race – but time was running out for them. Richard of Bordeaux (9-4) 'stole' £3,618.80 which left just one race.

The last race at any meeting is known to punters as 'the getting out stakes'; for the doctors it must have been quite unbearable to watch. Pegle was made favourite at 9-4 and now the stake was £5,222.15. Imagine it ... a £5,000 outlay to win £10 and total losses spiralling to nearly £17,000. Pegle was fourth and the doctors went home sadder, wiser and poorer. But, the two of them are paying off their debts to this day, which speaks volumes for their integrity and for the decency of the betting business as a whole.

Some would call this pair 'mug punters', a phrase to which I take exception. Just as there are lucky and unlucky owners, there are lucky and unlucky gamblers. But we talk of professional punters, so why not amateur ones, or uninformed ones? It is not to my credit, I suppose, that one of the world's greatest uninformed punters was a man who, over six or seven years, became a friend but ended up penniless. Tom Beard was a shirt-maker from Roman Road in Bow. He loved his horse racing; glorified it, but didn't understand the first rule of it. He would bet each way on three or even four horses in each race. In other words, he was so keen to make sure that he could back the winner of a race that he spent on it more than he could win by covering too many horses. Not much, just £2 or £3 a time, but no one can win like that and Tom was no exception. He would come into my office in William Hill's premises in Park Lane on a Saturday morning and ask, "How much this time, Ron?" I would say, "£187 I am afraid, Tom" and he would pay me, sometimes giving me one of his shirts. He never quite reached the point of using a shirt as a cheque as legend has it one punter did who kept his sense of humour if not his money, but Tom finished up 'boracic lint' (skint) and he went away out of my life.

Perhaps Tom should have remembered the advice I learned almost fifty years ago now: never follow a horse unless you have a bucket and spade in your hand! That may be an old racing tale, but there is more than a grain of truth in it. Many people will 'follow' a horse simply because they once backed it when it lost and wish to be on it when it wins – if it wins. Mostly, you will find that the horse lost on merit and will lose again and again. The ultimate irony generally comes, of course, when you have gone on holiday and the horse romps home at 20-1. No, only follow horses with a bucket and spade.

In fairness, that is only about 90 per cent correct. What you can sometimes follow is a horse that has already won. Few punters are aware that two out of three horses *never* win a race. So if you back one which is a previous winner, you start with a slight advantage. And if I tell you that two out of every three races are won by the first or second favourites, you will begin to think that this racing game sounds rather easy. And it is, always provided you know which those two races are! But quite seriously, if you back a horse that has already won and is the first or second favourite, then logically and mathematically you *must* increase your chances of winning.

These, then, are two of Pollard's Golden Rules; I never break them. Here are some more: always find time to study the weights for a handicap closely. On the flat, the handicapper will probably have allocated his top horse nine stone. The bottom weight can never race at less than seven stone – that is the rule. Yet some of those horses at the bottom of the handicap may well have been allocated only 6 st 2 lb by the handicapper, which means they must carry 12 lb overweight, or 12 lb more than the expert thinks they should be carrying. So never, ever back horses 'framed' out of the handicap.

Indeed, it is no bad thing to back the top weight if you must bet on a handicap – personally, I have always felt they are best left alone. The conditions of a race might specify that 9 st 7 lb is the highest any horse may carry. The handicapper, however, may well feel that a particular horse should be given 9 st 12 lb, but he is locked into the lower figure laid down in the conditions and therefore that animal will have what the expert considers a 5 lb advantage. Never forget either that up-to-date form, recent form, is always much more valuable than old form, and horses running again within seven days of winning are probably worth another crack, particularly in a handicap before the handicapper catches up with them.

I can actually give you one system that is guaranteed to make you money. There is only one snag – you may find it hard to get a bookmaker to accept the bet! It took us a while some years back to work out that this one was always costing us money, so we stopped it, and so did most of the big bookmakers. You simply put your stake, for argument's sake let us say £1, on the top horse in the handicap: you ask for £2 to be placed on the second horse, £4 on the third, £8 on the fourth and so on, but the key to this bet is your instruction to the bookmaker: "Stop at the winner." So if the top horse wins you have £1 on it. If the fourth one down wins you have lost £7 on the first three stakes but collect your winnings which will be £8 on at whatever price the horse is returned. The general rule is that the lower down the handicap you go, the longer price the runner is. As I say, work it out for yourself a few times – or try it with your local bookie, but you must instruct him to stop at the winner. You would not have to worry about your bookmaker's bills again if you could get that one on! It certainly cost us a good few pounds until we caught on.

Here is another piece of warm advice when it comes to two-year-olds. Always back a previous winner if (a) it is not favourite and (b) if the favourite has never won or never run. Why? Well, remember that two out of three never win and the favourite might just be one of those two.

But perhaps the best advice as a bookmaker that I can give is, "Never back each way." Each-way betting is for the faint-hearted: all you are trying to do is salvage your stake money. That is not the way to set about winning, and winning after all is what we are about. It simply isn't worth putting £5 each way on a 5-1 shot when you are getting just one-fifth of the odds for a place and then paying tax. Better by far to have two £5 win bets; bookmakers hate that, but love the each-way punter. You are looking for winners, so go for winners. But in doing so never forget that there is no such thing as 'a good thing'. Sir Gordon Richards rode a horse called Royal Forest against one opponent called Glendower at 25-1 *on*. It lost and was the ruination of thousands of bets. Not because your average punter will put a single bet on at such odds (that is for the really substantial gamblers who will put £25,000 on thinking that they can 'steal' £1,000) but because they would put Gordon into their doubles and trebles in the way that they did Lester and then Pat Eddery, and make it their banker in accumulators.

I do not suggest for one moment that my Golden Rules will make any one of you rich but I do believe they will help you to win more often because they all give you an advantage rather than take one away. And if you win, it keeps that buzz of excitement going that is so important to punters, big and small. I have always believed I was in a branch of show business. Having a bet can be fun for millions, a means of escape perhaps from a humdrum, day-to-day working life; it means entertainment and excitement and too many lives are lacking in both.

For just £1.75, for example, a working-class Joe can spread the entertainment and excitement over a whole day. Imagine it: he gets up, and over his cup of tea reads his morning paper. He scans page one and then turns to the sports pages. He sees that Cauthen is riding the favourite in the first, has another fancied ride in the second and in the big race is riding what Joe thinks is due a win, with a stable in form and the going just right for it. Joe spends so much time over this that he has to rush to get to work. Once there, he talks with his pal, who also likes a bet, and they agree over the coffee break that these are, indeed, three good choices.

At lunch-time, Joe slips out to the betting shop and has a 25p patent (seven mixed bets, comprising three singles,

39

three doubles and a treble) which costs him £1.75. By the tea break he discovers that the first two have won and he is now in a high old state of excitement. When his work is finished for the day, he can find out the result of the big race. A win, and he is a very happy man: he has won a little money and is able to go home and tell the wife what a clever chap he has been – always provided of course that he is one of those chaps who do actually mention their gambling to the wife! Is there anything else that would provide day-long entertainment such as that for just £1.75?

Betting has been my life for forty-five years or more but I am not basically a gambler – unless you wish to argue that I gambled with my employers' money most days of the year. I know as much, possibly more, about the business than anyone. I have seen them all . . . the high-rollers and the low, the titled and the humble, the rich and the not so rich. And I will tell you one thing about the majority of them: their gambling has more to do with ego than with money and greed.

Yes, of course there are greedy men about, those to whom money is a god and those who simply have to make a fast buck, as our American friends say. I remember when Mike Tyson lost his world heavyweight championship so sensationally in Japan early in 1990 to James 'Buster' Douglas, he had been 35-1 *on* to retain his title. One punter, taking the view I presume that it was a better rate of interest than he would get from the bank over twenty-four hours, staked 70,000 dollars to win 2,000. (The bank must have seemed a safer bet by the end of the fight!)

But men like that are exceptions; mankind will gamble because of his ego. It is about him being right and above all being seen to be right. To be a good judge, the better judge. To banter with his friends and fellow punters and to chide: "I backed it. I got 6-1. Don't tell me you didn't back it. Well, you bloody great fool!"

There are fine divisions, of course. When is a bet a gamble? When is it an investment? I would have no more than six, perhaps eight, bets a year. Generally these would be on a political situation, when I would reckon to know something that others didn't and I believed that other bookmakers were making a mistake with the odds. I considered these to be investments and was usually proved correct with a handsome cheque. But I do not *have* to gamble; a real gambler does.

When I wrote of high rollers, I meant really high. I have known Adnan Khashoggi lose £1 million in a night. He and his ilk will put £40,000 on the single spin of a roulette wheel with the chance of losing £1 million an hour. When a top-class croupier is at the table, there will be twenty-eight spins of the wheel every hour. At £40,000 a spin that is well over £1 million each sixty minutes. And fortunes fluctuate, steeply and rapidly, in both directions.

I loved the elegant Ladbroke Club in the heart of London's West End. There you could watch men win or lose a fortune on the spin of a wheel or the turn of a card and you could eat better than anywhere else in town. (Oh, that smoked salmon. I can almost taste it still!) One morning I left about 3 a.m. and asked the manager how we were doing. "Fine," he replied. "We are £400,000 up." When I rang him mid-morning it was a different tale. In the last hour of business we had lost half a million and we finished the night £100,000 down. But that is the betting business. You win some and you lose some, and why worry, provided there is a little left over to fight the next battle?

It pleases me to say that the betting world has been fun for me from my very first day with William Hill. It is a tough business but we have had a few laughs along the way, and that is what matters. I have been semi-retired for a year or two now, but from the day my war service ended and I walked back into William Hill's offices I have had few regrets about anything. It has been a wonderful life and I owe more than can ever be explained to William Hill himself. He taught me everything I know, gave me all my

41

experience and for nineteen years was my tutor and my mentor.

The contrast between him and Cyril Stein, who was to be my boss at Ladbrokes for twenty-seven years, was immense. They both loved to bet as distinct from accepting bets from others. The wagers between Bill Hill and old Bill Chandler had to be seen to be believed. And even in the early days of Cyril's reign as chairman, you would often see him, just before the 'off', dashing along the rails at a meeting trying to get odds a half-point better somewhere down the line! It was not in his nature to sit in a hospitality box and ask a pretty girl in a red uniform to place his bet for him. So there was a difference, for a start. Bill was a womaniser and Cyril was absolutely not; he would not have tolerated the sort of behaviour that Bill considered merely a minor part of his life's pattern.

If he had been in that hospitality box with Cyril, Bill would have smiled at the girl, invited her to place his bet, given her a £50 tip and asked what she was doing later while our Ladbroke man was haring up and down the rails. Bill could never resist, and few women resisted him. Even when he had nothing he talked big, and he spent big and he was big, in every way. After racing we would sometimes go off to the Embassy Club in London – Bill, Tommy Turner and myself. Before we had had our first drink almost, Bill would say to me: "There's a pretty girl over there. Go and say that William Hill is here and would very much like her to join him." We would tease Bill, telling him that the girl would have no idea who William Hill was. But I would go over and if, as mostly happened, the girl decided to join Bill, Tommy and I would simply disappear.

I remember only too well the occasion when I was supposed to be Hill's clerk at a race meeting and he had taken his mistress, Mrs Landa, with him. Suddenly and very surprisingly, Bill's wife Ivy arrived at the track. Normally, she would run the office while Bill was in the field but whatever the reason for her appearance Bill was warned within seconds, a message going along the grapevine like a tic-tac man reporting a sudden rush of money. Bill did not turn a hair. "Your job this afternoon," he said to me quietly, "is to keep Mrs Landa in the bar. No matter what she says or what else happens, she is not to come down here." It was another successful day at the races, though I fear Mrs Landa and I got rather tipsy.

Cyril would countenance nothing like this. He would not be involved and he did not wish those associated with him to be so involved. Married young, to Betty, a devoted father to his two sons and a daughter, he would become the most generous of sponsors to Jewish charities, and a sober-suited City gent who took an old-established but languishing company by its throat, carrying it into a modern era with immense success. In the betting business, the hotel world, and in the Square Mile of the City, Cyril is respected as a winner. But Bill was larger than life and he was the greatest odds-maker this world has seen and will ever see.

Lest you think I have hero-worshipped him and was blind to his faults, let me say that all his interests in life were selfish ones (women and horses, in the main). He could have played a far greater role in developing the book-making profession and integrating it into society but he chose to leave that task to others, like George Wigg. Hill was certainly the leader down in the ring where the punters gather for hand-to-hand combat with the bookies but he was never a leader of the industry. No, I was never blind to Bill's shortcomings, but I owed him much and he was for me the original likeable rogue.

When I came back from the Army I first worked in the Internal Course Department, where we handled all the sheets brought back from the courses by our Racetrack Representatives, which recorded every bet laid. The days of computers and machine book-keeping had not yet arrived, and every single item was written out laboriously by hand. Every bet was transferred on to individual accounts — and remember there was no legal cash betting except on the course, and even that was minimal. It was

43

all credit betting and the essence of our work was accuracy. If you didn't get it right, if the books did not balance at the end of the day, you stayed at your desk until they did. And there was no such thing as overtime!

Within eighteen months I became a Course Clerk, which was much better than being stuck in an office all day. My job was to record all the bets taken by our Representative, which would then be rushed back to the office from which I had just escaped to be transferred to clients' accounts by some other unlucky chap now sitting at my old desk. Every now and then I was allowed to be the bookmaker at lesser meetings, with a clerk of my own, and I would feel so proud of myself.

William Hill himself would stand at all the bigger meetings and there was no one to touch him. He was always the leader of the market. His true ability was in actually making a book, in thinking faster than anyone else. Let me try to explain: the mathematics of bookmaking are an exact science and Hill's mind worked at the speed of light. His ability was to see the way the market was moving fractionally before anyone else. He would appreciate precisely how much money was being laid perhaps thirty or forty seconds before anyone else and would realise, for example, that the favourite was about to be cut from 5-2 to 9-4. Such a market move dictated that as the favourite shortened another horse would lengthen in price. Presuming, for the sake of argument, that that was the 3-1 second favourite, its price would drift to 100-30 or 7-2. Hill's skill was to offer that second favourite at the higher price before any other bookmaker on the course, which meant that he would grab the first business, ensuring he had a better chance of making a bigger profit than the rest of them.

All bookmakers work to a tiny percentage of profit on a race; when a horse goes to 7-2 its next move could well be to 4-1. If the bookmaker takes money at 7-2 rather than 4-1 that horse represents 22 per cent of the book rather than 20 per cent. (Well, I did say it was an exact science!) Perhaps I can explain this in more simple terms, using

44

my 1990 Booker Prize odds as the example, although the six books could just as easily be horses:

7-4	*Amongst Women* (John McGahern)
5-2	*Lies of Silence* (Brian Moore)
3-1	*Possession* (A. S. Byatt)
7-1	*Solomon Gursky Was Here* (Mordecai Richler)
10-1	*An Awfully Big Adventure* (Beryl Bainbridge)
10-1	*The Gate of Angels* (Penelope Fitzgerald)

Each price represents a percentage of your book as follows: 7-4 is 36 per cent; 5-2 is 28 per cent; 3-1 is 25 per cent; 7-1 is 12 per cent; and 10-1 is 9 per cent. Those percentages add up to 119 per cent – the 19 per cent being your notional profit. The perfect book would be the one where a bookmaker has laid each horse to take out the same amount of money (hence the words 'notional profit') but in an imperfect world I regret you never see the perfect book! When a lot of money pours on to one particular novel or horse you have to adjust your prices accordingly and if the favourite hardens to, say, evens (a price which represents 50 per cent of your book) you can afford to lengthen one or two of the others to bring your book back to the 119 per cent you are aiming to maintain. Which, going back to the skill of William Hill, is what he was doing that much quicker than every other bookmaker, ensuring he had a better chance than them of making a bigger profit. To punters it no doubt sounds complicated: if they have £10 on a 4-1 shot that wins, all they are thinking about is £40 winnings; the bookmakers, however, see that 4-1 price as 20 per cent of their book. The proper way to make a book is for the bookie to lose if the favourite wins, to break even if the second favourite wins, and to win if any other horse, dog or novel wins.

Bookmakers can and do lose but if they can make a 3 per cent nett profit they are successful. As I hope I have explained, it is a question of mathematics and thinking quicker than the next man, which is where the laser-like

Hill was so good. At places like Royal Ascot it was an education just to watch him, let alone work alongside him. He would always arrive early and then, around one o'clock, perhaps an hour and a half before the first race, he would stand and start to make a book on the big race of the day. If it was Royal Hunt Cup day, for example, with twenty-three runners, Bill would go through the whole field, one runner after another, quoting a price on each and – quite incredibly – taking bets at the same time. I never saw another man do that with such precision. As he finished he would say to me, or whoever was his Clerk that day: "I think you will find that Horse A is in for £2,000, Horse B is in for £12,000, Horse C is in for . . ." and so on and so on until he had covered his whole book. Believe me, he was never very often much out.

Although he had health problems and lived on milk puddings and was never without a bottle of milk close to hand, Hill was a giant of a man in every way. Burly and bespectacled, he stood the width of a betting slip under six feet, was always smartly dressed, generally sporting a brown trilby. But had he been only 5 ft 2 ins tall he would still have had this immense presence. The moment he stepped on to those little wooden stools bookmakers use on racecourses William Hill commanded attention. All the other bookmakers would gather round as his voice boomed out "I will lay . . . I will lay . . ." and listened in the certain knowledge that this was the man who set the market.

One of my greatest memories was the first time I had 'attended' upon Bill. It was at Salisbury, and Pat Moore, his regular Clerk, could not be there. I was filled with this enormous trepidation, yet we had a quiet start and everything seemed to be going along serenely when Bill leaned down and said, "Get ready, then." Not sure what he meant, I looked up inquiringly and he said, "Right. We are going to have a go at this favourite. A real go. Don't you worry about anything else, just get every bet down in your book." Our quiet afternoon had come to an end.

The favourite in the next race belonged to one of the leading owners of the day, and it was a short price from the outset. Bill did not seem particularly perturbed about any liabilities; he was betting like a man who did not expect to have any. When, on every other board, it was even money, Bill was shouting from his little stand, "I'll go 5 to 4, I'll go 5 to 4" and everybody came, clamouring to get on. In their rush to get the better odds, people were knocking me over. "Don't worry," Bill shouted, "you will all get on. Don't knock my Clerk about. You will all get on."

Need I say that the favourite did not win? William Hill cleaned up around £20,000 on that race, and this in 1949 when the profits were counted in thousands at the end of the year, not in millions as they are today. It was not the first time, nor would it be the last time that I saw that sweet smile of satisfaction on Bill's face after a jockey had qualified for 'the usual' and Bill had won a packet. That afternoon he turned to Tommy Turner, who held whatever cash was taken, and said: "Give the Clerk a pony," and smiled down at me saying, "You've done well." All those he had promised "would get on" had done so – to their cost. Tommy, who was the son of a race-gang leader who had protected Bill in Birmingham in his younger days and had a job for life as a result, handed over my £25, which was three or four weeks' wages for me. Tommy Turner had seen it all before.

All the top bookies had a jockey on their books and when one thought he knew something that the others didn't, he would try to clean up, jumping in with both feet. Bill Hill and old Bill Chandler were fierce antagonists, with some bruising and at times quite breathtaking exchanges involving many thousands of pounds. Every now and then they would both lose, because the jockeys had their own little 'ring' and would sometimes carve a race up for their own benefit, without the courtesy of mentioning this fact to the bookmakers. But this was all an accepted, if not exactly acceptable, part of racing and betting by those in it at that time. When Hill had that real go on the favourite at Salisbury, he simply was not interested that day in knowing how much he stood to lose if the favourite won, which would be a normal concern. The favourite was not going to win – Bill had seen to that. He, or more likely a distant someone, had had words with the jockey, who would have collected 'the usual' (£100 on the winner, at whatever price it came in at).

Dorothy Paget was once the victim of just such a 'sting' and I fear that I was the distant 'someone' who played his part at Taunton in ensuring that a particular favourite did not win. Dorothy was an enormous woman, a renowned lesbian and a fearful glutton who would eat twelve lamb chops for breakfast and still wonder what was for lunch. She always turned up at race meetings with *two* Rolls-Royces, just in case one of them broke down, and if there was a place in the *Guinness Book of Records* for the person who set most beds alight with cigarettes in a lifetime, she would have claimed it.

Dorothy was also a great punter and when she thought she was on to a good thing would back it strongly herself and would always try to look after the interests of her all-girl staff. Ruth Charlton, an absolute charmer who would later marry Charlie Smirke, was her head secretary and Dorothy would say to her that she wanted £2,000 on her good thing and add, "Find out what the girls want, Ruth." Ruth would find out what 'the girls' wanted and the bet would be laid: £2,083 to win at 8-13! You can no doubt imagine the fury of a busy Clerk who had to work that one out!

On this day at Taunton, where I was working, Dorothy had a large bet on a hot favourite. A message came down the line for me to give a certain jockey £100. "He knows what it is for," I was told from Hill's London office. "He will be parting company." The horse did not win, for the jockey did indeed part company from his mount.

Hill's then set up a select group which was called the

'Mobile Squad'. Wherever the work was, we went; wherever there was a pressure point and help within the company was needed, we moved in. If, for example, we had been advertising our Derby odds and there was a sudden rush of betting, we would help out in that department. If the debts had not been collected, we made sure that they were. If the cashiers were under pressure, we relieved them. There was never a slack moment for this élite group, but it was a tremendous grounding in every side of the business: so much so that many of the directors of leading offices today were once members of the 'Mobile Squad'.

It was the end of a long apprenticeship as far as I was concerned. There was no area of the business that I did not understand and that I had not worked in.

In time though I had moved from the squad to be manager of the Accounts Department and I had to admit to myself that I was not enjoying it. I felt that I should be making more progress, but it was a bit like the dead man's boots syndrome where people wait for others to die so that they can move one more rung up the ladder. I did not like being in this position but there was a further complication that made me think it was time to move on. William Hill had acquired a new vice-chairman, a financial genius called Lionel Barber, who was a very difficult man to work with; indeed, if I were honest, I would have to say that he was impossible to work with. The crunch came when Barber asked me to undertake a special project for him and, delighted, I did so, spending literally weeks preparing it. When it was completed, I took it to Barber who, with no more than a cursory glance, threw it on to a table beside him and said dismissively just one word: "Bollocks." Essentially, my career with William Hill ended at that moment; I could not accept such behaviour from anyone and when I told Bill, he understood. Like myself, however, he was sad that nineteen pretty good years together were over in such a fashion.

Once more in my life, just as though someone was looking after me when I most needed looking after – that Chinaman on my shoulder again? – I spotted an advertisement in the *Sporting Life*. Ladbrokes were seeking a credit manager. I applied, met Cyril Stein and Richard Kaye, two directors of this old-established firm, and on March 1, 1962, started a new career that was to last the better part of thirty years.

It was like going back to Dickensian times. The clerks sat in little wooden boxes like booths where you cast your votes on polling day, with curtains across the front to preserve 'secrecy' when the rich and the titled rang in with their bets. For, remember, these were still the days of credit betting and you had an account with Ladbrokes at their Burlington Street offices only if you were in *Debrett*. If you were in trade, no matter how prosperous, you had no chance of an account with the firm that had a direct telephone link to Buckingham Palace for the regular Royal bets that would be struck, sometimes daily.

These illustrious clients were treated just like everyone else. There were no special deliveries, just an account, or a cheque if they had been lucky, in the post once a week to an equerry. And their commissions, like all we received, were written in our ledgers in hand, in copperplate with old-fashioned quill pens – a very different world indeed from standing alongside Bill Hill at Ascot or Goodwood as he boomed out to gentry and workers alike, "I will lay ... I will lay ..."

Just about the first question Cyril Stein asked me was, "Have you brought any names and addresses with you?" He meant, was I poaching any of William Hill's wealthier clients and I bristled at the very suggestion. "Certainly not. That is not my way of doing business," I replied. I told Cyril that if anyone whom I knew to be a good punter wished to get in touch with us, then I would say so and that would be an advantage to us; but, I insisted, "I will not do anything against William Hill." I have never doubted that my rather forceful reply earned Cyril's lasting respect, not simply for my integrity and my loyalty to an old friend and former employer but also because he realised at the same time that I would never let him down either. Our relationship was strong and we always had a good working partnership.

Don't get me wrong. I am not trying to suggest that I have always been an angel – I was not in the angels' business. I was brought up to be truthful and honest, to be respectful and to have a sense of responsibility (particularly to women), but from the earliest days I knew what was going on and at times I played my part in things which, while they do not happen today, were then an everyday part of bookmakers' lives.

There is a lovely old tale of a bookmaker offering a rather generous 8-1 on the outsider in a three-horse race. A punter laid £100 on it and went away. Then he returned for some more of the same, and this was repeated until he had £1,000 on at 8-1. The outsider romped home alone and the punter duly returned to the bookmaker to collect. "Why did you offer such long odds," he inquired. The bookmaker, shaking his head in disbelief, snarled: "Well, I own the damn animal." "Aahhh," said the punter slowly. And as he walked away with his winnings he smiled and added: "You weren't to know, I suppose, that I own the other two." An apocryphal story, clearly, but it does go to show the state of the game when I first joined it.

I am glad to say that those days are long gone, however, and racing today is cleaner than it ever was. The Jockey Club has its own security service, there are race patrol cameras including head-on recordings of each race, and every sort of modern technology is used to spot any wrong-doing, deliberate or accidental. But when you consider that our top jockey, Pat Eddery, can earn £6 million a year and that Steve Cauthen and Walter Swinburn will not be far behind that, where is the point any more in trying to pull a horse for a few pounds?

APPENDIX

These are the horses which ran as favourites at the Cheltenham Festival in March 1962, their prices and the amount that would have been staked on each one to win £10, a total outlay of £16,973.24.

Trelawny: 9-4	(£4.44)
Scottish Memories: 1-2	(£28.88)
Flying Wild: 11-4	(£15.75)
Big Diamond: 9-2	(£13.13)
Python: 9-4	(£32.09)
Brittas: 9-2	(£23.18)
Rupununi: 6-4	(£84.98)
Chaos: 3-1	(£70.82)
Another Flash: 11-10	(£257.52)
Willow King: 13-8	(£332.79)
Sandy Abbot: 100-30	(£262.07)
High Tempo: 2-1	(£567.83)
Mariner's Dance: Evens	(£1,703.48)
Pas Seul: 9-4	(£1,514.20)
Stenquill: 5-2	(£1,968.47)
Irish Imp: 11-2	(£1,252.66)
Richard of Bordeaux: 9-4	(£3,618.80)
Pegle: 9-4	(£5,222.15)

4

WHAT PRICE? ASKS THE PRESIDENT

There is nothing I like more than a quiet Sunday at home. A leisurely little gin and tonic around noon, having scanned all the Sunday newspapers, my favourite roast beef – just slightly pink – for lunch with a Yorkshire pudding that my wife Pat cooks so superbly, and a lazy afternoon watching any sport there may be on the box. That is what I like, it is not what I always used to get. Most weeks the telephone would disturb us several times during the day. The problem, if problem I should call it, was that all the leading Fleet Street writers had my number – the City desk men, racing correspondents, political experts, all the top news reporters and even the cricket writers; I had always made myself accessible to them. If they needed a quote on the likely winner of Miss World, the reason a Derby runner had suddenly gone out in the betting or why I had made Labour favourites for a particular by-election, they would always get one.

Sometimes they would mention Ladbrokes in their articles, sometimes not, but that never concerned me. I was always available, even on Sundays, because when our name did appear such publicity was priceless. Stanley Longstaff had been in charge of Ladbroke PR before me, perhaps the greatest publicity man I have ever come across; all I learned from him was to make my job much easier. He would be on Christian-name terms with all the leading writers, often recognising their voices before they had time to introduce themselves on the telephone. He would always try to get his copy used by the agencies, the Press Association or Exchange Telegraph, and Bernard Jones, the Racing Editor at PA was his great friend. "The Press Association is the lungs from which we breathe," was Stanley's favourite expression, meaning that if his story and Ladbrokes' name went out on the agency wire machines it would reach hundreds of papers throughout the land.

From Stanley, a most charming man, I learned that you could not buy the sort of publicity and promotion that accrued from editorial mentions. If I had an 'art form' it was to follow Stanley and never actually ask for our name to be used. You provided a service and if the company name was not mentioned, too bad; if it was, you expressed your thanks at some suitable juncture. So being available, night and day, seven days a week, to influential journalists and opinion-forming people, talking to them sometimes in confidence, earning their trust and respect and generally their friendship was a crucial part of the job for someone like me charged with helping to make what in fairness was a little-known company into a household name.

Ladbrokes had existed since the turn of the century, but had always had a low profile as befitted turf accountants with Royal and other titled clients. The thought of advertising themselves, never mind having the company name plastered all over the papers, literally horrified the old directors. Now 'under new management' as they say, with the dynamic young Cyril Stein taking them into a new era from 1956, publicity was to prove their lifeblood. Strangely, I never had any formal training in PR; I never went on a course or anything like that and nor would I have wished to do so. I am not sure there really is any real training that you can acquire – it is more seat-of-the-pants stuff. In some ways I suppose I drifted into it.

It really began in 1963 when I took us into political betting and earned Ladbrokes so much publicity in newspapers and on TV and radio throughout the land. The following year I was made a director of Town and County

Betting Ltd, the Ladbroke holding company which was to become Ladbroke Racing; I saw this as a reward for bringing a new dimension to betting, not to mention the badly needed cash flow from political wagers. Until then I had been the General Manager of Ladbrokes – now I became the PR Director. I made the odds for all sorts of things that created the publicity for which I was to become well known. The two things just happened; they simply went hand in glove. There are many different sorts of PR men and women around. For example, I would imagine Len Owen, the former Benson and Hedges Special Events Manager, to be a brilliant one – but you could not compare the two of us at all. The only philosophy we would have in common was the aim to promote our companies' names whenever and wherever we could with dignity and style.

A couple of years after our entry into political betting, when we were taking bets on almost any event, it was the redoubtable Stanley who was to come up with the truly brilliant suggestion that we should bet on 'Goldie', the African Golden Eagle which captured the imagination of a nation when it escaped for a second time from London Zoo. In February 1965 the eagle had flown to freedom and was at liberty for twelve days – twelve days of the most marvellous publicity. Television, radio, newspapers, magazines, photographers and cartoonists all had an absolutely wonderful time with it and now, ten months on, the bird had flown again. He or she – I am not sure which though I will lay two to one it is a he! – was bound to generate a lot of publicity once more and I wondered how we might cash in on it. I talked with Stanley and when he urged me to offer odds on Goldie's recapture the idea appealed to my sense of fun as well as PR. So, after Goldie had enjoyed four days of freedom and the publicity was hotting up nicely, I put out a story that Ladbrokes were offering 12-1 against Goldie being recaptured before midnight on Christmas Eve.

I am afraid that we were out of luck or perhaps I should say that the going changed overnight! The weather, which had been mild enough for December, suddenly turned very wet and then very, very cold. Goldie looked a pretty pathetic eagle on his lonely perch in Regent's Park. He was cold and wet and, as even the squirrels who might have provided the odd meal had hibernated, was getting ever more hungry. His keeper, Joe McCorry, had been tempting Goldie with all sorts of titbits which he cheekily snatched and then ate high up in the trees watched at times by as many as 5,000 people. Joe, who was deputy head keeper at the birds of prey section, was not happy at being out-witted and blamed the mass of photographers for 'clicking away' every time anyone got near the bird. But they did capture a marvellous picture, I remember, of Goldie swooping down on a little Cairn terrier that had the tem-erity to bark at him. Then, after twelve days and with the weather worsening, his keeper had the last word. He left an overweight rabbit out overnight as bait – and Goldie just could not resist. Down he fluttered to be recaptured just hours before our midnight deadline, in a blaze of head-lines and pictures.

We were the losers and had to pay out £14,000, but in the publicity stakes we were once again the winners. The whole nation had taken Goldie to its heart; wherever you went everyone was talking about Goldie, so we were indif-ferent to that £14,000. Our involvement had given a new dimension to the story, it supported my philosophy that betting should be fun and it won us world-wide publicity worth much more than our pay-out. Joe McCorry inciden-tally retired last year and Goldie died four years ago from cancer at the comparatively young age of twenty-six (they normally live forty years) at the Falconry Centre at Newent where he had been sent in his retirement.

When my own retirement party was being staged at the London Hilton in May 1989, I had long forgotten Goldie, but Cyril Stein had not. Among the gifts I was to receive that night was a specially commissioned solid silver eagle from Harrods weighing five and a half pounds. Although he had said little at the time, Cyril clearly saw the Goldie incident as a turning-point in our activities: from horses and dogs we were moving onwards, into other areas that were to make Ladbrokes not merely the most famous book-making name in the world but in some countries the only name people knew.

That silver eagle is a constant reminder of a long and enjoyable journey through life. It was a most generous gift and I say that not simply because of its monetary value. Like so many men, I suspect, whenever I am asked what I want for a birthday or an anniversary present I can only ever shake my head; I never know. It is always difficult to think of gifts for oneself and twice or three times as difficult to think of something personal for others. Cyril had clearly given my farewell present a deal of thought. It was an inspired gift and could not have been more personal. That is what I mean by generous and why I was so very, very pleased to receive it. The only way it will ever leave me is if Crystal Palace, my team for so many years, win the First Division championship; then my eagle will be bequeathed to 'The Eagles' of Selhurst Park.

The Goldie episode was a major publicity coup and one which illustrated the sometimes unseen value of my giving up those early Sundays to phone calls which might generate publicity for Ladbrokes. I had a saying: "When you are wrong you cannot afford to lose your temper; when you are right there is no need to do so". In other words, *never* lose your temper. And be patient. When a paper rings, keeps you on the phone for forty minutes and then uses three lines or even worse not a single line, shrug your shoulders, smile and forget it. That is why I say I rarely had a quiet Sunday afternoon. Yet on a particular one in July 1988 all was quiet. There had been no calls and it was just the sort of day I liked. I was in the frame of mind that, when the telephone did ring, I was more than happy to let Pat get up and answer it! "It's for you," she called out. "The White House wants you."

Believing that she was simply winding me up I said: "Oh, yes, the White House in Regent's Park I suppose." Yet when I picked up the handset, an American voice drawled: "Is that Mr Ron Pollard? This is President Reagan's office from the White House here." Reagan's aide then explained that David Frost had been in the day before and had mentioned to the President that I was betting on the American election. The President wished to know what the odds were on George Bush winning. I told him, was thanked profusely and then asked, "Do you mind if we ring again? The President really is keen to keep in touch with what you people are thinking and doing over there." I told him that it would be a pleasure and that they should call at any time.

A week later, again in the afternoon, I answered another call from the States (I suppose even the rich and the famous can take advantage of the cheap-day calls!) and was slightly taken aback to discover that it was not the President's office this time but Gene Pitney. "I don't know how old you are but I don't suppose you will remember me," he introduced himself modestly. "I sing a little, you know."

I certainly did know and tried to explain that I had enjoyed his music over many years, but Pitney was keen to talk my business and not his. He had rung, he said, only to have a bet on the American election. Were we still betting and, if so, what were the odds? He wanted to bet on Bush and I had to explain that while we were still betting, the whole world wanted to bet Bush, and the odds were now 1-8, so short as to be prohibitive and that it really wasn't worth his while. He thanked me for my advice and we said our goodbyes, leaving me to reflect upon two extraordinary transatlantic calls in a week and the fact that I had turned away a punter. It was not very often I did that, I can assure you!

We had been betting on the American elections for twenty-five years and they had proved, financially, very successful for us. Indeed, I have to admit that I had greater success in predicting the outcome of American elections than our own! But the PR value was also immense: when we wished to develop the company in America, the only bookmaking name that they knew over there was ours.

We would take bets on American elections from all over the place; from our own British punters who were game to bet on anything, of course, and from Americans in Britain, either working here or holidaying. Americans at home, like Gene Pitney, liked to bet with us as well, but the really big money, all the 5,000-dollar-plus bets, mostly came from Americans living in Switzerland. Barry Goldwater was an arch-right-winger, probably the original American 'hawk'. He would have declared war on anyone who drank Russian vodka, smoked Cuban cigars and expressed a dislike for Kentucky Fried Chicken. When he stood for President – against Lyndon Johnson – in 1964, he commanded the brash and popular appeal and almost all the headlines. Despite this, I did not believe that a man with such right-wing views could win, particularly at this point in American politics. We had seen McCarthy's witch-hunt against Communists and the country had hardly recovered from the shock assassination of the Catholic and popular John F. Kennedy. Could the No. 1 country in the world set such an example by electing Barry Goldwater to the summit of world power? I decided that America had more sense and laid long odds against Goldwater. It was too much of a temptation for some of his supporters. They took the odds and we took their money! My instincts had been absolutely spot-on, because it was an overwhelming Johnson victory.

Perhaps my most successful coup, both from Ladbrokes' point of view and from my own on this occasion, was in 1978 when I spread our net across the English Channel to take in the French Presidential Election. Giscard d'Estaing, the sitting, right-wing President, was not given much chance by anyone of staying in office; François Mitterrand, the Socialist, was a hot favourite with the French newspapers, the pollsters and the public to win. Once again in my life I was to be lucky. It was not my Chinaman who was to help me this time, but a friend who had married into a top French family. Even though they like to pretend that it isn't, being a part of the Establishment in Paris is just as important as it is in Britain. My friend was privy to what d'Estaing was intending to say in a major speech on the following Saturday, the day before the election.

It was generally felt by those close to him, my friend told me, that this speech would play a decisive role in ensuring another right-wing victory. So, even though all the polls were saying that Mitterrand would win, Ron Pollard predicted a win for d'Estaing. And I was right. The French newspapers conducted their in-depth inquests and among the many questions, several of them asked how it was that an Englishman came to know so much more than they did themselves. Well, now they know!

It was not often that I had a bet, but this was one of those occasions when I felt I had an advantage – that I knew something others didn't, and that other bookmakers were being a little foolish, or a little generous, with their odds. This French election was one such case, and another was the Kingston upon Hull North by-election in January 1966 when I would be banking a handsome cheque.

The two principals in this by-election, the only two who really mattered, were Kevin McNamara, a down-to-earth, Yorkshire-bred Labour man and the Conservative Toby Jessel, a public-school type who is now in a more natural habitat as Member of Parliament for Twickenham. An especially good friend of mine, a man with similar political views to my own, was Tony Howard, at various times down the years the political correspondent to the *Observer*, their Washington staffman and then their Deputy Editor. I would often seek his advice, and when I asked how he saw this by-election, Tony was quite contemptuous of Jessel's chances. "They will not wear a man like that up in Yorkshire. He hasn't a ghost of a chance against Kevin McNamara who has lived in Hull, been educated there and left Hull University to become a teacher there," was Tony's prompt and decisive reply.

It was our very good fortune to find that the chairman of Kingston upon Hull North Conservative Party, a very nice man indeed called John Hudson, was also one of the local bookmakers. Perhaps not surprisingly, he had made their candidate a firm favourite at 8-11 with Labour's man at evens. Having sought Tony Howard's advice, I acted upon it. I began with a chat with Mr Stein, explaining what I had gleaned from Howard. He agreed that we should have McNamara favourite at 8-11 with Jessel at evens, precisely the reverse of the local man. We also agreed that this was too good a chance to miss and that we would therefore go personally for what we called 'a nice touch'. Every time I went into Cyril's office from then on he seemed to be on the phone to John Hudson, having yet another bet on Labour. Meanwhile, I was also having my share!

I never did find out whether Hudson stood all those bets himself (which would not have surprised me) or whether he put them through his firm's books, but he certainly lost plenty to Cyril and myself, not having wavered in his belief that his man would win. Not long afterwards, his business was sold to William Hill.

Keeping myself 'informed' about situations, particularly in American and European elections, was at times mentally exhausting. I relied heavily on friends like Tony Howard, who would flit in and out of my life. Sometimes we would go months without speaking and then he would ring from the States to see what was happening over here, or I would ring him for his reaction to something, as with the Kingston upon Hull by-election. Another who flitted in and out of my life was David Frost, always a marvellous supporter, even though in our case we might go two or three years without contacting each other.

During the 1970 election, I remember David asking me to appear on his Breakfast Show. Over the weekend before the Thursday voting, Labour had been as short as 8-1 on to win. Then, on the Sunday, I took two bets totalling £18,000 to £4,000 from Michael Marsh, a director of Marsh and Baxter the ham curing and purveying company, and W. G. Turriff, boss of the construction company that bore his name, on the Tories to win. So I had to cut the Conservatives from the rather generous 9-2 that I had been offering and Labour came back to 1-4, still strong favourites. Cyril Stein was heading for Israel and he rang me from the airport. He was so totally convinced that Labour would win that he urged me to keep taking money for the Tories, regardless of how much we would lose should they happen to win!

On the Monday evening before voting, David and I met for dinner to discuss what we should talk about on his Breakfast Show on the Friday morning. I thought there would be only one possible subject: "When they have lost," I said to David, "they will ditch Ted Heath before you can blink." David agreed and I left, promising him a list of possible candidates and their prices the next day. Still though, despite the polls and my own beliefs, there was consistent betting on the Tories in the last few days and in ninety-six hours I had been forced to slash their price again and again.

By polling day Labour were only 5-2 on with the Conservatives at 7-4, a far cry from the 9-2 they had been a few days earlier. And, as history records, the Conservatives did win, which gave me an additional headache: what on earth did I now talk about on David Frost's show? Which was precisely the question David put to me when I arrived at the studios at the appointed hour. "What the hell, now?" I had no idea, unless to discuss how expensive it had turned out for Ladbrokes. And when Reggie Maudling, who was also due to appear on the show arrived, he seemed to have a similar dilemma. He appeared astounded by the Conservatives' success: "I don't know what we are going to do now," he said; "I never expected this." Words which suggested to me that I was right in thinking that the Tories were planning on a future leader, fully expecting electoral defeat and that Maudling at least had not backed his party to win.

Enough people had, mind you (and many of them at quite long odds) for us to lose around £80,000 which, although considerably less than Cyril Stein had suggested we should be prepared for, was nevertheless a significant loss. What I did not realise as I sat discussing the election result with David and Reggie Maudling was that this was only the start to a very Black Friday. For this was, coincidentally, the last day of the Royal Ascot meeting. Every single race was a losing one. Having got to bed very late the night before because I was watching the election results on television, risen at five o'clock to get to the TV studio, having 'done' our money all day to the point where the company was a quarter of a million pounds poorer than it had been twenty-four hours earlier, I was, to put it bluntly, 'knackered'.

And still it was not the finish. Worse was to follow for me personally as the main board of directors sat down with our election losses the main item on the agenda. They blamed me for them, and they wanted my head. Having become accustomed to years of success, forgetting that bookmakers can, in fact, sometimes lose as well as win, they were behaving like some members of Lloyds' were to behave some years later: because regular profits had suddenly become losses, they screamed "Foul" and wished to move the goalposts. In my case, they also wished to move me.

To his eternal credit, Cyril Stein sat and listened to the directors' demands for my dismissal and when they had finished their ranting said quietly, "If he goes, I go." Full stop; end of story. Not one of them was prepared to take on the chairman, or risk him walking out at a time when, thanks to my original political betting, they had recovered from near bankruptcy to become a prosperous company. What Stein understood, and the directors calling for me to be sacked did not, was that had it not been for our political betting, the company could never have survived its financial crises, and but for my gaining Ladbrokes so much publicity they could never have changed from a languishing company to one recognised and respected all around the world. I learned a lot from this little episode. There is an old saying, 'Evidence of trust begets trust', and I had just seen the truth of that. Having shown Cyril my sense of loyalty when I first joined the company, I never doubted his and was not really surprised that he showed it so forcefully. I did discover just how strong he was – the Board simply withered under his short but savage attack. It also went to show just how employees, even one like myself who had been made a director of the Ladbrokes holding company some time earlier, could be top dog one day and gone the next at the whim of a handful of small-minded people – small-minded people with short memories.

In spite of this financial hiccup, the huge profits political betting afforded the firm ensured its survival and encouraged us to look into other areas. What we had learned from our entry into the political sphere, offering prices firstly upon who would be the next leader of the Conservative Party when Macmillan was forced to step down, and then on the 1964 General Election, was that the public would actually bet on anything and everything. For years bookmakers had held the belief that their businesses centred upon horses and dogs. Indeed, in 1964 William Hill, who took his politics extremely seriously, gave me a fearful lecture about betting on it. Personally, I felt that there was nothing whatsoever wrong, provided it was done with integrity. Hill still disagreed, took me to task once more and for years left us to it, an open market place in which we operated alone, made a great deal of money and gained immense publicity.

Having succeeded with politics, we realised that we should be widening our spectrum of activity, and giving people other fields in which to bet. Our only problem was how to go about it. Help, as has so often been the case in my life, was at hand in the shape of a most unlikely man . . .

Douglas Bunn is the Master of Hickstead, by far the clearest-thinking person in the world of show jumping. He is a big man, a barrister, a former Joint Master of Foxhounds who still hunts, and dresses as well as you would expect a partner in a bespoke tailoring business in London's Savile Row, where you would be lucky to walk out minus only £1,000 for a two-piece suit.

Douglas is a medieval star in a modern world, a self-made man who lives his life as the Lords of the Manor did 150 years ago. Enter his beautiful home on his estate in deepest Sussex and you are waited upon by uniformed flunkeys in white gloves. That can be a little unnerving, I assure you. For all this, he is a businessman. He set up Hickstead in 1960, turning it into the home of British show jumping. In those early days he would stand near to the entrance to this picturesque arena on the London to Brighton road, cursing all the cars that went past the main gates and counting in, with a smile, all those which entered them!

This, then, is the man the public has in some ways to thank for being allowed to bet on just about anything, at any time and in any place. It was Douglas, with his razor-sharp legal brain, who brought to my attention the facts that opened the door to Ladbrokes creating a whole new world of betting. What he told me was that under the 1961 Betting and Gaming Act, you could bet at any one specific venue on seven days of any year from July 1 to June 30. In essence, this meant that if I staged a tortoise race in my back garden, I could invite people in to watch it, and to bet upon it and, more importantly, I could also invite them to bet upon the 3.30 at Newmarket, all without needing authority. More seriously, we could bet at snooker championships, golf tournaments or darts events – or, as Douglas was scheming, at show jumping.

He had seen this loophole in the Act and because he felt that it would add interest to show jumping if he introduced betting to his patrons who were, in the main, 'horsey' people – farmers, racehorse lovers and point-to-pointers, all of them used to gambling – he brought it to my attention. I was excited by what Douglas had to tell me; he clearly knew his law but I had to take the information to our company solicitor, Anthony Scott Tucker, at Stilgoes. After some research he confirmed what Douglas had told me. It was a thrilling moment. How it had escaped our attention heaven alone knows, but now Ladbrokes knew and other bookies did not know; we were about to turn the betting game upside down and inside out once more.

We were going to bet, on site, at cricket and golf, tennis and darts, snooker – and of course show jumping. The list was endless.

We saw this as a tremendous PR exercise. It is a fact that over 90 per cent of all betting is still on horses and dogs and while people at cricket or golf or snooker could now come in and have a bet on that event with us, they could also have a bet on the day's racing. This was important to us: it was a new service and it encouraged people to use a Ladbrokes' office rather than one of our rivals.

Ladbrokes as a company and I shared one great aim; we had to be first with everything new. If another bookmaker did something we were not interested in merely following suit; this was very important. Now, thanks to Douglas Bunn, we were again leading the way.

For some years, naturally, I did go to Hickstead to bet and at the Queen's own invitation we bet at the Windsor Horse Show. It seemed that, with her strong interest in the Turf, she wished to ensure that any of her Guards Officers at the show could bet on the horse racing! Later we attended some of the big county shows like the Bath and West, the Devon and Royal Shows, but we did not stay in it for long. While we obtained a few TV mentions, the expense far outweighed the income; there was very little business because of the way show jumping was set up. With thirty-six or forty-eight entries to an individual event or class it could last anything up to two and a half hours from start to finish. Something needed to be done to sharpen up the shows and I sat down with that maestro of the sport, Raymond Brooks-Ward, who commentates so splendidly at many of the arenas throughout the country and, of course, on the BBC.

Not too much seemed to happen without Raymond being involved. He was the head of British Equestrian Promotions and had as his side-kick David Broome, who was a leading rider of that era. We talked of the possibility of splitting an event into four heats, with eight or twelve competitors in each and the top three from each heat going into a twelve-strong final. While this would provide betting opportunities throughout a whole afternoon or evening, I also felt that it would be more interesting to the spectators. I knew that regular watchers, like the equestrian press writers, for example, had reached the stage where they would only watch a jump-off against the clock, so boring had it all become.

The show-jumping hierarchy, however, seem to have one foot in the last century and the other in their graves almost. Certainly they could see no further than the ends of their noses. They simply were not prepared to listen to the arguments or to consider any changes. Raymond Brooks-Ward and Douglas Bunn had done their best, but I came to the conclusion that it was time to leave show jumping to the horses.

However, this was not before I learned of one attempted coup, in which a dozen riders tried to take me for the sort of ride for which you do not require a saddle. It was at Devon, a country show, not one of the big ones like Wembley or Olympia, and I must say that I was satisfied in the end that it was done for a little Harvey Smith-style fun, rather than to take Ladbrokes for a lot of money. Led by Harvey, the twelve riders, who believed that between them they would produce the winner of a certain class, got together and organised just who should win. Then they had their bets with me. But they counted without two people: the Chinaman on my shoulder, who was always looking out for me, and a rank outsider whom they had omitted from their 'ring' – and he came through to win. I discovered the attempted coup only because Harvey told me of it later.

While I enjoyed my visits to show jumping and got on famously with some of the most likeable people in the sport like David Broome, Ted Edgar, Harvey of course and Alan Oliver in particular, who often advised me in the way that Godfrey Evans does at cricket, the world of politics was more my scene and it was Westminster rather than the Wembley arena that was to bring another milestone in my life.

In 1964, Harold Wilson had won a momentous General Election by just five seats. It was never going to be a big enough majority and, two years on, he was finding it extremely difficult to get any sort of positive legislation through the House of Commons and needed to go to the country to get a mandate to turn Britain into what I hoped would be a truly Socialist nation.

At Ladbrokes we were hopeful of another exciting period in the run-up to this 1966 Election and were not to be disappointed, although we little realised quite the avalanche of money that was to rush into our offices. Until this time, £1 million had never been laid upon a single event. Not even the biggest of betting mediums, the Derby and Grand National, had engendered such a figure and the £640,000 we had taken on the 1964 Election was, in fact, still the record. We wondered whether we might this time just crack the million barrier. To bookmakers, this was an awesome, Everest of a target.

As it turned out, we did not crack the barrier, we burst through it, and carried on taking people's money until polling day, when our accounts department calculated that we had just topped £1,600,000. The excitement we had hoped for exceeded all expectation and the day the millionth pound was actually laid was worth – well, it was worth another £1 million in publicity to us. Today, it would be impossible to target the person who actually laid the millionth pound; Ladbrokes have around 2,000 betting shops in Britain alone and if anyone did come up with such a person it would have to be a fake. The computer isn't made that could single out the one person as we were able to in 1966 when we had only twenty or so betting shops and were thus able to pinpoint the precise moment and the precise backer.

Television cameras, radio crews and newspaper reporters and photographers jammed our offices in Ganton Street, just around the corner from the world-famous

Carnaby Street, and the 'Million Man' was fêted, photographed, interviewed and finally given a free bet by a grateful Ron Pollard. It was a feat that has yet to be repeated. Other bookmakers, William Hill included, recognised that whatever their principles or feelings, they could no longer give Ladbrokes exclusivity with political betting; they desired their share of the cash and the publicity. I have no doubt that someone, probably Ladbrokes, will beat the £1 million mark again, for we came pretty close in the 1987 Election. With approximately 40 per cent of the market, we took £940,000 of the £2.5 million laid. Just as Christmas shopping is a 'record' every year, because people spend more as a result of inflation, no doubt in years to come our £1,600,000 will also be broken. But remember, that amount will then probably be worth £15 million.

Labour won by ninety-nine seats, eminently satisfactory to Harold Wilson (he half jested that England's World Cup victory had helped his cause!) and to Cyril Stein and myself as Labour supporters and the winning bookmakers. I had predicted a 101- or 103-seat majority and had they taken just one more seat I would have won an additional £50,000. But, I was not complaining about the result either financially for Ladbrokes or politically for myself. Although Wilson was, in my opinion, to let down his true Socialist supporters in the long term, this was a moment of joyful anticipation.

I was now spending more and more time at the House of Commons, meeting all sorts of people. Gerald Nabarro, a wonderfully extrovert Conservative MP who sported a quite magnificent moustache became a great mate. He would ring me and say, "Ron, I will have £100 on our chap in the Rugby by-election. By the way, you can tell the papers!" As a self-publicist, he was in the Bernard Docker class, but it did not matter. He wanted what I wanted, if for a slightly different reason. Gerald would introduce me to a host of other Members, and I would lunch at the House with him when he would encourage others to ring me. I still have the menu from one lunch there in May 1966

– it was 10s. 6d. (52½p) per person, which shows how times change!

On another, later, occasion, I was invited to lunch at White's Club, that haven of Conservatism and the high and mighty if ever there was one (its members include HRH the Prince of Wales, the Dukes of Atholl and Argyll, and sundry lesser noblemen). In all my years I could never have envisaged stepping through the front door of such an establishment, yet here I was in 1975, taking wine and sitting at the same table as all these arch-Tories, all in the way of business. Try as I might, I simply cannot recall now who had invited me (although I do know that he had to pay), but I well remember another Tory MP joining us while we were still at the bar having a drink.

He inquired what the odds were on Mrs Thatcher to win the election for the Conservative Party leadership that was by then under way. "Fifty to one," I responded, only to be told: "I would be very careful, if I were you." I was a little alarmed at this, because it was clearly meant as a genuine warning; furthermore, this was White's Club and members here were likely to know something that I did not. As I pondered this, my antenna went up to the red alert mark and, lunch over, I hurried back to my office and immediately cut the odds on Mrs Thatcher to 20-1.

If even that price looks slightly ludicrous today, you have to remember that the Conservative Party had been dominated by male leaders like Pitt and Disraeli, Churchill and Macmillan, not working-class girls from corner shops in Grantham, even if this one was an honours graduate of Oxford University. However one looked at the situation, it just was not feasible that she could beat Ted Heath, who was a figure of some stature, particularly in Europe. Never did I think I would be so grateful to a Conservative MP, but I was. That man in White's Club certainly saved me a lot of money with those words of caution. Even though I clipped the odds there were still people who backed Maggie at 50-1 and a lot more at 20-1, but it might have been very much worse.

By 1987, when the 20-1 shot had been Prime Minister for about eight years, I was an experienced and established TV and radio performer. There were times when I was on the box on a regular basis and I did not think I could be surprised or alarmed by anything that might happen to me. I was wrong. Quite out of the blue I was approached by Andrew Jennings, chief researcher to ITV's World in Action programme (and another marvellous chap with similar political views to myself!).

Over lunch he asked if I would be prepared to appear in the World in Action programme they were planning from the Conservative Party conference in Blackpool. After a little argy-bargy over my fee, I agreed. Anything for a laugh, I said, and a few days of sea breezes would do me a power of good. However, things were not quite as I had envisaged them. Instead of simply calling the odds on who might succeed Margaret Thatcher as leader (she was under siege that far back), a bit player in the programme, it transpired that I was to be the centrepiece of it all; the star.

I had arrived at Manchester Airport and was met by Andrew Jennings. As we were being driven to Blackpool, he said: "Let me tell you a few things about interviewing." I was puzzled. Interviewing? What, I asked, did he mean by that? Andrew explained that the idea was for me to interview MPs and other delegates to the conference, seeking their opinions upon who would be, if indeed there was to be, the new leader. I was absolutely terrified at the prospect. There would be a world of difference, I feared, between being the interviewee as I had so often been in the past, and being the interviewer, which I had never been. Then Andrew dropped another bombshell: my first interview was to be with Michael Heseltine.

My recollection of Heseltine was of seeing him, on BBC, storming off after the Westland affair and of reading about him whirling the Mace around in the House of Commons, to be known thereafter as 'Tarzan'. It was with considerable trepidation, therefore, that I approached him at a fringe meeting to ask if he would be a candidate should there be an election for a new leader (and this, remember, was in 1987 – not 1990 when he was considered the 'assassin' of Mrs Thatcher for standing against her). He was courteous throughout the interview, although he played what was to become a very familiar straight bat to any searching question, and I left after the interview very much happier than when I had arrived. I shall always be grateful to Michael for that; had he been awkward, he could easily have destroyed me and would certainly have made subsequent interviews very much more difficult.

Looking back, I found myself pleasantly surprised at how well some of the interviews went, with John Biffen, Teddy Taylor and particularly Kenneth Clarke. We even visited a fortune-teller along Blackpool's famous 'Golden Mile' and her prophecy was to agree with mine – that Kenneth Baker would emerge as the next leader of the Conservative Party. These were pre-John Major days, of course, and I had been rooting for Baker from the day I reached Blackpool, chalking him up on my board, which was shown several times during the half-hour programme, as a 4-1 chance. It was most satisfying when a World in Action poll, taken among delegates at the Conference, put Baker at the head of the list. But Heseltine was an outstanding choice in the event of the Tories losing the next election and electing a new leader subsequent to that. When the programme came out the following Monday, I had to admit that I was delighted with my performance and its whole presentation. Strangely, though, no one has asked me to do another. I wonder why! Perhaps I should go back to Blackpool and ask Gypsy Rose Lee whether that was also in the stars!

What I do not need the gypsy lady to tell me is that it was a brilliant PR scoop. World in Action is a major programme; it has a vast audience, comprising many of what newspapers call A and B readers. As Stanley Longstaff had told me so many years before, you simply cannot buy that sort of promotion and publicity.

5

THE NATIONAL: SEVEN GLORIOUS YEARS

The detractors of bookmakers are many and I feel we at Ladbrokes have often been quite unfairly denigrated down the years. Whatever we did, some people would look for a reason to criticise our honourable intentions. I think we proved in 1974 that we had then, as now, the good of the community and the racing areas particularly in mind when we bought Lingfield racetrack in Surrey, one of the prettiest courses in the country and a most splendid circuit for a Derby trial. When it looked as though it was going to be closed we agreed with Cyril Stein that it would be tragic if it did not exist. With not a little persuasion from the Epsom trainer, John Sutcliffe, who turned out Specify to win the 1971 Grand National, we agreed to buy the whole Lingfield estate for £500,000 and run the racecourse. Rather aptly, one of the properties we took on was called Carewell Lodge, which was used as a training centre for Ladbroke executives.

When, shortly after, Ladbrokes were asked if they would step into the growing crisis over the future of the Grand National by purchasing Aintree, we at first refused because we had no real idea what it would entail. It was clear that something had to be done if the Grand National was not to die but others – including the Horserace Betting Levy Board – were reported to be interested and I think we expected action from them or perhaps the Jockey Club. Aintree had been in considerable decline for many years.

Money was not spent in updating the place and finally the Topham family, whose name was synonymous with the National, sold out for £3 million to a man called Bill Davies – certainly not a racing man but a property developer who ran a company called the Walton Group. As far as I could ascertain at the time, he expected to be given building permission for the course after local elections, only to find that the wrong party won.

He was left with a white elephant and not an idea as to how he should handle the situation. His way in 1975 was to increase admission prices dramatically. As a result, the attendance slumped to only 10,000 and you could have played a game of football in the area behind the County Stand. When he came to count the takings, Davies must have had a shock because not that many actually paid to get in. The regulars simply 'jibbed in' – giving the gateman a fiver for himself instead of the £20 Davies was seeking. It was a perfect demonstration of how not to run a racecourse and it was clear to me, as I watched the Irish horse L'Escargot beat Red Rum that afternoon, that unless the course changed hands we had seen the last Grand National.

My view was then and remains today that all the press speculation about running it at another venue was rubbish. The National was unique to Aintree, it belonged there; it could not be run on any other course. At Ladbrokes we talked constantly of the problem. We all felt that the race was a part of our heritage and had to be saved at all costs. We wondered if we could possibly lease the course and manage the whole event. It is impossible to say now whose idea that was; I think it just derived from the lengthy chats we held among ourselves during the summer. In the November we entered into secret discussions with Davies, the prelude to an horrendous time with certainly more difficult negotiations than I had ever endured. They left us drained physically and mentally, and saw headline after headline predicting gloom and doom for the Aintree course and its big race.

Although we were still reluctant to purchase outright, we

did begin these negotiations with an offer of £1.5 million to buy Davies out completely. This was rejected and so we offered to lease the course at £125,000 a year, only to be told that he required £200,000, plus a share of the profits. It was clear that he wanted to get back his outlay of £3 million as quickly as he could – but everyone in racing was telling him that racing could not pay for his mistakes. My dear old friend George Wigg put things into fine focus for Davies as the bitter battle went on when he said, almost ramming the words down the man's throat: "When the shadows lengthen and your hair has turned grey, you may regret that you have gone down as the man who killed the Grand National." The noble lord was merely summing up what all the newspaper headlines were stating – that it looked the end for the National. Cyril Stein said that he 'loved the race' more than any other, adding: "The National must be saved. I personally will be delighted, whether we run it or not. I will be very sad if there isn't one because I feel that if there is no race in 1976 there will never be another one."

It was probably because of our deep feelings for the event that even when times were at their darkest we kept discussions open. Only once did even we think that all was lost. Finally, after two hours of talking in Davies' Mayfair offices in early December, we thought we could get a deal at £180,000 – a small drop from the £200,000 Davies had been insisting upon from the outset. We left the room for a private discussion and agreed that if that was what it was going to cost to save the National, then we would pay. We trooped back and in happy frame of mind at last told Davies we would pay him £180,000 and the share of other monies he sought. When he replied: "No. No. I am not taking £180,000," we were stunned, we thought that was what he wanted. Davies simply would not budge. Now in considerable anger, we stormed out. "You cannot deal with the man. We have done our best," fumed Cyril – and he never spoke a truer word. In racing terms, as we put it at the time, what in the afternoon had been an odds-on bet that we would be saving the Grand National, and organising its running at Aintree the following April, was in the evening long odds-against. The back page headline in the *Daily Express* summed it up perfectly for us – 'National takes a nosedive'.

All sorts of stories now started to creep into the papers. Corals and William Hill were alleged to be thinking of a bid, but we never ever took that one seriously. (They were simply sneaking in on the publicity.) There were reports of 'secret consortiums' and inevitably all sorts of suggestions that the National could be run at Haydock, Doncaster, Newcastle or even Sandown. I actually ran a book on this – probably to retain my sense of humour. Can you imagine it, the National which had always been run over thorn fences at Aintree being staged at a park course like Sandown, beautiful though it is?

Behind the scenes, however, we maintained our links with the Davies advisers. The National simply had to be saved.

Sir Desmond (now Lord) Plummer who was chairman of the Levy Board also continued talking to Davies and on December 22 the Jockey Club gave the bearded Liverpudlian an ultimatum. If he did not submit satisfactory arrangements to them within seven days, they would run a 'National Steeplechase' at Doncaster instead of the Grand National at Liverpool.

Whether or not they would have carried out this ultimatum I am not sure – but it served to frighten Davies. We had left our offer on the table and so, at the eleventh hour, we were back in the Walton Group offices talking money. This time Cyril took the view that time was not simply running out – it had run out. If John Hughes, our chosen Clerk of the Course, was to be able to plan the meeting and have a National that Ladbrokes would be proud of, we had to do a deal that evening. So, around six, Cyril was back in Chesterfield Street to offer everything Davies had been demanding from the outset. We proposed a seven-year deal (we did not wish to go on longer, not being sure

76

how much money might be needed to get a safety certificate for the rundown County Stand). In that seven years we would manage the race, but not own the course; and we would pay £1.5 million for the right to do so.

Eventually, around seven, Cyril came bursting into the Ladbroke Club, where I had been waiting for him. "We've done it. We have done it. Organise a press conference." "When for?" I queried. "When do you think for? Tonight," he retorted. "Get them all here – radio, TV and newspapers." And in a hectic hour or so I arranged for all the TV cameras and the newspapers to be at the Ladbroke Club for nine o'clock and ensured that BBC got enough in advance for their Nine O'Clock News.

It was the most incredible task that we set John Hughes. With Christmas and the New Year upon us and the race that no one thought would ever take place just thirteen weeks away it was really unfair. But he never once complained; he set to and from the moment the press conference was over until the race was run on April 3, he did not stop working.

I hardly need to say of course that the Grand National was a huge success. In our first year we halved the entrance price and lifted the crowd from 10,000 to 42,000 and by the end of our seven years the crowds had risen to 64,000. That was a tremendous effort on our marketing men's part because we knew we were never going to see again the massive pre-war six-figure crowds. Television had put paid to those; people now had a better and more comfortable view at home with the BBC's quite brilliant coverage. With those pictures being beamed around the world to over 700 million viewers it meant that Ladbrokes' name was known everywhere, which was to be very important as they grew into an international company.

I enjoyed going to Aintree each year immensely, but it was always hard work for my Press Officer, Mike Dillon, and myself. Mike particularly, having come from Manchester and knowing lots of people up there, did a lot of local radio broadcasts and I would have television and my regular Radio Four programme on the morning of the race. We would stay either at the Adelphi or the Atlantic Towers and would rise very early and go straight to the morning gallops at the track. The fresh, early-spring sun glinting across the course would exhilarate you for the rest of the day, and we always had our little flask with us! We would go back for breakfast and then always return to the track for eleven. It was hectic but it was marvellous.

That first year, 1976, was marked for me by two events – Cyril Stein's dilemma as to whether he could attend and by the 14-1 victory of Rag Trade. As one of Britain's leading Orthodox Jews and a man who devoted himself to raising money for their special charity, the Joint Palestine Appeal, Cyril would never do business deals or travel except by foot on the Sabbath. Yet he felt it so important that he should be there on this occasion that he agonised over what to do. He finally solved his problem by booking into a tiny hotel near to Aintree (in some considerable contrast to the five-star splendour of the Adelphi, I must say) and walking to the course, where he was inundated with congratulations for 'saving the day'.

Rag Trade was ridden by the underrated John Burke and was trained by that lovely West Countryman, Fred Rimell, who never rode a National winner but trained three (he also had Nicolaus Silver at 28-1 in 1961 and Gay Trip, ridden so well by that master horseman, Pat Taaffe, at 15-1 in 1970). The real romance of the race came via the owner – Mr P. B. Raymond, better known as Mr Teasy-Weasy, the Court hairdresser. He had suffered greatly over the years from cancer and it was a joy for me to see him and his lovely wife in the winner's enclosure, even though it meant that Red Rum was once again consigned to second place.

It was Red Rum's year in 1977, a day when grown men cried for joy; a day that belonged to him and him alone. He won for an historic third time and at the incredible price of 9-1. It was an absolutely wonderful National and how Rummy's dear old owner, the octogenarian Norman le Mare, survived the day, I do not know. If people had had any faith at all, they would have made Red Rum a hot favourite. Just think about it: he had won in 1973 and '74; carried 12 stone in 1975 and run second as the 7-2 favourite: and in 1976, with 11 st 10 lb, he had again been second at 10-1. His record was impeccable and he showed what he thought of those odds of 9-1 by carrying 11 st 8 lb and winning by a ridiculous twenty-five lengths. I was so elated at seeing history made, so excited at being there when a horse won the Grand National for the third time, that I stormed into the Press Room immediately after the race and shouted, "We have lost a quarter of a million and I don't care" (only to be told later by Mr Stein, "Let us hope it doesn't happen too often"). It will always be one of my great memories, even though as a race it was pretty uneventful, being won by such a margin.

What a truly wonderful horse Red Rum was. He could only produce his great performances at Aintree. You would see him there, whether he was in the race or in the parade of old champions that now graces National Day each year, and he would look as though he owned the place; indeed, even his trainer, Ginger McCain, had a different step when he walked across Aintree's vast acres. He is a big man, Ginger, and yet he seemed to grow by a couple of feet as he strode through the gates.

There was another fine race in 1978 when three horses went for the winning post with only one length between them, but there was not to be the excitement of the previous year. How could there be? Lucius was to beat Sebastian V by half a length with a 50-1 outsider, Drumroan, third. This was a splendid training feat by the Northerner, Gordon Richards who was making his mark as an outstanding NH handler.

I seem to remember that the BBC's Cliff Morgan had a good celebration the following year. Cliff, later to be honoured personally by the Queen with the CVO, was a good friend of the Rugby-playing John Douglas who owned Rubstic and Cliff had been freely tipping this one to win from early morning as he flew into Speke Airport. David Montague's Zongalero was second and a really good Aintree horse, Rough and Tumble ridden by Johnny Francome, the all-time great jockey who was never to win a National, came third. I had to content myself with watching this 1979 race on TV. I had gone up to Aintree but I was then called back to London in a hurry, I think because a by-election had been announced by Jim Callaghan. I remember listening to the radio in the morning and hearing Judith Chalmers telling the nation that "The Grand National will not be the same this year; Ron Pollard isn't here." What a lovely girl!

There was never a bad National, but it would be fair to say that 1980, when I was back in my usual place, was a little lack-lustre. It was saved, perhaps, by becoming the Grand Inter-National – Ben Nevis was American-owned, although trained by Tim Forster at Wantage, and was ridden by an American amateur, Charlie Fenwick. Who was second? John Francome again on Rough and Tumble, but Ben Nevis was a very comfortable winner indeed; John was never in with a shout. The Pilgarlic came third and there remain two pleasing memories: the crowds were now over 50,000 and it was a good year for the bookies. Ben Nevis started at 40-1 and while there were a few very nice little touches, it was a much nicer earner for us!

No one could have dreamed of the drama and the romance that 1981 was to bring – the year of Bob Champion and Aldaniti. It was the most emotional day in horse racing, never mind Grand National history. You could not have written the script – we had to write that afterwards when our Ladbroke film company produced that tear-jerking epic *Champions* which told the story of Bob and his horse. Bob had been a cancer victim and yet, with immense courage, had conquered this killer disease. To ride a horse at something like thirty miles an hour around any racetrack you have to be fit. Bob doubted that he had the strength to get around the four and a half miles of formidable Aintree fences: The Chair, Valentine's and

Becher's most famous Brook. But he had dreamed through all the agonising treatment hours of riding in the National again and here on this spring afternoon 'The Impossible Dream' was about to be fulfilled. Taking part was the aim – winning was not something to be considered seriously. And yet the public had taken him to their hearts. They backed him in their thousands and Aldaniti – who had also been nursed back to health having broken down with leg trouble at Sandown the previous November – was down to 10-1 by the off.

As the two of them came to The Elbow the cheers from the huge crowd were deafening. We were watching the impossible happen. The tears were streaming down my face and I was not alone. There wasn't a dry eye to be seen. Every single person around me seemed to be crying with joy for Bob Champion. It was the most emotional moment sport can have ever known. As I say, it was not a story any writer would have dreamed of scripting beforehand, but what a memorable film it made when we got around to it. I saw an early release in a little film theatre in Wardour Street – and we all cried again. If anyone has not seen *Champions* I can only say, go to the video shop and see if you can hire it. It is magnificent and there is some wonderful music in it too. It is a shame that a sequel was never produced, for that could have shown how Bob, with his new motto 'Life is for Living', launched himself into a new career as a trainer and into raising vast sums for other cancer victims with selfless dedication.

Hardly surprisingly, much of the day's glory was stolen from Aldaniti's trainer Josh Gifford and owner, Mr Nikki Embiricos, which was a pity because he had been a very good supporter of National Hunt racing and he deserved his success. The 'rage' that year had been Spartan Missile, another marvellous horse that typified those who made the National such an event year after year. He was a good old hunter and was to be ridden by his owner, Mr John Thorne. He was not exactly a slimline farmer and he did go on a diet, but there was a little campaign for a professional jockey to be given the ride and hopefully a better chance of winning. But John was determined to be in the saddle himself and, starting at 8-1, he and Spartan Missile ran second, beaten by four lengths. Whether a jockey like Francome would have made any difference to the result one will never be able to say. I am only glad that we had the result we did and a sporting occasion that will never be forgotten and is unlikely ever to be equalled. I for only one would never wish it to be.

Despite all the money we had spent – and it did come to nearer £4 million than the £1.5 million we intended to invest – and all our efforts, the truth of the matter is that after six years Aintree was still run-down. It was and remains a crying shame that the course is used for three days' racing only each year and that, in reality, is just one day; for while the standard of racing has been dramatically improved on all three days, there is only one that has the magical attraction and that is Grand National day. No matter what we did to stimulate interest on the first two days, we had only limited success. I only hope that the Jockey Club can see their way clear to giving Aintree back the November fixture it used to have; it deserves that support at least.

As we came to our final race the seven years seemed to have flown. It was with considerable satisfaction that we were able to announce that 64,000 people had paid to watch the 1982 event and I derived some pleasure from the fact that Frank Gilman, a Midlands farmer whom I had known for many years, owned the winner. Frank was one of those lucky punters; he had a five-figure bet on the Tories to win an election some years before and they did. Now he was backing his own horse, Grittar, and that won.

Ridden by an amateur, Charles Saunders, Grittar started at 7-1 favourite and had been my tip to anyone who cared to listen for some weeks. Like John Thorne, Frank also trained his horse and he clearly did a good job. He beat Hard Outlook, a 50-1 outsider ridden by Anthony Webber, by fifteen lengths and a long way back third was Richard Hoare on Loving Words.

Because of the ease of Grittar's victory, it was not a particularly memorable end to our seven years, but I looked back on them with enormous satisfaction. Had it not been for Ladbrokes – and Cyril Stein in particular – Aintree would by then have been a car park and a part of our national heritage would have been lost. We had enjoyed some fantastic publicity and become known throughout the world thanks to television; we had savoured some truly outstanding moments and great races; and we had built up a splendid relationship with News International who sponsored the Grand National through their *News of the World* and *Sun* newspapers for virtually the whole period that we staged the event. We had an unhappy year with Colt Cars, who took over in 1979 and whom I found to be particularly difficult people to deal with.

I got on famously with Rupert Murdoch, who owns papers here, in Australia and in America. If we ever land on Mars and find a newspaper there, I will lay 2-1 it is owned by Rupert! He and his executives, Bruce Matthews (who is now the boss of SIS, the racing satellite service that Ladbrokes partly own) and Sir Larry Lamb who went on to edit the *Daily Express* after making the *Sun* such a huge success and is now retired in deepest Devon, were tough to deal with but never went back on their word: once they settled on something, it was done. Whenever we had to negotiate, they would invite us to lunch at one splendid restaurant or another in the West End. Larry, who was an expert on Bordeaux vintages would select the wines for lunch and always ask, "Shall we have an experience today or a bargain?" loving nothing better than to find a decent bottle that he considered the restaurant had underpriced. Magnificent they were too, just as the *Sun* were magnificent sponsors. But I do believe that they had a good return for their money.

In the way that I was later to evaluate darts and our involvement with that sport, so Murdoch could evaluate his links with the Grand National: racing sells newspapers, and they were being seen to be the leaders of their industry when it came to supporting that sport.

We set aside a very large room in the County Stand right over the winning post for News International and their guests and I looked after them personally, making sure that they were comfortable, wanted for nothing and that if people wished to bet they could do so without fighting their way down to the enclosure.

I found Rupert a very nice gentleman indeed (even if events at Wapping did later disillusion me a little). He would come up and put an arm around my shoulder and say: "Take me down to the paddock and show me what is going on." And then he would always ask me, "Well, what do I back?"

As the 1983 Grand National drew near there seemed a gigantic void in my life. For seven years I had been absorbed into the frenetic organisation and had played a major role on the day itself. Now, suddenly, I was in a vacuum. I knew I had to go to Aintree, if only to see how someone else ran the event, but I didn't have to go there to work and deep down inside me I felt that if we were no longer involved and I had no responsibility, then I did not wish to be there. So it was with a slightly heavy heart that I travelled up to Liverpool with my wife and my mood did not improve as I wandered around with nothing to do and not knowing where to go – you can actually tire of guzzling champagne. But Lady Luck was with me when I ran into Rod Gunner, who was the right-hand man to show-business impresario Robert Stigwood. Good old Rod had horses with Jenny Pitman, who was running Corbiere in the big race, and he invited Pat and me to join the party in his box. Who did we find ourselves standing next to when the National started but Jenny herself. If only I had had a camera with me as I watched her during Corbiere's run from the last to the winning post, I could have made a small fortune from a newspaper. As Greasepaint, over from Ireland with Clem Magnier up, battled it out with Ben de

Haan and Corbiere, Jenny's face showed every emotion that a human being can endure. As Corbiere passed the post, a 13-1 winner with three-quarters of a length to spare over the 14-1 Irish horse, it was pandemonium; she was in tears and the box erupted.

Jenny had to rush down to the winner's enclosure and the world was able to share that emotion as she was interviewed on television. Then the party really started! Those few hours made it more than worthwhile for me to attend Aintree in 1983 but I have not been back since: I simply do not feel as though I am a part of it any more.

Certainly the National is unique but until I was involved in it I would have looked upon it as a handicap, not to be confused in any way with the top-class racing you would see at Cheltenham. I think that position has changed a little in the past ten years or so; the standard of racing there has improved quite considerably thanks to sponsorship and there are now some high-quality fields. I have always enjoyed National Hunt racing but I do like to see good horses, which is why I have not missed many Cheltenham Festivals, but I would have to think long and hard about whether I saw this National or that one; basically I used to go there only to bet in my early days when I was out in the field. The alterations to the Liverpool course, particularly the changes to Becher's where horse and rider cannot land up in the drink any more, have in my opinion downgraded the race. But the Grand National remains a tremendous test of bravery for the horse as well as for the man. Anyone who thinks the horse doesn't know what is going on knows nothing about horses. You only have to look at Red Rum. He knows precisely where he is the moment he goes through those gates and begins to behave as though he is Royalty. And is there a man alive who would deny that he is just that – the King of Aintree?

6

ONE-HUNDRED-AND-EIGHTY!

There are many reasons why companies pump money into sponsorship: to increase their public awareness, to develop good community relations or perhaps even to satisfy the whim of a chairman's wife! We spent the better part of £4 million on the Grand National over seven years, because we wished to protect the interests of racing and something that we considered to be part of the nation's heritage. We went into the Boat Race almost by Royal command; into snooker and golf because we thought there was the possibility of a little exposure on television; into darts because it equated with our business, and into the Booker Prize because I was turning over a new leaf! No; I jest. We went into betting on who would win the big book prizes for the same reason we entered every other arena – to win publicity for our company, to be the pacemakers of our profession and to make some money if that was at all possible at one and the same time.

The exception, the one that was different, I suppose, was the Boat Race. British institution it may have been, but I was always against our sponsorship of this two-horse affair up the River Thames and so were most of the Ladbroke executives. It was not right for our image, I doubted how much co-operation we might get from the BBC who had televised it for ten years and, while we had run a book on the race for a time, I certainly did not see any extra business being generated by our becoming sponsors. I considered it a non-starter – but Cyril Stein was insistent.

We had staged a charity night gala dinner at our Caesar's Palace Casino in Luton which actually raised £10,000 for Boat Race funds and was attended by Princess Margaret, whose former husband Lord Snowdon once coxed Cambridge. While some of the biggest names in show business were entertaining us, Her Royal Highness slipped Cyril a real Mickey Finn: "Why don't you sponsor the Boat Race?" The event, founded in 1829, was in rough water. Apart from the BBC fee there was little income. Spectators, who sometimes numbered many thousands, paid nothing to stand on the riverbank, yet the costs of putting it on were escalating.

The boats were costing £2,500 apiece and Alan Mays-Smith, who had rowed for Cambridge in 1955 and was now the London Representative, which meant he acted as secretary to the Boat Race, had been desperately seeking funds. He approached over forty firms without reward and when the Princess spoke to Cyril in 1976 there was a genuine fear that the 122nd Boat Race might well be the last. Mays-Smith must have been a very much happier man than I as he stood on the towpath on the day before the race drinking Ladbrokes' champagne which Cyril poured to celebrate our £20,000 a year sponsorship. I could not see us getting that sort of money back even if Oxford (hot favourites at 2-5) were to sink. I was not a bad judge, although we struck gold in 1981 when Sue Brown became the first girl to take part in the race. Every paper, including the *Financial Times*, had stories about this pert and tiny twenty-two-year-old from Honiton who was making history. What is more, she was doing so on merit. More than thirty men had aspirations at coxing the Oxford boat, but Sue was chosen as the best of the lot. There wasn't a lot of her, at 5 ft 2 ins and 6 st 8 lb, but she insisted that she was going to be the boss, although she would try not to swear at her crew! Pictures of her being hoisted high by 6 ft 7 in fellows were lapped up and used everywhere. But

that was our one stroke of good fortune. The rest of the
time we managed to manufacture a few 'rows' that made
the papers, but the BBC were generally as unhelpful and
argumentative as I had feared. They seemed to do their
best to ensure that their cameras never quite picked up the
sweaters, T-shirts and anoraks I had designed and which
carried our name, even though it was quite small. And they
were most insistent about what advertising signs we could
– or more importantly we could not – put up along the
route.

It was a desperately frustrating time. We stayed as sponsors for a decade – but we never had a fair deal. The BBC
seemed to operate double standards. You were told, "You
cannot do this . . ." and "You cannot do that . . ." and
then you switched on the TV set the next day to something
like Ski Sunday only to find the screen full of advertisements, far worse than anything you ever envisaged. Perhaps the worst part of it all was the inability to talk with
anyone who mattered about your problem. The Boat Race,
like the Grand National, could well have died but for Ladbroke intervention and money, but instead of saying
"Thank you" many people were looking for hidden reasons
for our action.

There were those in the media who then – and indeed
to this day – refused to give credit to sponsors or mention
them in their programmes or in their newspapers. Thank
goodness there were one or two who took a much more
rational view: that without big sponsors there was no big
sport, and without big sport they would have nothing with
which to fill their sports pages. Whenever you tried to
discuss any of these problems with the BBC, however, you
could never speak with the person who actually made the
decisions; you were dealing only with the people who said
that they had their orders from higher up – from people
you never saw. Whatever they do, BBC Sport does marvel-
lously; certainly no one as yet does it better. But they do
seem to get caught up in swirls of bureaucracy.

The one 'story' that summed up the experience for me

was in the year, quite early in our sponsorship, when I was marooned with the *Financial Times* reporter on a boat that had broken down. I was invited to follow the race in that flotilla of launches and cruisers which meanders in the wake of the boats, and ours conked out. Thank goodness there was a sufficiency of alcoholic beverage aboard, for we were not on dry land for a couple of hours or so and at the best of times I am a very bad sailor.

I am not much of a golfer, either, but when we were invited to consider betting on the game I thought we should experiment. Lewis Rowe was a superb marketing man with John Player. He saw the value of having betting on events and was as keen as I was for the name of his company to get into newspapers. It was, therefore, a happy coming together of like spirits when he invited Malcolm Palmer and myself to be his guests at Turnberry for the John Player Classic. He had arranged for a tent to be erected for us but there was no real money about – just small change. This was no more than I had expected, but it fed my ego to be able to say that "I was first" when anyone talked about betting on golf. And anyway, there were far worse places that I could have been. The Turnberry is a fine hotel, and golfers are among the nicest people you will ever come across in sport. We were eating good food, drinking nice wine and generally enjoying ourselves. No one could have made us more welcome than Lewis and his team. The two things that I most remember about those few days were learning from Harry Carpenter just how much it cost to televise a golf tournament. Then (in 1971) it was around £20,000 so I suspect it is ten times that amount today. The second and greatest memory of Turnberry was waking one morning to find the tented village no longer there. Gales during the night had devastated it!

Years later, in October 1979, I was to be devastated myself by watching the World Matchplay Championship at Wentworth. In a marketing exercise for some luxurious houses they were building in Scotland, which even then were priced at £71,000, Bovis were offering one as a prize for a hole in one at a specified hole. Wishing to 'insure' against paying out, they asked me for odds. I offered them 40-1 which on reflection was a little generous – but then we learn from our mistakes – and they invested £1,000. The event was being televised and it was my misfortune to turn the set on in my office just as they were showing Isao Aoki, one of the many Japanese players who have become favourites on the European circuit, play a tee-shot early in the day. I could not believe my eyes. Aoki struck the ball and it bounced on the green once, then a second time and a third before disappearing down the hole. At no stage did it run along the green. I went up to see Peter George, the managing director of the Racing Division. "Good morning," he said brightly. "Not really," I replied. "We have already lost forty grand."

I suppose I still had not accepted that golf was not really for me when in the early 1980s I went to see John Jacobs, who is now a famous coach, but had been a Ryder Cup player and then the captain, and who was a power behind the scenes in those days. I explained that Ladbrokes were prepared to sponsor the Ryder Cup at home and across the Atlantic, but even though I offered £180,000 we were rejected. That idea actually came from Cyril Stein, and it was not until some time later that I realised that he was even then involving us in America as part of his grand plan for the future.

My final disillusionment came in 1988, when I had discussions with Ken Schofield, the Scot who runs the PGA European tour so brilliantly, about betting at their tournaments. I think Ken once worked in a bank, and he certainly had a Scottish shrewdness when it came to money. He would let us bet at only eight tournaments (and golf was not like cricket, where we had permanent marquees at the Test grounds) and he wanted a fee and a share of the profits; I am not sure of the precise figures now, but it certainly was not viable as far as I was concerned, and I was quite happy to see William Hill try to make it so.

If golf was to find me constantly bunkered, darts was a

bullseye. The equation I referred to in the introduction to this chapter simply meant that it added up: darts meant pubs, pubs meant betting, betting meant Ladbrokes, and Ladbrokes would mean darts. That, anyway, was my thinking when I first moved on to the oche.

It all began when, on a cold day early in 1971, Peter Thompson, our Marketing Director, and myself met Olly and Lorna Croft to discuss how Ladbrokes could help the London Darts Organisation. Olly and Lorna are big people in every way, but by far the biggest part of them is their heart. They are successful in their business life (Olly is a high-class tiler) but that business has always suffered as a result of their devotion – for over twenty years – to darts. Without them there would never have been a British Darts Organisation which now spans the world. I was pleased for Eric Bristow when the Queen honoured him with an MBE. But without Olly and Lorna there would not be a darts set-up as we know it today; no one would have ever heard of Eric Bristow or anyone else. A knighthood for Olly, who formed and still runs the BDO, would not, in my opinion, be amiss. I immediately admired their honesty and sincerity – they had an ability to speak plainly. When we asked where they might wish to lunch, Olly said he had noticed a Henekeys pub just around the corner; that would do. So we had beer and sandwiches there and began a business relationship that lasted for nearly two decades and a friendship that has lasted even longer.

I know that Olly thinks highly of my involvement in his sport – in fact, at my retirement party he presented me with a wooden plaque in appreciation of 'all his help and friendship over sixteen years'. I treasure that plaque, which sits alongside the photographs of Mum and Dad, my grandfather and one of myself and Neil Kinnock together. Olly has also been quoted as saying that he learned a lot about betting and life from me and that I was good for darts. Well, meeting Olly and Lorna was good for me.

Our first event was a Festival of Darts at the Seashore Holiday Centre we owned at Caister, near Great Yarmouth. This incorporated a British Matchplay Championship and was a huge success. Being staged in September, it helped to fill caravans at the centre that might otherwise have been empty. (I used to stay in one, and so did Olly and all the players – and they were pretty luxurious!) It also gave dartsmen and women a focal point – a championship of which they could be proud. And when we took £50,000 over the bar in five days, I think I knew we were on to a winner. But I must say that while most darts players drink endlessly there has never been the slightest bit of trouble – and there are a lot of sports that would like to be able to claim that.

The British Matchplay is an invitation event to the top eight Players of the Year, so I came to know all of them pretty well. Ten men have shared the title among them since 1976, when Bill Lennard's was the first name to go on the trophy. Rab Smith won in 1977, and then John Lowe, who has gained such a following at Caister, won the first of his two titles (1978 and 1985). The genial Cliff Lazarenko, always accompanied by his father and a gentle giant if ever that phrase fitted a man, won in 1979 and the eighties were started off by Jocky Wilson whom I have always considered one of the truly great dartsmen, in 1980 and 1981. Eric Bristow foiled his hat-trick bid in 1982, won again in 1983 only to miss out himself on a three-in-a-row success when Mike Gregory took the 1984 championship. Bristow's name was being inscribed on the Cup again in 1986 though, to make him the only man to claim it three times. Dave Whitcombe was triumphant in 1987 and the next two years belonged to the lean and scholarly ex-civil servant, Bob Anderson, who shot to the top in such a very short space of time.

It was a proper turn-up for the book in 1990, I can tell you. In the near twenty years I had known him, Olly Croft had never once had a bet. He had no objection to his officials and players doing so – he simply wasn't a gambling man himself. And yet here he was, the day before the 1990 Matchplay was due to start, joining myself and my colleague Dave Seeley at our betting position with a £20 note in his hand. "Well, what is this all about then?" I asked, only to be told that he wanted to have a bet. "A bet! You must be joking, Olly." But he was not joking. He told me that he thought he knew a man who would come through to win. "You have him at 6-1 but I suppose you will give me 8-1?" I assured him that I most certainly would and Olly handed over his money saying, "I want £10 on Alan Warriner at 8-1 then, please." I asked if he wished only a tenner, not the £20 and Olly said, "Yes, I want £10 change, please." He must have set a world record, becoming the only man to have one bet in his life and one win! For Alan Warriner took the title in the most exciting darts competition I have ever seen.

A nurse in Lancashire, Warriner had an eight-hour drive to reach Caister the day before his first-round match – hardly an ideal preparation. That opening match was the best of only five sets and he was playing Peter Evison, who had won the British Open the previous year. Alan beat him on the very last game. In the second round he was matched with the quite phenomenal Phil Taylor, the favourite and a man who, in defeating John Lowe in his opening match, averaged 32.77 per dart – a quite unheard of scoring rate. This time it was the best of seven games and once more it went to the very last one before Alan won. Now the 1989 winner, Bob Anderson, stood between Alan and the title and Olly and his winnings. In his second match Bob had, by his own standards, fumbled his way through, but now that form was behind him as he stormed to a 4-2 lead; it was the best of nine games and he required just one more to retain his championship. But Alan, not inhibited in any way, came back at him winning – for the third successive match – 5-4 in the very last game.

This was, I have to say, a pretty memorable event – but then I have a host of memories of our annual stay with general manager Rex Evans and his wife Jackie (Pat and I have missed only three of the fifteen championships). Perhaps the one I remember best is of Leighton Rees, who may have so far failed to win the title but did win himself a bride who then had to spend a part of her honeymoon at Caister. It was lovely to watch them both, oblivious to everything and everyone about them!

Alan Glazier, perhaps the world's best left-handed darts player, became a great mate; he was known around the world as the 'Ton Machine' because of his unerring route to 100, which in the early days of darts and before players made such an art of scoring 180 was considered to be the certain path to victory. Putting one dart above the treble 20, one below it and then the third smack in the middle was Alan's particular penchant. Had he not decided that his skills could earn him a lot more money across the Atlantic he would have become far better known at home than he is.

One of the great showmen of the game does not actually throw a dart – not in competition anyway. Many will recognise his voice, yet for £10,000 would not be able to put a name to it. Mister One Hundred and E-i-g-h-t-y himself is actually called Tony Green who has quite a talent for saying what needs to be said in the best possible way. Tony has become just as much a character as Bristow or Lowe or Anderson. The way he lets the words 'one hundred and eighty' bounce across a crowded hall whenever a player makes that magical total has become an integral part of the entertainment, a talisman almost to the game. Some see him as a joke figure. That is quite wrong. As a presenter and compere, whether on television or merely as the Master of Ceremonies to a small show, he is first-rate. Unassuming and courteous off-stage, he is quiet and a good listener; I am slightly surprised that he has not achieved more – but I suspect that the best of Tony Green is yet to come, perhaps in another sport, or even in another walk of life. He may well make a very good administrator in the future and he may become a good broadcaster (BSB did give him a chance to see what he could do as a commentator), but whatever he does I hope that 'signature tune' of his continues to be heard when those darts thud into that little treble-20 slot.

If you were to conclude from all this that I love darts and the people in it, and enjoy betting on it more than on any other sport, you would be correct. There is always a special thrill to be at the Winmau World Masters and then the British Open each December. Thousands enter the latter, playing with or alongside the big names and being treated just like them. It is a little like the FA Cup when the minnows take on the giants and sometimes, as in the Cup, there are surprises. Although normally you expect to see all the top names come through, it is a difficult event to bet upon, because anyone and everyone can enter and there are something like 1,700 games played before they reach the last eight.

If there are cynics who doubt the fact that I have a spirit guide and the trust I place in him, let me tell you a small story that may dispel any such disbelief. On the last Saturday of 1990 I was due to represent Ladbrokes at the Websters' British Open at the Horticultural Hall in London. I had no idea who had reached the last eight – the matches had gone on long into the night, much too late to be carried in the papers. Nor were they on Teletext. As I was going up the escalator at Victoria I received a very clear message: "Mike Gregory will win today." I had no idea whether Gregory had even won through and when I reached the hall I scanned the order-of-play sheet and was pleased to see that he had. Not that I had any doubts, really; when people ask for 'evidence' of my Chinaman's help, it is difficult to recall incidents down the years – it has generally been a gentle awakening or realisation, not a vivid or mind-bending pronouncement. Yet here without doubt was a message from the other side, perhaps the clearest I had ever received.

I sought out Olly Croft immediately – it was barely half-past nine in the morning – intent on having my tale authenticated. "You know that I have a spirit guide?" When he replied that he did, I said, "Well, Mike Gregory will win this tournament today." On paper it looked a tall order: Gregory, a thirty-four-year-old from Poulton in Gloucestershire, had to beat Guy Harvey, which was certainly within his compass, but would then meet either Bob Anderson or Peter Evison in the semi-final.

Harvey was duly despatched and Anderson played out of his skin to beat the World No. 2 to set up a dramatic semi-final clash. Anderson won the first set and in the second had two clear chances to win, yet each time he threw it was as though the hand of God was preventing him from doing so. Thus surviving Gregory went on to reach the final, where he proved too much for John Lowe and won a high-scoring match 2-1. Once again in my life, I had been helped by the unseen Chinaman on my shoulder.

Sadly, I cannot praise the administrators of snooker in the way I have those who run darts. Ever since the big money from television came into the game, there has been nothing but argument and intrigue which was bred as far as I could see from greed; everyone seemed to be worrying whether the next man was getting more out of the game than he was.

It says much for the players that snooker has managed to survive in spite of the officials who in my opinion all too often were putting themselves before the game.

Just as sadly, it has to be said that we moved into snooker sponsorship because I felt there was an opportunity for us to get some TV exposure, yet before my judgement was seen to be correct I had pulled us out of it. I was the first in the field and threw it away and obviously this was a big mistake.

We had sponsored the England v. Rest of the World tournament, and Thames were putting it out at some unearthly hour and not when I wanted it – after their ten o'clock news. Although I was an extremely good friend of their Head of Sport, Sam Leitch, a most splendid sports journalist who moved from newspapers to television to extend an already quite brilliant career, he would not listen to my arguments. When I consider how many hours of televised snooker were to come in the years that followed, at least I know that my instincts were right in the first place – there was to be exposure for snooker sponsors; but it was still a mistake on my part. My trouble was that I was just a little too impatient, but at least we stayed in to bet upon snooker which has given me many happy years among some of the nicest sportsmen you could wish to meet.

When we were first involved the 'top guns' were John Spencer and Ray Reardon, gentlemen both and very good players. But the greatest talent I saw was in a young Irishman called Alex Higgins. When he was playing at his best he could achieve shots that no other player would attempt. Alex was a punter who bet the way he played – fearlessly. I like to think that we have remained great mates and whatever the media have had to say about him and his headline-laden lifestyle, he has always been most honourable and trustworthy in all his dealings with me. If only he had had more self-control away from the table he would still be at the top of the tree and would most certainly have won the World Championship more than the two occasions that he did so.

Barry Hearn has made a huge success of his life and helped a lot of snooker players to fame and fortune. I have had an immense respect for him – and his judgement – since he telephoned me to seek very big odds on a fifteen-year-old one day becoming world champion. The name of that young man? Steve Davis. I had a very nice chat with Barry and then declined to do business with him because I took the view that he knew more than I did about this young prospect. I think I was right! Steve has turned out to be a supreme player but above all a great ambassador for his sport.

Snooker betting has grown since those early days and has developed with ever more different types of bets being offered. It is not without its dangers, however. If I had to offer one piece of advice to any bookmaker who was betting on the sport today, it would be to show extreme care when betting on the early rounds of a tournament that does not carry ranking points. It is dangerous to give any participating player the opportunity to obtain more by losing than he would get for winning.

If Ladbrokes and I owe a lot to snooker, so too does a young man I mentioned a little earlier in this book – Mike Dillon. When I first met him he was the manager of a Ladbrokes shop in Manchester. I had travelled north to bet at a snooker tournament, and he had been instructed to look after me over the few days I was staying there. When I stepped from the train he was waiting for me and was to impress me greatly. He was off to a good start when he greeted me and said that he had heard of my reputation and he wished to learn as much as he could from me! The tournament ran on until past midnight on the first evening, and I decided to put a little pressure on him. Giving him a list of telephone numbers and the revised betting, I told him to ring all my newspaper contacts with the latest odds and then be with me at the Piccadilly Hotel by nine in the morning. Mike measured up. Although he had had a long and tiring day, he made all the calls and was with me, bright as a button, at ten minutes to nine.

We spent a few great days together. Mike is a genial type, always smiling and joking, never given to even a tiny grumble, and always smartly dressed. I knew then that Ladbrokes had found a star for the future, without realising that he would become my Racing Press Officer. But when Malcolm Palmer moved on to Corals, Mike came to work with me and we have been close for more than a decade. I could not have had a more dedicated, loyal and hardworking partner.

Obviously, that England v. Rest of the World snooker tournament sticks in my mind but not, I have to say, simply because of my folly in getting out of sponsorship so fast. At the end of 1976 I met Patricia, the lady who was to become my wife, and when early in January, we staged that event at the Holiday Inn in Swiss Cottage, I asked her to be my guest for the evening. When it came to the prize-giving, I invited her to present the trophy to the 'Most Promising Newcomer'. She handed it to Cliff Thorburn, who was later to become world champion. Two good decisions out of three on the one night was not too bad, I feel, when I look back on them!

I did not do too badly either when it came to judging books. For ten years now I have run a book on the Booker Prize and I have picked the winner just about every other year. (Much to the surprise of the *Sunday Express* Literary Editor, Graham Lord, I have actually named the winner of *their* annual award three times out of three!) Not all writers appreciate having odds quoted on their word-smithery. Philip Kerr, whose own book *The Pale Criminal* was published in 1990 (but did not win the Booker Prize!) wrote that 'the whole affair is reduced to vulgar spectacle by the presence of Ron Pollard who chalks up the odds on each writer as if he were down by the rails at Kempton Park'. Kerr, who I suspect would like to see an end to literary awards, let alone betting upon them, thought it entertaining for the majority, but added 'just imagine how you would feel if your lovingly crafted novel, representing two or three years' work, was knocked down to the 6-1 status of rank outsider'. Mr Kerr is certainly entitled to his opinion, but I have to disagree with him. Not all authors are disapproving and remote; some actually have a bet. Others join the fun and many have become friends. I do not see that any harm is done by my laying odds, and only last year one author rang me and asked if I would read his effort and tell him what odds I might offer were it entered for the Booker award.

Simon Rose took the view that his book, *Filthy Lucre*, with its humour 'base and Tom Sharpe-ish', was unlikely to win the Booker Prize, and I had to agree with him. I said that I thought 100-1 would be the correct odds.

So there is another side of the coin and I have certainly never heard the book companies complain; they like the publicity generated, the exposure which has been obtained in papers that years before would not mention the Booker Prize or any of the many other literary awards. As in so many other fields, betting has helped to promote books and their authors.

Just over a hundred books are entered most years for the Booker Prize (publishers can enter three new books annually, and can additionally put forward any previous winning author if they so choose). The five judges have to read them all. It takes several months for them each to reduce that number to six, and then, on a given day in September, they spend several hours considering which of their individual choices are to make up the agreed short list of six. That is when I join the game. Publishers rush their short-listed copy to my home by taxi or courier and I then spend a couple of days half-reading and scanning them before I put out the odds in time for the Sunday papers. One or two of the book critics, like Penny Perrick of *The Sunday Times*, will call me to give me their feelings about the six selected and obviously – because they are professionals – I will always bear in mind what they have to tell me. But I have my own criterion: I believe that any book has to be 'a good read' if it is to win anything, and so their advice is generally channelled in that direction.

I try not to let the name of the author influence me, even though I look upon Kingsley Amis as the Lester Piggott of the books world. If there was something that with another jockey in the saddle would be at 7-2, you would make it more a 9-4 chance once Lester had climbed aboard. And when David Lister wrote in the *Independent* that Brian Moore would be my Pat Eddery, I suppose he was about right!

My normal method is to read the first sixty or so pages, then the same number near to the centre, and then the final sixty pages. That is generally enough for me to fix the odds but twice now something has really started to command my attention and I have had to read it right through. It first happened with Brian Moore's *The Colour of Blood* and last September (1990) the same thing occurred: although it was not to win, I simply could not put down *Amongst Women* by John McGahern. Unless I think something is terribly lightweight, I try to read all the books fully later and it is only rarely that I have to amend the prices. Generally, only weight of money for a particular book would cause me to do that.

One thing I have never done is to offer prices before I have seen the books. Other bookmakers who have followed Ladbrokes into this field do so, but I think that is very unprofessional; I did not make a book on Miss World before seeing the girls and so it is with the books. I also use a precisely similar process to Miss World to find the favourite for the Booker Prize or the *Sunday Express* award: I decide which of the runners will *not* win.

I settle on the three novels that could do so and discard the three that in my opinion could not. Only once has that really let me down – the year *The Colour of Blood* by Brian Moore did not win. It won everything else in sight but not the Booker, and I still believe it was the best book I have read. I feel a sense of responsibility when I am making a book, because I am aware that sales of books can be affected by being short-listed for the Booker Prize and that my odds may have a further effect. I was delighted that *The Colour of Blood* became a tremendous seller and won so many other awards because, let's face it, everyone likes to feel right. Similarly, when Booker hold their magnificent annual dinner at the Guildhall each year, I am interviewed by the BBC. Getting such promotion for my firm means only that I am doing my job, but when a PR man says all he wants is promotion for his company, do not believe him; PR men like to be seen and they like to be heard, particularly on television!

When it came to sponsorship of racing, Ladbrokes were front-runners. There is, in fact, only one older sponsored race than the Ladbroke Handicap Hurdle at Stratford-upon-Avon and that is the Whitbread Gold Cup which is run at Sandown. Ladbrokes had been associated with the county of Warwickshire from the day Arthur Bendir founded the firm and named it after the Warwickshire village that he came from. When the Stein family took over in 1956 it was the natural thing to do to sponsor this race at Stratford (the nearest track to Ladbroke) and since then their sponsorship has grown and grown, and will continue so to do. Apart from the particular requirement upon a company which makes a profit out of racing to support that industry, there is a substantial amount of exposure to be had for very little outlay and this has grown since SIS beamed racing into just about every betting shop in the land. That is a big audience.

Had we set up a sports marketing company, as I at one time thought we might, I would have advised many businesses to put money into horse-racing sponsorship; at some tracks it would be very worthwhile, costing as little as £500 or £1,000. SIS apart, there is often the chance of national television coverage and every major newspaper prints the racecards each day, with the name of the sponsoring company. I do not think you can get better value than that.

Years ago the season started with the Spring Double, the Grand National and the Lincoln, and ended with the Manchester November Handicap. The winter months were very quiet, with the bosses going away to Barbados or the Canaries and there would be very little betting activity until the following March. Traditionally, the high-profit periods were the first thirteen weeks of the Flat season and the last eight. Ladbrokes sponsored the first major handicap of the season, the Lincoln, which was once run at the course of that name but then switched to Doncaster. This sponsorship was a quite deliberate strategy in the sixties: if the public had been half asleep during the winter, they would wake from their hibernation to hear and see only one name at the start of the Flat – Ladbrokes. We followed this through by sponsoring at the first meeting of the season at racing's headquarters, Newmarket, where Captain Nick Lees was a most superb Clerk of the Course. He was a man after my own heart – he recognised the value of good PR – and Nick has always looked after us famously. We sponsored the two major races at that spring meeting, the Craven Stakes and the Nell Gwyn Stakes, both Classic Trials. The latter was great fun. We would dress up lots of lovely ladies in Nell Gwyn costumes and they would give away oranges. The girls loved it – and so did the public.

We also sponsored on the third day what was then called the Abernant Stakes, named in honour of a great sprinter. Lady Beaverbrook, who has been such a staunch owner for so long, had a marvellous colt called Boldboy, which was trained by Sir Gordon Richards. This horse won the Abernant three years in succession and immediately after his third victory I said to Nick Lees that we would sponsor a race to be called the Ladbroke Boldboy Stakes. To this day the Boldboy is run at the Craven meeting, still attracting some of the best six-furlong sprinters there are – a fitting memorial I think to one of the great sprinters of all time.

After Newmarket we would appear at the Epsom spring meeting – a joy for any racing man. Epsom is a part of the United Racecourses group managed so ably by Tim Neligan and I would only say that if all racecourses were run his way (Kempton and Sandown are a part of the empire) racing might not be as subsidy-mad as it is. Next stop was Chester, for the Chester Cup meeting. I loved going to this beautiful and ancient city. Racing there is unique; the course is not much bigger than the Wembley greyhound track and racing can be viewed by looking over the wall. We were the only sponsors at Chester for a long time, sponsoring a race a day, including the Chester Cup itself.

As at Newmarket and Epsom, we were looked after superbly in Cheshire by the Clerk of the Course, Captain Charles Toller, and Lord Leverhulme, the Senior Steward, who allowed us to entertain our guests in a marquee on the lawn by the side of the paddock. It is a wonderful three-day meeting, and now that the new stand has been built to replace the one destroyed by an arsonist, Chester's future looks assured. How the BBC can be so shortsighted as to have dropped television coverage there is beyond belief.

Lingfield was our next port of call. This picturesque, tree-lined course on the Surrey-Sussex border is important for more than just its aesthetic look: with its undulating track and its tight, left-hand bends, it is perfect as an Epsom testing ground and several Derby winners ran their final trial over one and a quarter miles here. Lovely, lovely Lingfield. It was perhaps the most pleasant place we ever went to in the springtime, dining after racing at the restaurant I consider the best in the country, the Gravetye Manor at East Grinstead. Simply writing about it makes me feel very contented! And it was here at Lingfield, when Ladbrokes bought the place to save it from becoming another housing estate, that I had the most remarkable lunchtime with the Queen Mother.

At the top of the stand there is a small dining-room – it probably holds no more than sixteen people. It was normally my custom not to eat until I had made sure all was well, and had seen the first race. As I wandered in, I could see that the only empty seat in the whole place was next to the Queen Mother. Now there was a problem! But the Queen Mother looked up and smilingly invited me to "Come and sit with me," so I went to join her with a quiet "Good afternoon" and my thanks. Before I sat, though, I decided to get myself a drink from the bar at the far end of the room. The Queen Mother said: "If you are going to the bar perhaps you would get me a gin and Dubonnet." Before I had gone a couple of paces she called after me, "And go easy with the Dubonnet." I took her gin back and although she had finished her meal and was ready to watch the horses, she chatted happily about racing for quite a time. It became apparent that Lingfield really was a favourite spot for Her Majesty. It was always a pleasure to welcome her to Lingfield, for she had been a tremendous supporter, particularly of National Hunt racing and is without doubt the most loved lady of the Turf.

That was the end of our springtime sponsorship, but I

had as much affection for Ayr in September as I had for Chester and Lingfield. For some time we had been looking for a race in Scotland and when I heard a rumour that Burmah Castrol might pull out of the Ayr Gold Cup I asked Bill McHarg, Clerk of the Course, for first refusal and in 1977 we were delighted to take on not only that wonderful race but to sponsor on each day of their four-day meeting. A true Scottish gentleman is Bill. Apart from controlling Ayr for so long, he is still Managing Director of Hamilton and I doubt if anyone quite realises the debt the whole racing world owes to him; his achievements for racing in Scotland during a difficult period were truly outstanding with many problems over rates and he ran his courses on a shoestring and quite superbly. I went to Ayr at my own expense last autumn, and will continue to go simply to see Bill and his son David for a few days, to enjoy their company and the warmth of their welcome. It is good to see David following so meticulously in his father's footsteps. David has inherited a great depth of vision and sees the future of racing with clearer eyes than most. If he sometimes tends to run before he can walk that is a good fault and will be put right with the passage of time. Bill is likely to have retired by the time this book is published, and no man better deserves to be sitting down, with feet up, contemplating a race well run.

One of my great beliefs was that Ladbrokes should be associated only with the best and at Ayr – thanks in great part to Malcolm Palmer's foresight – we took on the Ayrshire Handicap on the Saturday; what a magnificent race that is today. Malcolm always believed it had the potential to become a big-betting race, as big as the Ayr Gold Cup, and he was right. Owners now wish to run their horses in it, jockeys like to win it and the punters love to bet on it. It really has become established not only as one of the biggest but one of the best.

Unfortunately not everything we were to do had quite the same appeal. While I was battling for the established races, the big trials like the Craven Stakes, to supplement

major handicaps our trading people were fighting for
events without the glitz. They did not want us involved
with these other races – they argued in our sponsorship
committee meetings that handicaps attracted twice the betting turnover and that that was where we should concentrate. I was virtually a lone voice in wishing us to be
associated with only the best and slowly but surely I lost
the battle.

I remember when many meetings used to finish with
maiden and plate races (which have a valuable part to play
in racing, giving chances to horses that have not won to
do so) but our trades people pressed for us to sponsor only
handicap races. They wanted these to be the last ones of
the day, with the maidens and plates either switched or
dropped, because "more people would stay to watch and
more people would gamble", and so Ladbrokes set aside
£100,000 to sponsor such last-race handicaps. There was
no publicity for them, no TV coverage and no ante-post
betting such as we gained with our big races like the Oaks
and the Derby trials, but they were proved right – we
increased our turnover. All the same, I was saddened by
the desire to lose an identity with only the finest in racing
which I felt was important for the image of the company.
That was probably why I so enjoyed our entry into Irish
racing!

It was Mike Dillon who pressured me into this Irish
connection. For some considerable time I had been looking
for one particular race that we could sponsor; a major race
worthy of being called simply 'The Ladbroke' and which
would be the richest handicap race in Europe. Mike said
that the Sweeps Hurdle was available and urged me to take
it over. Although we had established ourselves in Ireland
with property and our betting shops, I would have to admit
that I was not over-keen – but Mike kept at me. It was run
in the winter, when nothing else much was happening, and
would therefore get all the media attention, he argued. I
was finally sold on the idea and in 1986 we negotiated
a five-year contract for this £50,000 handicap hurdle at

Leopardstown which has been a tremendous success and will I am sure continue to be so throughout the nineties. It has pulled big crowds, and is a wonderful betting race, which the punters love. It is now Mike Dillon's pride and joy. He has a fabulous relationship with the Irish, and specifically with Tony Corcoran, the Clerk of the Course at Leopardstown.

I have no doubts that Corcoran, still a comparatively young man, is destined to go far in the administration of Irish racing. Certainly he has ensured that Ladbrokes have had an enormous benefit from their Irish connection.

Of course, the company has always had its own and its shareholders' interests at heart, but I feel proud to have been associated with a sponsorship programme that has at the same time advanced and enchanced the sporting traditions of this country.

7

THE MAN WHO GAMBLED £100 MILLION

Some people may drink too much, others eat too much. And there will be those who gamble to excess because, in every walk of life, someone, somewhere, crosses the barriers of sense and reason. You will recognise those who drink too much – sooner or later they will fall down in a bar. It is not difficult to spot those who eat too much. But how do you tell the compulsive gambler; the one who gambles beyond his means? More importantly, if you do suspect such a person, how do you stop him?

Just imagine yourself as a bookmaker, running a shop in a small market town somewhere in Britain. You know your customers, just as the local butcher or publican knows his; you probably exchange the time of day quite regularly with them, in your betting shop or even if you meet in the street. One afternoon just such a client walks in for a few bets. By the end of the afternoon he has lost £50. You possibly know his circumstances, and that £50 is too much. In other words, he is in too deep. What do you do? Do you, when he asks for a tenner on a 6-1 shot in the last race of the day, refuse him because that is the kind and decent thing to do? After all, a publican should by law refuse the alcoholic another drink if the licensee thinks he is drunk. But that most certainly is not what you do as a bookmaker: you take his £10.

If his horse wins (and you do not know whether it will or not) he will have cleared his day's losses and be left with a small profit. Where would you stand then had you refused to take that winning bet? Are you so conscience-stricken that you hand him what he would have won? Of course not, you take the bet because that is the way the business is, the way life has to be.

I never feel sorry for gamblers who lose. They could just as easily win my money as lose their own. That is what gambling is about. Do not think that I am without compassion. I have as much as the next man, and would have every sympathy with a mother and her children affected by a man who does not know when – or how – to stop. But mostly you will never be aware of a problem and even if – as in my imaginary little story – you do recognise that there is something wrong, there is little you can do about it as a bookmaker. I related in Chapter 3 the tale of my shirt-making friend, Tom Beard. If I had refused to take his bets, there were plenty of other bookmakers around he could have bet with; and who was I to suggest what he could, or could not, afford? Many would quickly take offence at the suggestion.

None the less, I am all too conscious of the fact that there are compulsive gamblers, the ones who cannot handle it, those to whom betting has become an obsession. While I cannot speak for every bookmaker in the land, I suspect that there are very few indeed who would wish to take advantage of such people, whose real need is for help. I was always happy to try to give some of that help whenever the Church's Council for Gambling asked. The Council was run by a marvellous man called the Reverend Gordon Moody. It is an organisation something like Alcoholics Anonymous, I suppose. They run (at least they used to, and I presume it still operates) a house in London where compulsive gamblers could go for rehabilitation. I would often go and talk to them there and they had my sympathy, not because they were gamblers or losers but because many were incurables, unable to help themselves. Mr Moody would also hold Sunday evening talk-ins at Southwark

Cathedral for those who were either afflicted or companions to the addicted.

I remember one July Sunday in 1970, Gordon Moody (who himself had an addiction he could never cure – for chocolate biscuits!) had asked me to join Bill Deedes, then MP for Ashford but later to become a most illustrious Editor of the *Daily Telegraph* and Lord Deedes, Eric Morley of Mecca and Miss World fame, and A. W. Taylor who I seem to remember represented the Tote. We were being questioned about the relatively new commercialisation of gambling and the problems it posed for society in general and the compulsive gambler in particular.

I pointed out, gently, that betting had not necessarily increased during the eight years since the Act came into force. Prior to the Act no one knew how much gambling there was; it had mostly been done illegally and no one as far as I knew had ever monitored it. "As for compulsive gamblers," I added, "there are some sitting in this Cathedral this very night."

You could feel the animosity diminishing as they realised that, even in an audience of 'Gamblers Anonymous' they were just that: anonymous, until they stood up and admitted they were compulsive gamblers. No doubt relatives themselves in many cases had been unaware until the carpets, furniture, or in dire cases even the family home itself were being sold off. Just as you can never tell a book by its cover (and as the man who sets the odds each year for the Booker Prize and the *Sunday Express* Book of the Year, I can certainly testify to that) you should take no notice of how a person looks, or the clothes he wears, particularly when it comes to gamblers. They are to be found in all sorts of dress and in all sizes.

Joe Sunlight was an outsized gambler who dressed like a tramp. He was an architect, responsible for the Sunlight House Building in Manchester. At the end of the forties he must have been among the top half-dozen high earners in the country. He earned £50,000 a quarter; I know that because on occasions he used to give me his pay cheque.

Now, I know that I have said I dislike the phrase 'mug punter', but Joe was another role model. He would have six – yes, *six* – bets in a single race and that is the surest way I know of losing money. We used to have a saying that if Joe won, the Queen would have no soldiers; in other words, it was not a possibility. His bets were what we called 'top of the book' which meant that William Hill stood all Joe's wagers himself – they did not go through the firm's books. It was a guaranteed income for Bill because he never had to pay out.

Unlike Joe, no one could accuse Terry Ramsden of being other than stylishly dressed as he gambled away an estimated £100 million in the eighties.

Terry Ramsden was the biggest loser of the latter-day gamblers and could even be the champion all-time loser. He was certainly the biggest ordinary punter – by which I mean a working man, not a member of High Society with inherited wealth – who ever existed. Once a major owner (he had a Classic winner, Katies, in the Irish One Thousand Guineas) he was also a chairman of Walsall Football Club. Above all he was a wild, wild gambler. He had a regular Yankee (that is, a four-horse combination comprising eleven bets) and by regular I mean just about daily.

Sometimes he would have a £1,000 Yankee, which would cost £11,000 but there were times when he would have a £5,000 one, which meant a lay-out of £55,000. Over a period of years, betting in this way, on both horses and dogs, was to lose him an estimated £100 million to bookmakers at large. I was very sorry indeed when, in 1988, he owed Ladbrokes so much money that I was forced to take the action that ended with him being 'Warned Off'. I tried to protect and help him to the very last, organising a deal and preparing a letter for him to sign agreeing to pay us a certain amount each month. Time and again I warned him of the consequences of not paying if he did sign the agreement and time and again Terry assured me that it would not be a difficulty for him. Yet we did not receive a single payment and we were left with no other option. His debt was so huge (around £2 million, if I remember aright) that I had to report him to Tattersalls' Committee who then reported him to the Jockey Club. His warning off was inevitable, which meant that he could no longer bet, attend race meetings, own horses or even go to the stables or watch the gallops. That is how severe the penalties are if you are 'reported' and the Jockey Club warns you off. Severe and, I suspect, so shaming that one does not wish to be seen by one's friends until the debts are cleared.

The tragedy of Terry Ramsden was that he was a clever man – too clever you would have thought to get himself into such a mess. He was a working-class lad who by his own labours had made enough on the Japanese money market to be able to spend over £100 million on his gambling. He simply wasn't clever enough to know when to stop or how to behave when he was offered a lifeline.

Another wealthy man who I will call only Mr D.H. got himself into some considerable difficulty and his co-directors surprised me one morning by turning up at my office with a cheque and a proposition. The cheque was to clear his debts; the proposition was that if they did so – and I was warned that D.H. could not do so – his account must be closed. They were adamant that, under no circumstances, would he be allowed further facilities. That, I said, seemed fair enough and deep down I knew that I had to agree. It must have been a shock, not to say an enormous embarrassment, for this London businessman to find his fellow directors ganging-up on him in that way, but the shock treatment worked. He certainly never had another bet with Ladbrokes and I learned later that he had 'kicked his habit' and was able to walk straight past a betting shop.

Some months ago there was a very rare story in the newspapers of a man, in total contrast to Terry Ramsden and Mr D.H., having his account closed for being too successful. I simply did not begin to understand why that should be. Years ago it could happen on occasions that someone could win too consistently for a bookmaker's well-being. Betting always has to be equable and – believe it or not – sometimes it is not. There were once shrewd 'specialist' gamblers who ambushed bookmakers with wagers that should never have been accepted.

No doubt there are plenty who may try to dispute it, but it is a fact that 73 per cent of all money wagered is returned to punters, though not necessarily the same punters. However, there were one or two specific bets that were loaded in the punters' favour. There was the handicap betting that I mentioned in an earlier chapter. And then there were specialists who would bet only on two-year-old races with between eight and twelve runners. The betting on these might normally run something like this: 4-6 the favourite, 3-1, 6-1 and 12-1 bar those three; the 'specialist' few would always bet each way (at a quarter the odds then, not one-fifth as it is today) on the third favourite. Without rigging the odds there was very little chance indeed of the bookmaker ever winning if he took this bet, so those who betted exclusively this way would have their accounts closed. Bookmakers are just as much in the business of making a profit as Marks and Spencer or Harrods; certainly they are not philanthropists. With the place odds now one-fifth, that bet is no longer so viable and there seems little point in closing accounts these days when people can go from shop to shop and bet as they wish.

Perhaps some of the most cunning betting I ever witnessed was performed by J. S. (Jack) Gerber. A South African millionaire several times over (a sugar man, I believe, not diamonds) he was, despite his wealth, normally just a nice steady backer: £100 and £200 bets, always at the tracks and generally on Fridays and Saturdays. Just every now and then, however, Jack would set himself out to knock the bookies sideways and his successes could be swift and quite spectacular. One particular coup was in the Stewards' Cup at Goodwood in 1953 with a horse which I think he owned in partnership with trainer Fred Armstrong called Palpitate. Its price was 100-6 when, at a given signal from Jack shortly before the 'off', a team of workmen he had brought with him moved straight down the line of bookmakers on the rails. Jack himself came to William Hill, placing £600 to win £10,000. We should have guessed then that something was up, for this was a Tuesday. But it was all too quick for us. Such was the volume of money that, while he had been laid odds of 100-6, Palpitate was returned at 5-1. Before anyone had realised how they were being – quite legally – stitched up, Gerber's team had placed £18,000 that was to bring him £300,000 – at that time a very considerable amount of money. Jack Gerber was a very different sort of punter to those who would ring up every day with their doubles and trebles; he might not have another gigantic bet for a couple of years – thank goodness!

It was easy enough to know when His Excellency the Maharaja of Rajpipla was 'having a go'. This Indian aristocrat had immense wealth – indeed, he was reputed to be among the world's richest men – but a £2 bet was normally his largest. And whenever he lost, my goodness – you have never seen a man so miserable. His wife had no such inhibitions. She was a cheerful gambler and £500 or £1,000 would be her regular bet. It was with some surprise therefore that we received a call from His Excellency placing £100 on his own horse, First Consul in the Stewards' Cup at Goodwood in 1950. At first I did not believe it; I felt a mistake must have been made taking his bet down so I insisted upon a check being made. The only way we could do this without an embarrassing phone call to ask him directly was to send his voucher around to his home by hand. I knew that if we had made a mistake he would pretty soon let us know. But it appeared that it was what he wanted so I immediately asked myself just how miserable might he get if he lost £100. Logic told me that he did not expect to lose; such a cautious man must know his horse was laid out to win. If the Maharaja was having £100 on a horse, then Ronald James Joseph Pollard was having his share. I took a look at First Consul's credentials – a four-year-old carrying 8 st 13 lb, and trained by Fred

Armstrong – and decided to place £20 (a huge bet for me, more than twice my weekly wage). First Consul duly won (at 100-9) and while another couple of grand probably meant little to His Excellency, £330 meant a heck of a lot to me.

I suppose I was pretty unique because unlike most bookmakers I am not a natural gambler; I would only bet when I thought I knew something, like the Maharaja's wager, that put the odds in my favour. Few are like me. Bookmakers are constantly betting against each other, generally backing their own judgement.

One of the most successful bookmakers of all time was a woman, Mrs Helen Vernet. She was a lady after my own heart and had she still been alive her first reaction, like mine, would have been to contact the chap who had had his account closed 'for being too successful' with an offer to accept all his wagers. Mrs Vernet was a quite fearless gambler who, after she became the first and only female ever to appear on the rails at tracks with the bookmaking élite, became a director of Ladbrokes in the thirties, earning £50,000 a year. A one-time actress (she always vehemently denied ever being a Gaiety Girl) she was beautiful, brilliant and never less than charming. Her story would make a fascinating book; a larger-than-life personality who loved and lost (twice officially, but almost certainly several times more), lived and worked with respect in a man's world for nearly fifty years, and drove – quite regally – a four-in-hand through Hampton Court and Richmond Park.

Her father, a Scottish nobleman, had died when she was thirteen, leaving her £8,000. By the time she was twenty, Helen had managed to gamble the lot away. Because of poor health, doctors said she should acquire a job in the open air. "Be a veterinary surgeon," it was suggested. She chose, instead, to take bets on racecourses, having learned to her cost that this was the safer side of the ropes. At first, working from the Members' Enclosures, her only clients were her friends.

Soon, as her fame spread, she was taking business from

the rails bookmakers. She did not seek it out; the punters looked for her, but the railsmen were none too pleased all the same. It was Arthur Bendir who sorted the problem out. Arthur was the founder of Ladbrokes, back at the turn of the century and prior to the 1914 war he was the boss. His was an inspired thought. If they could not beat Mrs Vernet, why not invite her to join the Ladbrokes board? And that is precisely what he did. Mrs Vernet accepted and she represented the company on the rails until the year before she died in 1956, aged seventy-nine.

There have been half a dozen women bookmakers since, I would guess, but never one to touch Helen Vernet. I actually introduced one to Ladbrokes – but it was purely a PR gimmick. We were always looking for ways of getting our name into the newspapers and we did so once more when I took on Judith Groves. She was young, blonde and very attractive. I trained her myself to take bets and then installed her at Epsom. Since 1924 Ladbrokes have had the exclusive right to bet in the Epsom Grandstand on all three levels.

As I say, it was intended as a gimmick and Judith did not last too long – but while she did last we were very successful. The newspaper photographers liked the look of her and so did the customers; she did plenty of business for us.

Speaking of females, there have been many weird and wonderful ways of seeking winners over the years, but trust a female to come up with one that takes some beating to this day. Brooke Sanders was a leading lady jockey in the seventies (and is now a successful trainer at Epsom). I recall one year when Ladbrokes were sponsoring a Lady Jockeys' Championship in Malta, Brooke saying to me in the paddock just before the start: "This one has the goers today, Ron." Quite what she meant, I am not sure; a gut feeling perhaps. Anyway, in a desperately close finish, Brooke won by a neck – which I have always put down to her jockeyship – and I had cleared my expenses for the trip. I seem to remember a few journalists drinking at the Hotel Verdala in Rabat and putting all the champagne down to my room, so it was a pretty handy win! That was the day I turned up in the ladies' changing-room to be confronted by a dozen naked and near-naked jockettes. Concerned about Brooke, whom I knew had been taking pills in an attempt to lose weight quickly, I was taking in a couple of bottles of champagne to celebrate our little success and to help her in case she was dehydrated. "Sorry girls," I said cheekily. "Do excuse me." And I left ... after we had all had a little drink, of course. Wonderful girls, those lady jockeys; brave, splendid horsewomen who loved their racing, and always full of fun. We shared many marvellous moments together in Malta. So, too, did some of the journalists we used to take with us, but those stories are best left untold, I suspect.

William Hill (who was a very good judge of form, incidentally) would often 'have a go at a favourite'. He would say, "This horse cannot possibly win on this track over seven furlongs – we'll have a go at this one." That is not making a book, of course, that is gambling pure and simple.

In my early days the Course Clerks were no different to their bosses. These were the élite of the betting world, respected by the bookmakers on the rails for their skill in getting down every bet laid, however hectic the business in the build-up to a race, and they were paid commensurately. Pat Moore was one such man – Clerk to William Hill and probably earning £100 a week even in the fifties; gambling was in his blood and he liked nothing better than to take on his rivals with his own money. In 1948 I was still working in Hill's Internal Course Department when Pat landed a real gamble in the Cambridgeshire. A keen student of form, he had decided that, carrying only 7 st 4 lb and with a weight-claiming apprentice on board, the Pat Beasley-trained Sterope was a cinch. He was very friendly with the trainer's wife, Lady Beasley, and she confirmed his feelings. They were both right and Pat won £70,000 as it stormed home at 25-1. A short, tubby little man, Pat came back from Newmarket triumphant. We were all around the big mahogany table in the Internal Course Department waiting on this evening for the course notes to arrive as Pat burst in. They were not the course notes he threw on the table – they were those big old white fivers. He kept putting his hands into his deep pockets, pulling out these notes and scattering them all over the table. "We've done it today, lads," he kept shouting; "we've done it today."

Indeed he had. But there was still work to do, for even if it had been Pat's lucky day, it had also been a busy one at the track. By the time we had recorded the mass of credit bets on to their respective accounts it was nearly eleven o'clock. "Come on, all of you; I'll buy you a drink," said Pat, and we rushed for Rayners, our nearest pub. As we were going in a couple of sailors were coming out. They looked astonished, as well they might, as Pat pressed £50 on to each of them. "Have a drink on me," he invited them as we poured into Rayners where Pat bought everyone a drink and thanked them for their labours. Then he turned to me and said, "Right. We're off to the Embassy Club." It was a tremendous night. Generously, Pat also gave me "a few quid – a small thank you for staying so late to work on the course notes", although upon reflection I do not think I received quite as much as the two sailors! And I later discovered that Pat had bought Lady Beasley a very expensive bracelet for her encouraging words of advice.

A year later, Sterope won the Cambridgeshire again. This time he was burdened with 9 st 4 lb but now he had Charlie Elliott aboard and – again at 25-1 – once more he carried Pat's money. This time Pat collected £40,000 but the tale has, I fear, a sad ending. Pat was not to keep his £110,000 winnings. Some time later he was introduced to what he thought was a good investment, a football pools business in Hong Kong. Somehow, I think someone saw him coming, because Pat lost everything.

The Cambridgeshire and the Cesarewitch, two sporting and most competitive races, form the ever-popular Autumn Double; many are the punters who double up horses, generally at good prices, from these two races in the hope of making a late-season 'killing'. One of our regulars, Jack Hallsworth, actually linked them with the St Leger with striking success in a £1 treble. Indiana won the Leger, Grey of Falloden the Cesarewitch and Hasty Cloud the shorter race of the two. Hallsworth took 25-1, 33-1 and 16-1 respectively and his cheque totted up to just over £15,000. We counted ourselves fortunate that he had not had his usual £5 bet!

I doubt if anyone will ever match the legendary 'Gilroy Double', however. Dudley Gilroy was racing manager to a wealthy American, A. K. Macomber, who owned two French-bred horses that were to run in the last two big races of the Newmarket season. Forseti, in the Cesarewitch, and Masked Marvel, in the Cambridgeshire, were not strongly fancied because in 1925 French-bred horses were looked upon with some suspicion; the British thoroughbred was considered invincible. Gilroy asked Ladbrokes if he could have a £100 double and Arthur Bendir offered him 500-1. This was accepted and when they both won (at 25-1 and 100-8, respectively) Gilroy received a cheque for £50,000, then, and for a long time to come, the record pay-out on a single bet.

The man who was to break that record was Bernard Sunley when he won almost £70,000 on Santa Claus in the 1964 Derby – a clear case of Christmas coming early for once for the builder and property tycoon who was one of the heaviest gamblers I have ever known. He had his big wins, but one year he dropped over £1 million, mainly to Ladbrokes. He always wanted to be seen as the biggest punter of his era (that ego syndrome again!). He and Bernard Myers were friends of a sort. Certainly they were friends to us poor bookmakers, for they would try to 'outbid' each other when they were betting. Dickie Gaskell, the hugely popular Ladbroke Representative for so many years now, can dine out on the hilarious tales of the way these two competed against each other to see who could wager the most. Myers would wait until Sunley had laid his bet, then sidle up to Dickie and ask: "How much did Bernard have on, then?" He would be told and promptly make his bet £100 higher! Sunley would get his own back in exactly the same way. I have often wondered whether dear Dickie sometimes upped the ante a little, thus getting a larger bet than was actually necessary for the two adversaries to be No. 1. If he did it was no more than they both deserved, squabbling like three-year-olds over who had the most jelly babies.

Sunley's record win on Santa Claus has been bettered many times since – inflation does that in betting just as in everything else – but he was at times a reckless gambler. He laid out £30,000 on a 7-1 *on* shot to win some £4,000; he lost £30,000 when he backed Mill House to beat Arkle at Cheltenham (it did, but that had been the year before!); and at Royal Ascot in the sixties he was £50,000 ahead after the Hunt Cup on the Wednesday but lost it all and plenty more during the following two days. It certainly wasn't boring when Bernard was around.

Now let me tell you of the bookmaker who lost and did not give a damn! The 1949 Derby had everything: a supreme winner, a finish that will never be bettered and a fascinating twist in the tale.

From his earliest days, William Hill had wanted to own a stud and breed a big race-winner. In 1949 he owned the Whitsbury Stud where David Elsworth trains today and the star of that stable was Nimbus, owned by Mrs M. Glenister but bred by William Hill. Nimbus had won the Two Thousand Guineas, hacking up to give Bill his first Classic success.

Your view of having a Classic winner depends upon which saddle you sit. Jockeys will claim that without a driver the bus doesn't move; trainers will say that horses, like engines, must be properly tuned; and owners argue that without their big cheque-books there is no big event. But each and every breeder from the Queen down will tell you that breeding a winner, and particularly the Derby winner is racing's purest success. Bill Hill would not have argued.

However, before the race he doubted whether Nimbus

would get the one-and-a-half-mile trip around the undulating and tightly turning Epsom course and, ever the practical betting man, Bill backed Amour Drake hugely to win. Amour Drake was one of two highly fancied French colts – Val Drake was the other – and Lord Derby had a very good horse indeed called Swallow Tail.

The race promised much and we were not to be disappointed; it was, I believe, the greatest Derby ever. Charlie Elliott, on Nimbus, jumped off in front (there were, of course, no stalls in those days) and would make every yard of the running. As they approached the furlong pole, Swallow Tail, with Doug Smith aboard, was battling on the outside of Nimbus but, I suspected, tiring. Rae Johnstone, on Amour Drake, tried to go through between them but found his way blocked as Swallow Tail drifted slightly to his left. Forced to back off, Johnstone decided to go on the inside. Now the three horses were being driven to their limit past the cheering hordes on the rails and the hundreds on the open-top buses.

The jockeys would have seen none of this; their eyes were riveted on the winning post ahead, their minds on the desperate job in hand. Their bodies were taut and balanced, their whips in almost perfect unison going to and fro, just brushing the sweat-covered sides of their mounts. It was Swallow Tail that faltered; minutely, but enough for the experienced eye in the Grandstand and for Charlie Elliott and Rae Johnstone to be aware. If Nimbus was to lose now, he would have to concede the lead he had held from the start; for two furlongs that lead had been only a matter of inches but an inch was the difference between being a winner and being a loser. He did not concede. He held on to win by a head from the French horse with Swallow Tail just a further head away third. It was the first year that the photo-finish camera was in operation; it merely confirmed that which our eyes had told us.

I was still standing next to Bill Hill; we had watched every stride of the race together in absolute silence. We had not exchanged a word and were almost unaware of the noise from the crowd. But now we were being engulfed by the cheering and the shouting. Not awaiting the evidence of the camera, people were racing across the grass towards him, to the man who had bred the Derby winner yet was showing less emotion than any of the 100,000 gathered on Epsom Downs that afternoon. Not one of them knew then, and I doubt if anyone else knows to this day, that that head victory by Nimbus over Amour Drake had made the difference of £1 million to Hill. Convinced that Nimbus would not quite stay the distance, he had backed Amour Drake to win. Bill still said nothing. There was a benign smile – of self-congratulation, perhaps, or for those who were milling around, clapping him on the back and pumping his hand – but not one other sign of emotion.

We were never displeased when regular clients had a good win. Sometimes we would have a small drinks party for them in our boardroom and if that was not possible, Cyril might send telegrams of congratulation. One such recipient in 1966 was Ian Maxwell-Scott, a close friend of the missing Lord Lucan. Ian was one of our regulars, and often to be found at The Clermont, a plush gambling club in Berkeley Square.

Owned at that time by John Aspinall, zoo proprietor, high-roller and man about town, The Clermont was the haunt of old Etonians who would spend many days and nights playing blackjack, roulette and mean games of backgammon for huge sums. Early in September, Maxwell-Scott called Ladbrokes from the club to have a dozen bets on four horses. Only two of the bets went down (a £50 win and £25 place bet on Waterloo Place) which cost him £75 of his £705 outlay. After that he was sliding down the rainbow and there really was a crock of gold at the foot of it. Rockemar (at 100-8), Common Pond (100-6 at Doncaster), and Renwick (9-2 at Fontwell) were backed variously to win and to be placed, some at Starting Price and some at the Tote return; the two long shots were paired three times in doubles and were finally put in a treble with

Renwick. Maxwell-Scott's total winnings were £40,699 — a jackpot by any standard. I am told that the party in Berkeley Square was long and loud enough to drown any nightingale.

Among the great and the good of the gambling world has been the Packer family, Sir Frank and son Kerry. Frank was a multimillionaire newspaper magnate who rather liked a punt and with whom I did a little business every now and then. It was, therefore, a matter of regret that I did not meet up with Kerry, the son who was to turn cricket inside out in the seventies, particularly as he now appears to be an even bigger gambler than his father.

Kerry is a living legend 'down under'; when he bets on the horses there he will wager anything up to a million. It does not surprise me when they claim his bookmaker retired early! But Kerry seems much more a casino man these days. He runs a couple of polo teams in Sussex and finds solace from their defeats at The Clermont, Crockfords and the Ritz Casino in London. In the spring of 1990 he was reputed to have won £4.5 million at the tables in eight days. At The Clermont alone, playing blackjack at £25,000 a time, he won £2,400,000 and if that isn't reasonable compensation for losing a couple of polo games, I do not know what is!

I said we do like to see the big winners occasionally, but that was a bit much even for such a big spender. What no bookmaker likes, however, is the embarrassment that comes when people think they have had a winning day when they have not. You really would not credit the number of honest, thoroughly decent folk who genuinely believe they have had a different bet to the one they actually laid. The greatest boon to our lives at Ladbrokes came with the installation of a Thermionic system for recording every telephone call to our Harrow headquarters. It was worth its weight in gold because it saved us (and many clients) from a great deal of embarrassment.

We would send out an account in the normal way for money owed, then get a call from the customer to the effect that he had expected money from us. "I had an each-way bet on this one," was the normal argument. I always told such callers that I would check, knowing full well what the answer would be. Sometimes when I rang back to say that they had quite definitely had a 'win' bet only they would accept; mostly, they continued to argue. "Well, would you like to come in and listen to yourself?" I would inquire, explaining our system. That then normally settled matters – but one day a particularly well-known sportsman (and a firm friend to this day whose name appears elsewhere in this book) said that he would like to come in and listen, so sure was he of what had been said.

Whenever this happened, the pattern was always the same; it was no different this time. The client would look astonished at his recorded voice and the instructions he had given. Up into the air would go his arms, or around my shoulders as happened on this occasion. "Ron. I am so sorry. I could have sworn I had it each way." He genuinely did – but he hadn't. And while I always felt that no one should have doubted our word in the first place, the recording system at least produced irrefutable proof and allowed long-standing and affable relationships to continue. As I say, there was never any real intent to avoid payment, just a genuine doubt as to what the bet had been.

When I used to get a regular Sunday afternoon call to my home from a Greek industrialist based in France where he owned several horses, I had no such recorder. So the moment Constantin Goulandris had placed his bets, which ranged from £10,000 to £30,000, on the day's French racing (about which I knew virtually nothing) I would ring the telephone operator and ask her to record the time of the French calls. While Goulandris had his big wins and his big losses and would never ever have considered pulling a fast one I had to be sure, in fairness to my company, that all bets had been placed before the start of racing. I would scrawl his instructions on a piece of paper, which I then put on the top of the television set and I did not know until the following day whether we had won £15,000 or lost

£100,000; and not even the next day if I forgot the slip of paper on top of the TV set and went off to work without it.

It's been great fun dealing with the high-rollers but in so far as anyone in my business can take pleasure in paying out, it must be the most fun when the little punter strikes it rich.

Among the small punters I can remember who won big, perhaps George Talbot was the most notable. The 16-stone retired dock worker got his fun each weekend with a bet we had introduced called 'Lucky 7 Bingo' – so named, I suspect, more because we then owned Lucky 7 Bingo halls rather than for the fact that it involved seven horses, though it was later renamed 'Lucky 13' because it involved 13 bets. On Saturday, August 8, 1981 George went into his local shop in Portsmouth, as he did most Saturdays on his way to the pub for a lunch-time pint, and spent £1.30p on the 13 bets on his coupon – six doubles, three other doubles, two trebles, and five- and seven-horse accumulators. He paid the tax (precisely 13p), handed over £1.43p and went off for his drink. That evening we announced that a mystery punter in Portsmouth had won £100,000 for £1.40p. George sat baby-sitting with his grandchildren, too busy to check his coupon. It was not until the Monday that he realised he had won; he had actually gone into the pub again on the Sunday lunch-time and said "Good luck to him" when other customers started to talk about the "big winner from Portsmouth". We kept his name secret for a day, so that I could go down to see him and set things up for a big announcement.

Having of course made sure that there was a TV crew in town, waiting at a hotel for us, I took him off for a glass or three of champagne and to talk about the publicity. George stunned me by saying he did not wish for any announcement and certainly no publicity. As for him going on television, I could forget the whole idea. It was not the first time we had come across this problem. We knew how to handle it. By the time we had drunk a couple of bottles,

George and I were on 'Ron' and 'George' terms and had done a deal. He would give the TV company whatever they wanted and I would get Willie Carson to give him his cheque at Newbury races on the following Friday afternoon. The camera crew were called in and a case of champagne ensured that Willie (coincidentally, but quite splendidly, wearing the Queen's colours) handed George his £100,000 cheque.

It transpired that Willie had always been George's favourite jockey and had actually ridden the last winner in the jackpot bet that brought him his fortune; he was not complaining, however; he bought himself a new bungalow and a car, bought his children and grandchildren presents, and spent his reclining days in comfort and happiness. A 'lucky 7' winner indeed.

8

THE LIFE I LOST AS A MEMBER OF PARLIAMENT

My greatest regret in life is that I have never been and will now never be a Member of the House of Commons, even though I am perhaps the only man to be offered a seat by all three of the major parties. I used to feel the gods were decreeing that I should have a political career when I was born just a few yards across the River Thames from the Palace of Westminster; but it was not to be. I spend a lot of time at the House of Commons and meet a lot of MPs and I have been able to feel that I was playing a role with both my closeness to Labour leaders and my political betting. Indeed, the Mandrake Column in the *Sunday Telegraph* in March 1966 said of me that I was 'one of the most powerful personalities in politics'. I have never personally seen it that way because, while politics are dear to my heart (and I have hope that I may yet be of help to a Labour government), political betting was simply a part of my job and, as I have said, never once have I allowed my sympathies or desires to influence my judgement. The integrity of political betting had to be protected at all costs and anyway, no matter how much I would have wished to see a Labour government, to suggest that they were hot favourites to win an election during the eighties would have been an expensive folly indeed.

Whatever influence you have, whatever role you may play, the one thing that really counts is to be an elected Member of the House of Commons. And that was the first thought that excited me when, in July 1966, Labour offered me the opportunity to contest Stroud, safest of safe Tory seats. I knew that newcomers sometimes have to fight the no-hope seats to prove themselves before getting something winnable . . . but Stroud? I talked with my old friend Tony Howard, who commented: "Bloody cheek. They cannot expect you to win that one."

He told me to try to get somewhere where I had a better chance, but I thought about it and finally and very reluctantly, because I suspected that my opportunity might be gone for ever, declined. To my astonishment, a second invitation came my way – from the Tories of all people. Gerald Nabarro, with whom I had become very friendly (we shared a common aim – to get as much publicity as possible), invited me out to lunch "to talk about standing as a Conservative candidate".

Gerald even brought along a Brigadier who, it appeared, was to be my agent. I did not have the courage to tell him that not only could I never stand for the Conservatives, I could never even vote for them as I disliked all his party stood for. I settled for the easy way out. I was, I told him, now so deeply involved in my political betting, and that it was so important to my employers, that I felt my political career would have to wait. It was a deal easier telling one of David Steel's publicity men that, much as I appreciated the suggestion, I was not a Liberal and therefore could not stand as a Liberal candidate. Years later David Steel and I got to know each other quite well, but if I was to become an MP it would be as a Socialist or not at all.

Basically, I was never financially equipped to take what, as it turned out, would have been a considerable risk. I could presumably have stood and won in 1966 when Labour had a ninety-nine seat majority. But from that year on, one could so easily have been ousted. With no finance behind me, the important thing was to keep a job that I did well, paid me reasonably well and was one that I actually very much enjoyed; dreams of office had to be pushed to the back of the queue when there was a mortgage to pay, food and clothes to buy.

There was one further factor that influenced me considerably. In one of our many discussions, Tony Howard suggested that I may have 'tainted' myself; that if I contested a constituency my opponents were certain to throw at me the fact that I was a bookmaker who bet on politics; that my interest was commercial rather than one of concern for the electorate. He did not think that was worth the risk. As far as I was concerned there would have been no Member of that noble House who would have cared more about his constituents' well-being than me, but I valued Tony's advice and, as usual, I took it.

But I still had a job to do for Ladbrokes and with a direct line of communication to Harold Wilson through Percy Clark, I still had an influence. Percy was the Prime Minister's Press Secretary; he fulfilled for Harold the role that Bernard Ingham undertook for Margaret Thatcher. If I wanted a message passed to the Prime Minister or wished to seek a favour (such as requesting that he mention the Ladbroke prices on whichever TV channel he was appearing that evening) I would ring Percy. If an answer was required, I would have it within two hours. If it was simply a request, Harold never failed me; he would always manage to slip in somehow that he was heartened by the way the polls were going and the amount of money being laid on Labour and the fact that the Ladbroke price had hardened. Tony Howard discovered that my telephone was being tapped, presumably because of this regular communication with No. 10, but I never worried about it. There was never anything said or done that could compromise or embarrass anyone.

For all his favours and his kindnesses, Wilson was a disappointment to me and, I imagine, to all true Socialists. Even as Prime Minister he seemed to have this desire to be subservient, whether to the Trade Unions or to the Governor of the Bank of England. He is an old man now and if you look back on his Downing Street years I think you can see that, deep down inside himself, he was never that confident about his own abilities. It was watered-down Socialism that he practised to ensure that he remained in office.

I am also fearful that Neil Kinnock might feel compelled to dilute Socialist principles to retain power once he attains it. It may well be that the British electorate does not wish for my brand of politics and if that is the case then they will presumably keep voting for the Tory Party. But I do fervently believe that any political party, and most specifically my political party, has to be true to its birthright. I pray that the next Labour government will feel just as deeply as I do that this is the way forward: passion and conviction, not pragmatism and dilution, are the heart-beat of the Labour Party.

For twelve years of government, Conservatives have had the benefit of North Sea oil and falling commodity prices throughout the world, yet they are taxing us at a higher rate than in 1979 and on their own figures concede that the poor have got poorer — and that there are more of them. It is time Labour had a chance, although I accept that Socialists like myself are unlikely to see the society we wish to see in the foreseeable future because when they win the election they will be confronted with a set of problems unprecedented in times of peace.

There is little doubt that Margaret Thatcher had to go even though the manner of her departure was so bizarre. She represented a monumental failure. In my view she failed herself, her party and her country. She had fostered the 'I'm all right, Jack' society and ignored the problems of the poverty that pervades all our larger cities. We cannot accept, as we approach the twenty-first century, our young people living in cardboard boxes in the doorways of shops that sell a pair of shoes at a cost of a month's social security. We must turn away from greed and look at need. It is essential that Neil Kinnock and the next Labour government do not let the working class down as Harold Wilson with his majority of ninety-nine did twenty-five years ago.

We must always remember that, to the Tories in power, money and profit are God. I recall at the Bank Rate Tribunal many years ago Lord Kindersley admitting to selling sterling short in Hong Kong and making money by so doing saying "What I did may have been anti-British but it made good sense to me." An honest Tory admitting that money comes first even if the action damages the country. The CBI and the Institute of Directors are very fond of laying the blame for inflation at the door of the workers, claiming that increased wages mean increased unemployment. But do those two bodies have any comment when company chairmen and group board directors award themselves gigantic rises, often 50 and sometimes even 100 per cent? Of course not. Yet these are the same directors who will go to profit-plan meetings and wage negotiations and leave with big smiles if they have managed to limit the workers who have laboured hard throughout the year to 5 per cent rather than the 8 or 9 per cent they sought. That, they say smugly, was a good morning's work. Yet when some of those same directors lead their companies into insolvency or liquidation, you can rest assured that only the workers thrown on the dole will suffer – the bosses never will. What hypocrites these people are.

One man who would have agreed with every word of that little speech was Hugh Gaitskell. He was much more to the left, particularly on education, than many might have imagined, and I believe that he would have made a magnificent leader and a truly great Prime Minister. His death was a tragedy not only for the Labour Party but for the whole country. He held the party together during one of its many 'warring' periods and I am convinced that he would have dealt with the Trade Unions, not as Thatcher did but much more firmly than Wilson. I met Hugh several times and he came to Hornchurch when I stood for the Council. Before he died he apparently gave instructions for the file he kept on me to be passed on to Jim Callaghan (now Lord Callaghan). I discovered this when, not long after joining Ladbrokes, I took Cyril Stein to meet Callaghan at his offices near the House to discuss the Labour Party attitude to a Betting Tax. "I know all about you," said Jim with a smile. When I asked what he meant he told me, "Mr Gaitskell left me your file." Cyril seemed suitably impressed.

Nye Bevan was a lifelong atheist and he held a simplistic attitude to life that I was never going to change. I did not spend much time with him but I do remember one long conversation about spiritualism and life after death. Nye insisted that the most important thing was life itself: it had been given us, so enjoy it while doing what one could for others was the gist of his argument. As for an after-life he insisted: "I didn't worry before I got here, boy, so why should I worry about where I am going?" There was no answer to that!

An MP after my own heart in every way was Ian 'Mik' Mikardo. As with Bevan, there has never been any retreating from his profound views; nor has there been any wishy-washy 'Liberal-Socialism'. Mik is of the red-blooded variety. Over the years I was to talk with him many times about the odds on varying events and I do believe that he became the closest thing to a licensed bookmaker that you could find in the precincts of Parliament.

I clearly didn't teach him all I know – he was a far better MP than ever he was a bookie! Mik has been one of the genuine personalities to adorn Westminster for more than thirty years. Another was the aforementioned Gerald Nabarro. He sat on the opposite benches to Mik and he was a vastly different man to the bluff left-winger. Gerald was quite unique and – politics apart – we had so much in common that we became firm friends. I don't think Gerald ever realised that I was not of the same political persuasion as himself and there were times I suspect when even his fellow Tories wondered precisely where his loyalties lay, for he was a constant thorn in their side. Nabarro made his name in the fifties by attacking anomalies in the Purchase Tax Regulations. He would point out that the tax on underpants was 'x' but the levy on 'long johns' was 'x'

plus 'y'. There were some hilarious moments and the public loved him for it.

There was nothing wrong in what he was doing (pricking the bubble of authority is always a worthwhile pastime) even though it irritated members of his own government but there was a vitally important second purpose to it, and that was drawing attention to Gerald Nabarro, MP. He was a great self-publicist; he probably received more letters than any other Member and he simply loved to see his name in the newspapers. You always heard Gerald first and saw him some moments later: he was a marvellous companion and when it came to matters of publicity we were a splendid partnership: he would lay a bet, one of us would tip off the newspapers and both of us would receive a mention!

Being involved so closely with sport I always endeavoured to maintain a close relationship with the Minister for Sport. Only one has filled that role with what I would call real distinction: the Rt Hon. Denis Howell, PC, MP.

It is with considerable pride that I have always been able to count him among my two closest friends in Parliament. Denis was a sportsman himself, being a Football League referee. He married his love and knowledge of sport to a shrewd political ability that was crafted in Birmingham. Big city politics can be just as tough, just as bitter as those in Westminster and Denis had a magnificent education in how to win political battles. Come rain or shine (remember how, when Harold Wilson made him Minister for Drought during one terribly dry summer it promptly poured!) Denis always knew what to do and when to do it. It was a brave man who took Denis on in debates on sporting matters — he has always been a master of his subject. In this respect he was helped quite considerably by two aides: his first personal assistant was Vic Shroot and more recently Patrick Cheney has been his right-hand man. They have been invaluable to him. Denis does not intend to stand at the next General Election, but I do hope that his vast experience will not be lost to the Labour Party.

My other confidant was George Wigg (later, of course, to become Lord Wigg). I first got to know him well when he was on the Tote Board from 1961 to 1964. Most might suppose the Tote and bookmakers to be sworn rivals – but George and I were never that. He would ring me up to talk politics or confer on racing problems and I would go to his home at Clapham Common where we would talk for hours. No one has ever said anything about me that I appreciated more than when George, during an interminable political discussion one day, said: "Ron, there is no doubt about you. You are a bloody good Socialist."

Mind you, I will not easily forget either just how infuriating George could be; a real devil. His favourite times for a phone call were early morning and late at night. "Just wanted to catch you before you left for the office," he would say and if you were only half-awake and not answering his questions sharply or shrewdly enough, he would bite your head off. "You haven't done your homework," he would bark; "you must do your homework." Even at six in the morning you should be doing it as far as he was concerned and so it was hardly surprising that he got a very high standard out of those who worked for him. People did not have to like George Wigg – and many did not – but he certainly commanded their respect.

The Jockey Club were among that number forced to respect him when he became the first President of the Betting Office Licensees' Association (BOLA). He had very few friends at Portman Square because George never hid his dislike of non-elected, autonomous bodies; and when it came to self-perpetuating, non-elected bodies, the Jockey Club ranked fractionally higher than even the International Olympic Committee. I have to concede that while I once may have shared George's lack of enthusiasm for the Jockey Club, I have changed my mind: today I think they do a very good job indeed. If they were voted for by everyone within the racing industry or were all paid officials, there would not necessarily be an improvement. Sorry, George. I think we are now well served by the Jockey Club.

A strange and amusing thing to all who knew him was that Wigg was a man besotted by security; by MI5, phone-tapping and conspiracy. He did not know where they were, but there were always daggers about! No matter where you were, whenever he called he was concerned about security. "Are you alone?" he would ask in an exaggerated whisper. "Can anyone overhear us?" And then: "Are you sure there is no one about?" It was hardly surprising, then, that a man so obsessed by security should have played such a role in the Profumo scandal.

In many ways Wigg was an influential figure in guiding racing into its healthy state of the nineties. When BOLA was formed nearly thirty years ago, it was to look after the interests of the mushrooming number of betting shops, both large and small. He did this magnificently. He represented the interests of the bookmakers, the Levy Board (for five years he was chairman) and the interests of the man in the street. He understood them, he related to them, felt himself one of them – and so, while he was basically the figurehead of a bookmakers' protection association, the ordinary punters also had a voice. He was always thinking about them, and speaking up for them.

The bosses of the big betting concerns, men like Cyril Stein and Peter George from Ladbrokes, William Hill's Len Cowburn, and Bob Green, the managing director of Mecca, all came to rely on him absolutely. They would seek his advice, knowing that it was sound and to be trusted. No man played a greater role this century in integrating bookmakers into society than George Wigg; believe me, that is no overstatement.

It may sound ludicrous now, but Ladbrokes and William Hill did not immediately go for the High Street shops in 1961. There were early doubts about their profitability; worries that drugs and crime might become associated with them but, as we now know, and the Government came to recognise, there was to be no more trouble, no more robberies and no more violence at betting shops than there was at banks and post offices. Because of this, the Government recently amended the Betting and Gaming Act, allowing shops to be carpeted, to have television sets installed and tea and coffee to be served. This was their way of saying that betting shops were responsibly dealing with the public and should therefore be treated with respect. George Wigg helped lay all these foundations.

Thirty years ago the very suggestion of men like Peter George and Len Cowburn going to meet the Home Secretary to discuss the Levy would have produced a horse-laugh. But, thanks in great part to Wigg, that is exactly what does now happen. And even though he had been a member of the Tote Board, George saw the unfairness of the Tote Bill which the Government tried to foist upon us. This would have given the Tote a priority in the High Street, allowing them to open a shop next door to an existing bookmaker's premises. George advised on that and – with a little help from one or two other Parliamentary pals – we managed to have that Bill stopped at the Committee stage, thank goodness. There is no doubt that Wigg's death was an enormous loss to the whole industry. Personally, I lost a true friend; I miss his companionship and his conversation. Damn it, I even miss those early-morning and late-night telephone calls.

Without realising it at the time, Ladbrokes played a most significant role in having the on-course betting duty abolished. In 1982 we were sponsoring the winter greyhound Classic, the Golden Jacket, at Haringey, and I asked Neil Kinnock if he would present the trophy. He was more than willing, but wondered if he could bring his wife, Glynis. Could he bring Glynis, indeed! We all had a drink in the office of Ernie Farrant, then the general manager of Harringay. There was myself, my wife Pat and son Christian; Ernie, of course, and Charles Chandler who was the boss of the NGRC. Neil surprised me by not simply talking about the sport, but stating that in his view people should be positively encouraged to go racing. To do this, he said, the next Labour government would abolish the on-course tax on racing. I could hardly believe my ears. I had long been campaigning for this very abolition. How did I now make capital out of this forthright view by the Labour leader?

As luck would have it, the race was being televised and the man in charge of the ITV operation for the World of Sport programme was Gary Newbon, a friend of mine and a good professional journalist. When I told Gary what Kinnock had said, he asked if there was any chance of him repeating it – on air. I agreed to ask Neil, and the result was that he confirmed on television all he had told me. He also backed the winner of the Ladbrokes' Golden Jacket that afternoon. It was called, suitably, Amazing Man!

Once it became clear what the Labour view would be, Tories led by Sir Charles Morrison were able to lobby the Chancellor for the abolition of what I had always considered an iniquitous tax and Nigel Lawson announced the measure in his next Budget.

So although that was one bit of good to come from a Tory government, if you suspect that I had had enough of the Thatcher era, you would be perfectly correct. I was not alone, either. As the voting in the first ballot showed when Mrs Thatcher faced another challenge for her place as Tory Party leader and Prime Minister in November 1990, there were many Tory MPs who also wished to see the back of her. The difference this time of course was that she was challenged not by a stalking horse as in 1989 but by an ex-Cabinet Minister of substance in Michael Heseltine. Events had moved swiftly after Sir Geoffrey Howe's speech in the House of Commons explaining his resignation as Deputy Prime Minister – a speech described to me by Denis Howell as "the first time I have seen a public execution!"

When I heard that Heseltine was to stand, my mind flashed back to the World in Action programme I did for ITV in 1987 and his reply to my question, "Will you be a candidate for the leadership?" "You must make up your own mind. You have a free choice." He was right; I did have a choice and I exercised it by leaving him in my list of possibles at that time. However, when the first ballot became a straight fight between him and Margaret Thatcher, I made the Prime Minister favourite at 1-2 with Michael 6-4. I did so because I felt that she would win on the first ballot and there was indeed a great deal of money for her to win, including two wagers of £20,000. But the real surprise of that first week was the continuing support for Douglas Hurd, the Foreign Secretary, whose name was not even on the voting papers. In fact, by Friday, November 16, he had been backed down from 6-1 to 7-2 and Heseltine had drifted to be the outsider of the three at 5-1.

It was then that I realised that even if Thatcher did not win on the first ballot, Heseltine's goose was cooked, and I said precisely that on Granada Television in a programme called Granada Upfront whose editor, by a strange coincidence, was Charles Tremayne who had produced the World in Action programme three years before. After considerable fluctuation, the closing odds for the first ballot were 2-7 Thatcher, 11-4 Heseltine, 10-1 Hurd, 20-1 bar to become the next leader. It was a great surprise when Thatcher failed to win on that first ballot by just four votes even though she had defeated Heseltine overwhelmingly, but it tells us much about Tory MPs who, in order to save their own skins, will ditch a leader who has never been beaten in a vote and who has won three elections. What fair-weather friends they proved to be, though maybe justice was done, as they were as uncaring about her as she had been to the aged, the poor, the sick and the disabled.

If I say I got it wrong again on the second ballot, that would not be quite fair to myself, for while we opened our book with Hurd and Heseltine bracketed together at 5-4 with John Major at 5-2 I could not buck the market. There had been a lot of people backing Hurd during the previous week and now the early money was again for Hurd and also for Heseltine.

I began to wonder if 1963 was going to happen all over again, with the Tory hierarchy having decreed that 'that woman' had to go now saying that 'that man', the Hon. Member for Henley, had to be stopped at all costs, coming

138

up with a 'safe' stop-gap like Hurd for a couple of years and then giving Major his chance. But if, as Harold Wilson declared, a week is a long time in politics, two days is a long time when it comes to political betting. On the Friday (November 23) John Major was all the rage. He was backed to win over £100,000 at all prices down to evens and the closing prices when Conservative Members came to vote were Major a very hot favourite at 4-7, Heseltine 11-8 and Hurd at 10-1. At the end of it all, Ladbrokes had taken £396,000, finishing up about level. It seemed a far cry from that first Tory leadership battle which I bet on in 1963. Was that really twenty-seven years ago, I kept asking myself!

What did amaze me was to be reminded by Ian Wooldridge that I had actually predicted that John Major would succeed to Margaret Thatcher's crown in an article he wrote for the Festival of British Racing programme called The Sport of Kings in September 1989. Ian assures me that it is there for all to see on page 40. What I find even more amazing is that John Major has actually become Prime Minister with the votes of 185 Tory MPs and Margaret Thatcher becomes an ex-Prime Minister with a seat on the back benches having had 204 Conservative Members vote for her. They really are a strange bunch!

But it is not for me to complain. I never liked Margaret Thatcher, her party or her policies and I was glad to see her go. To say more would, perhaps, be churlish. She once forgave me for something and while I cannot forgive, I can at least show some restraint. I had the temerity to ask her if she would have a go on a skateboard at the Ideal Home Exhibition. Skateboarding was a current craze at this time in the seventies and Jim Callaghan had been pictured on a board the week before – just a bit of fun and a good publicity picture.

I shall never forget the look of disdain she gave me or the stinging words: "Me on a skateboard. I should think not," when I asked Mrs Thatcher if she would similarly perform for a few moments, just for a photograph. She had clearly forgiven or forgotten when, in 1989, I had my formal retirement party at the London Hilton; she and Neil Kinnock both signed a bottle of House of Commons whisky and sent it to me – by a motor-cycle DR from the House – not only as a farewell gift but also, surely, as a testament to the integrity of political betting over the last twenty-five years. That bottle will never be opened. I shall keep it as a treasured reminder of all my many years around the political arena.

9

CRICKET, LOVELY CRICKET

Politics has always been the great love of my life, but cricket, lovely cricket, has been the great escape. It has entranced and entertained me. I played it, I watched it and finally I had the happiness of being able to work alongside it. The Oval, a homely Test match ground set in one of the poorer parts of South London, is the home of Surrey County Cricket Club and my spiritual home. It has figured in my life since my earliest recollections. It was there that I spent five wonderful days as the guest of my headmaster during which Len Hutton scored 364 runs against the Australians. And it is there, more than fifty years on, that I still sit betting on cricket with cricketers and cricket fans, in the corner of the Long Room that has become virtually my own.

The parallel between John Major, the Prime Minister, and myself – when it comes to this great game of ours, at least! – is uncanny. When I read of his young days in South London, I could hardly believe it was not me that they were written about. It appeared to be a carbon copy of my youth, although mine began, I suppose, more than a decade earlier.

He walked to The Oval as a nine-year-old from Cold-harbour Lane in Brixton; I walked there from Peckham. He won a cricket bat from the *Evening Standard* for the best bowling performance of the week when he was around twelve; I won one from the old *Star* for a best-of-the-week

141

bowling feat – only mine was a Jack Hobbs bat. He used to sit and watch from the old wooden benches at square leg – those in front of the Archbishop Tenison School – which was exactly the place I would choose, except that I liked to sit on the grass (and how sad it is that the youngsters of today can no longer do that). Like him I would sometimes also wait until late in the day when we could get in for nothing, but that, I guess, is where we set off at a tangent. He became a Conservative, a Chancellor and Prime Minister; I became a Socialist, a bookmaker and PR director, and a would-be politician. Yet, because this is the way of the true supporter, we will both support Surrey until our dying days.

I shall always remember those long-ago days when the London evening newspapers (there were three of them then, of course – the *Evening News*, the *Star* and the sole survivor, the *Evening Standard*) offered bats for the best performances of the week. I was a slow bowler and one particularly fine effort in 1938 – and for the life of me I cannot remember how many I took for how many and against whom – was submitted by my schoolmaster. To my utter astonishment, my name appeared in the *Star*. You cannot begin to understand the thrill it was to see my name in print. And then, wonder of wonders, a Jack Hobbs bat was delivered to my home.

I had never seen Hobbs play, but the older men at The Oval would sit and talk in considerable awe of his batting exploits for Surrey in years past. To own a Jack Hobbs bat, then, was really something. My headmaster, Mr George Hirst, seemed almost as thrilled as I was. He called me into his study at Peckham Central School to congratulate me and told me he was so pleased that I should bring such honour to the school that he was intending to take me to see the Australians play the Test match against England at The Oval. "Would I like that?" he asked. Would I? It meant sitting on a seat rather than on the grass, but it also meant that I would see my hero of the hour: Eddie Paynter. Nothing was going to keep me away!

Quite how Eddie Paynter, of Lancashire and not a Surrey player, came to be my favoured player is something that I cannot really explain; I can only suppose that it came through reading newspaper reports and being gently channelled down the Paynter road by a cricket writer who perhaps idolised him. Anyway, here was my chance to see him in a Test match – not something to be missed. So Mr Hirst and I sat there for a couple of days awaiting the arrival of Paynter while Hutton – now, sadly, the late Sir Leonard – piled up the runs. Eddie was padded up for two days and then, when he did reach the wicket, he was out for – a duck! My despair at seeing him out like that outweighed the immediate enjoyment of watching Hutton score his then world Test record 364. I have to say that I still feel the disappointment to this day, and I was upset a few months ago to learn (too late!) that the ball Eddie hit for six out of the Brisbane ground to win the Ashes and the infamous 'Bodyline' series in 1933 was sold at auction by his son for £4,400. I would gladly have paid that for such a memento of my boyhood.

But perhaps a more important event in my childhood took place on July 31, 1937. It was a Bank Holiday and a quite splendid one. It was the first day of a three-day County Championship match between Surrey and Nottinghamshire at The Oval and I remember it as yesterday because it was the day I had my first bet. I find it fascinating now – and perhaps even significant – that my first bet on anything was on cricket.

I was in my favoured place on the grass, close to the boundary rope. Fielding near to me was Joe Hardstaff, a prolific scorer for Notts and England. I think he must have been a very nice man as well as one of our finest batsmen because he began a conversation with me during one lull in the early play. "I bet we will have three wickets before lunch," he teased. "I bet you don't," I retorted staunchly. "All right," said Joe, "I bet you an ice-cream." No matter how many times I look at *Wisden*, the fact remains that Surrey let me down: they did lose three wickets before lunch – Sandham caught for six, McMurray run out for nine and Gregory out for five, clean bowled. What *Wisden* does not record is that I had to do without an ice-cream that Bank Holiday Saturday.

Just before the players returned to the field from lunch, I went to the kiosk and spent my only thruppence on a cornet; this I handed to Joe when he returned to his fielding base and, with due ceremony and what appeared considerable relish, he jolly well ate it. It was the start of a long career in the betting business and I was to lose much more in the years ahead, but never did paying out hurt quite as much as watching Joe Hardstaff eat that ice-cream!

Forty-four years later was to come the most memorable wager in cricket history when two Australians bet against their own side in what will for ever be known as 'The Botham Test' or 'The 500-1 Test'. Again I was to suffer the agony of paying and this time it was a lot more than a thruppenny ice-cream. It might even have cost me my job as the PR director at Ladbrokes, but it helped to forge one of the more remarkable partnerships in cricket: that between myself and Godfrey Evans, my adviser on the game for twenty years.

Loving cricket as I do is not the same as being an expert and when in 1971 we decided to give cricket betting a 'go', we needed someone to guide us. One of our most respected clients, even in those days, was Colin Ingleby-Mackenzie, a charming, well-heeled, well-educated (Eton), swashbuckling ex-captain of Hampshire who was with merchant bankers Brown Shipley and today heads their insurance broking division. Colin knew cricket, he knew racing and he knew enough about gambling to be a shrewd and winning punter. I could think of no better person to advise me and I invited him to join us. He wrote back regretting, "because of business commitments", that he could not do so and suggested that we talk with the former England wicket-keeper, Godfrey Evans. It turned out to be an inspired choice.

Thomas Godfrey Evans, CBE, seventy years of age (in

August 1990) but going on fifty-five, kept wicket for England ninety-one times and scored 2,439 Test runs with centuries at Old Trafford in 1950 against the West Indies and at Lord's in 1952 against India. He had 1,066 first-class 'scalps', 219 of them in Test matches, the fourth best in Test history. For almost a decade he was a vital England player and for Kent he was simply an institution. Of him, John Woodcock, cricket correspondent to *The Times* for many years, wrote: 'I do not believe it is humanly possible to keep wicket any better than Evans used to do for England in Australia . . . he was faultless from start to finish.'

It transpired that Godfrey had actually spoken to William Hill when they met on holiday in Montego Bay some time before I contacted him and had suggested that they bet on cricket. His idea had not been welcomed then and thus it was with some alacrity that he accepted my invitation to lunch to discuss that very possibility. We met at the Ladbroke Club in Mayfair, ever my favourite watering hole, and he very quickly agreed to my proposition. Godfrey always liked his little punt, but I pointed out that I needed an expert to guide me on cricket problems – not on what he thought was a 3-1 chance! I would fix the prices, I insisted, even though we were not quite sure at that stage what we intended, other than the desire to bet on cricket.

What became abundantly clear was that you need to ask an awful lot of questions before you start offering odds and those questions will vary as to whether one is dealing with a five-day Test or a one-day match. You need to know such basics as how good a wicket it is; whether it will turn early or last the duration of the game. Do the batsmen go for the runs or prefer to get well set? On such questions and many, many more depend your odds.

The number of runs scored during a session will depend to a considerable degree upon the number of overs bowled, although having two forceful batsmen would obviously become a factor. If, for instance, the West Indians are involved you would not expect twenty-eight overs in a two-hour session — the figure to which I normally work — but a couple of Indian leg-spinners operating for two hours as we had at times during their last tour would be an entirely different matter. On the first period of the first day of a Test match we bet in groups of ten runs (1-10, 11-20, and so on to 71-80 or more) and I now work to two and a half to three runs per over. It is remarkable how many times in a season that between 71 and 80 runs are scored in the opening session of a Test; we generally have that as favourite because in a five-day match the openers are hardly likely to gallop along. But if someone thinks that the batsmen will score at a run a minute and that there will be between 121 and 130 runs scored before lunch then they can have 12-1 on that belief.

I always change the odds after every innings, and generally after each session and these are dictated solely by the state of the game. If I was a betting man (which I am not, really) I would put my money on the score in the first two hours of a Test being 76 for 1. But just suppose that the batting side was 68 for 4 at lunch, then the odds would change dramatically, depending upon two factors: whether it was a bad wicket or whether it had been one bowler or another breezing through the opposition's top batsmen. If it was the former I could envisage the team being all out around tea-time; if it was that one fast bowler with the new ball had taken three or four quick wickets but that batsmen Nos. 5 and 6 had stayed together for an hour or so, then there would have to be different odds. In short, there are an infinite number of options to be sorted out.

After nearly twenty years at it I was beginning to think that I had mastered the business and knew most of the pitfalls, yet only in June 1990 we had a sharp reminder that things can go very wrong if you do not ask the right questions. We were betting not at a Test but at the Benson and Hedges quarter-final at Trent Bridge where the scorecard showed a D. A. Leatherdale down to bat at No. 11 for Worcestershire against Nottingham. Godders suggested that we put him down at 50-1 to be top scorer, but because the last man in is never much of a batsman and in one-day cricket frequently would not even reach the crease, I said we should offer 100-1. "He won't even get a knock on this pitch," I argued, and up he went on the board at 100-1.

I would not say that we were besieged, but there were quite a few Worcester fans coming in to have a bet on this outsider and if the unexpected were to happen, we stood to lose quite a lot of money. Alerted, and slightly alarmed, Godfrey rushed away to ask a few questions. Master Leatherdale, it turned out, was not a No. 11 at all; he was an up-and-coming young batsman who would normally appear at No. 5 or 6. If he was promoted in the order, it appeared that he might well get runs – and the Worcester fans had not been slow to appreciate that fact. As it happened, Leatherdale did not get in to bat. Tim Curtis, Martin Weston and Graeme Hick knocked off the runs. Most people, perhaps not surprisingly, had backed Hick to be the top scorer and I don't think anyone had anything on Weston, yet it was he who scored 99, helping to ensure that Ladbrokes had another winning day. But we did not celebrate or even go home happy. We always try to be professional in everything we do but this time we had made a mistake that could have been costly – and we knew it. As we reached the car park to drive home, Godfrey quietly admitted his carelessness: "Sorry about today, Master. I didn't do my homework." No one is more critical of our shortcomings than Godfrey and I are, but that was an end to that little affair; the mistake had been recognised and it would not occur again, of that I could be quite sure.

From our very first meeting, Godfrey and I had forged a bond that grew only stronger as the years passed. He was, and is, an open, honest man who for want of a better phrase calls a spade a spade. Cyril Stein happened to be in the Ladbroke Club on the day of our first meeting and I introduced Godders to him; like me, Stein realised that we were in the company of a unique man. People talk lightly of 'legends' but you have only to walk around any cricket ground with him to know that no other description suffices.

He has been retired thirty years, yet boys only nine or ten years of age will still queue for his autograph; mature and successful businessmen in the hospitality boxes that you find at most grounds today, will welcome him effusively. I doubt if there is a box-holder on any Test ground who doesn't know Godders and there certainly isn't one who doesn't expect him to make an unscheduled appearance at some stage during the match for 'just a little g and t then'.

Ted Dexter, another of the cricketing fraternity who likes a little gamble, once called us "an unlikely combination" but the truth is that from the first day I have never considered the moment when Godders, looking like some Dickensian refugee with those extravagant side-whiskers of his, would not be my partner. He grew those mutton-chop whiskers, incidentally, because Graham Hill, once one of Britain's great motor-racing drivers, told him that if he wished to remain in the public eye after retirement he should acquire something by which he would be recognised. My belief is that the twinkling eyes, the ever-present smile and that jaunty walk would always give him away without him needing to look like an Old English Sheepdog.

We had our good days and our bad ones, but the worst two we ever spent were during that Headingley Test match in 1981. Once more the Ashes were being contested: Australia won the first Test at Trent Bridge and the match at Lord's was drawn. This one was marked by Ian Botham getting a 'pair' and immediately renouncing the captaincy with which he had been honoured amid considerable controversy. The third Test was mid July at Leeds and Mike Brearley, restored as captain, spent two days fretting, while Australia spent most of them compiling 401 before declaring. The irrepressible Botham had guaranteed his skipper five wickets "if you keep me on"; Brearley kept him on – for forty overs! – and Both actually delivered six. Nevertheless, the Aussies seemed in a strong enough position and it looked positively rosy for them on the Saturday evening as England, bowled out for 174, were invited to follow on. They then lost Graham Gooch for a duck, the Essex man thus having the rare misfortune to be out twice in the same day in a Test match.

Having been home for the Sunday, I drove back up to Yorkshire on the Monday morning, feeling that it really was rather a waste of my time. The Aussies were heading for an overwhelming victory – everyone was agreed on that in all the newspapers. The Leeds public were not renowned for turning out in huge numbers on a Monday in such circumstances. Add those two points together and it was clear that I would not be doing much business and might be better employed in London. England began the day 222 behind and their position – and my depression – steadily worsened: 2 for 18, 3 for 37, 4 for 41. Before tea any vestige of hope appeared to vanish with the (reluctant) departure of Geoff Boycott. Bob Taylor came and went and Graham Dilley joined Both with the score at 135 for 7 wickets.

Godfrey agreed with my reasoning: we should book out of our hotel room and head for home. England would have lost before we were halfway down the M1. If there was anyone left on the ground foolish enough to want a bet, he could have 500-1 on an England victory. I could just as easily have said 5,000-1 but thank God I did not do so because two of those so-called 'mug' punters that I like to say do not exist had a bet on England at 500-1 and won £10,000 between them. Those two 'mugs' were fast bowler Denis Lillee and wicket-keeper Rod Marsh. Like so many Aussies, they were real gambling men: neither could resist what they saw as a bargain.

They sent the team coach-driver over to place their bet and when news of their big win inevitably leaked out of the dressing-room, there was a huge row, with allegations of cheating and throwing the match. The lads made it crystal clear that they had done their damnedest to win, wanted to win and had a bet only because the odds, in a two-horse race, seemed too good to miss. That apart, it has to be said that it was also a good 'insurance' for them.

The players were due a bonus if they won the match; if by any chance they lost, Lillee and Marsh would still be financial winners.

Godders and I were in blissful ignorance of all this as we steamed down the M1 towards Newport Pagnell where I was to drop him off. We tuned in to Test Match Special on Radio Three to find unexpected English resistance: Botham and Dilley were hitting out. It could not last. Could it? Godfrey and I exchanged glances once or twice; we did not need to say anything. At this point it was still only a question of asking ourselves whether England could make the Aussies bat again, which had seemed most unlikely as we set off on our journey south. Yet in eighty frenetic, momentous minutes, Dilley (smashing 56) and Botham put on 117 runs to push England ahead. In homes and offices all over the country, TV sets were being switched on with everyone (and I was among them!) asking breathlessly: "What's the score? We can't really do it, can we?" The buccaneering Botham, intent upon expunging all memory of his dreadful experience as captain, was proposing that he could, that England could, with the greatest Test innings he would ever play and was, perhaps, ever played. Between tea and the close he scored 106 runs, his century coming off 87 balls. Fast bowler Chris Old, on his own Yorkshire strip, stayed out there with the hero of the hour while another 67 runs were added. Last man in was Bob Willis, who would claim his own fanfare on a climactic final day yet to come. No batsman, Bob, but a dogged fighter who was to see Botham through to the close, enabling England to fight that one last dramatic day.

I had dropped Godfrey off at his Newport Pagnell home. "Well, Master . . ." he said. His words tailed off but there was nothing much else he could say. When I reached my home I rang him: England, at 351 for 9, would go into the last day – the day Godfrey and I had cancelled – 125 runs ahead. I was fractionally more conversational than he had been. "Bloody hell, Godders. If we have this one wrong we will take some stick," I said to him.

I slept uneasily, I must admit. I *knew* that I had not made a mistake: if England's nine, ten, Jack could score so freely, surely Australia would get whatever target they were set comfortably enough? And that target was modest indeed when play did resume the next morning. Willis was out quickly and Australia needed only 130 to win. It should have been a doddle, but now Willis tore into them with his finest performance for his country. The easy target for Australia became an Everest and Bob Willis took eight wickets for 43 runs, Australia finished 18 runs short. England's was the first victory by a team following-on this century and it so demoralised Australia that they lost the next two Tests and with them the Ashes.

I also lost a lot of money (£21,000 on the game) and for a while a little self-respect, I suppose. Everyone thought we were idiots – or almost everyone. My most gratifying moment of that whole affair came with a phone call from a Yorkshireman who knows his cricket, Len Cowburn, the chairman of William Hill. He rang Peter George, then Managing Director of Ladbroke Racing, to say: "Don't blame Ron for those odds, Peter. I would have thought 5,000-1 would have been nearer the mark." Little did either of them know that those were the odds I might very easily have offered on that fateful fourth day!

That telephone call made me feel a little better, but in fact it mattered not: when the news of two players betting against their own team came out, another million pounds' worth of publicity echoed around the world. Much of it was desperately unfair on the two players. Lillee and Marsh were nothing if not patriots; not for a single moment would they have considered trying to lose any match, let alone one against the Poms. It was simply that, to a gambling Aussie, the odds were so good that they could not be missed. And they were, of course, proved right for once.

What I did not discover until I started writing this book was that there was another well-known chap who celebrated with champagne that night – Don Mosey, erstwhile member of the famous BBC radio Test Match Special team.

151

I gather he had a tenner on and knowing his cricket like any good Yorkshireman, decided, as did the two Australians, that the odds were too good to be missed!

When I think about it, it is a miracle that people like me who spend a lifetime offering odds do not end up with ulcers or in a mental home, but all a person such as me can do is be as professional as he can and take the consequences, whatever they are. Mind you, there can be times when you are not necessarily master of your own destiny.

I have told how, in the way of having a little fun, some show jumpers tried to rig the result of a minor event at Devon. They still lost, but it does go to show how vulnerable we can be. I remember very clearly, shortly after we started betting on cricket, an incident which at the time I thought to be just another joke. Indeed, it probably is apocryphal, yet it could have had nasty implications had the rules not been swiftly changed. At Lord's, where Middlesex were playing Surrey, we were doing very little business (even in the early seventies county games were poorly attended) and what business there was was on one man to score a century: Peter Parfitt.

We were offering 10-1 and the only bets we were taking were a quid here, £2 there and a few fivers – all on Parfitt. When he was in the nervous nineties, so the story related to me went, Peter told the umpire that he was "getting a bit twitchy". He said that all the lads in the dressing-room had their money on him to get a century and he added, "I dare not let them down." "Don't you worry," the umpire is reported as replying, "I have had a bet on you as well." Peter reached his ton, we paid out with a smile, and when the story was first told I laughed with the rest, not taking it at all seriously. It was clear, however, a year later when we were renegotiating our contract at Lord's that the story had received a wider audience. It was suggested to us that betting on individuals was "not in the best interests of the game". Remembering the story – on which Parfitt, now an accomplished after-dinner speaker, has dined out for years – I wasn't too sure that it was in the best interests of

Ladbrokes either, so we quietly dropped such betting. But not, unfortunately, before we were really skinned by two more Aussies.

Depending upon circumstances, 10-1 is about the right price on any individual scoring a century and when the Australians were here in 1972, that is what we offered on the Chappell brothers at both Lord's and The Oval. Greg (and his supporters) celebrated his 131 at Lord's with our money, and then we came a real cropper. At The Oval, where the final Test was being played, 10-1 were again the odds being offered for either of them to score a century; if anyone wished to back them both to score 100 in a double, those odds were 109-1. A very large number of Australians did just that and cleared us out. The Chappells put on 201 in Australia's first innings, Ian scoring 118 and Greg 113 and those who had £10 doubles picked up £1,090 apiece. It was a bad Test for Ladbrokes – we lost nearly £20,000, most of it on the Chappell boys.

One man who has been a good friend to many of the Aussie tourists over the years is Charles Benson, at that time 'The Scout', the senior racing correspondent on the *Daily Express*. Charlie is a sporting punter, a friend to many of the great gamblers from the aristocracy, a man who knows his cricket and tennis as well as his racing and who is a very good client of ours. He not only bets for himself; he will often place large amounts for his friends, like Robert Sangster. On that day Charlie backed both the Chappells individually to reach three figures and to this day will recount volubly his regret at not joining those who had them doubled up! But at least Charlie has one marvellous memento of that innings: Ian gave him the bat with which he scored the runs, and one of Charlie's sons is still using it – to good effect, I gather.

Perhaps my favourite tale about Godfrey goes back to the World Cup of 1975 when we were at The Oval (where else?) betting on the Australia-West Indies match on June 14. That splendid sports writer from the *Observer*, Hugh McIlvanney, who loves his horse racing and his gambling, stopped at our corner of the Long Room to ask how we were doing. Quite straight-faced, Godders looked at Hugh and said: "Oh! I've been a bit out today. I said that Australia would last 53 overs but they lasted four balls more. I also said that they would get 185 runs and they got 192. That kind of thing gets me a bollocking around here." We all burst into laughter and Hugh duly recorded the story in the following day's paper, with the fact that the West Indians had won by seven wickets.

Life was always like that with Godfrey – good fun. It would not be quite true to say that he and I never had a row but, as in the Trent Bridge car park, after admitting that he hadn't done his homework, the next morning we will carry on as grown men should, as though nothing untoward has occurred so that our friendship continues untarnished.

I feel so lucky to have known Godfrey. We have shared times in the doldrums and days of success. I have learned more and more about cricket from him and he has learned a lot about laying odds from me. So much so, in fact, that now when we are cross-examining each other, doing our homework and seeking the answers to all the many questions we consider each day, Godfrey will have the temerity to suggest that my 3-1 offer should be only 5-2! It has been a wonderful partnership and a wonderful twenty years and I would not have wished to spend twenty years betting on cricket with anyone else. Among those roaring successes we shared was a day at Edgbaston, the Warwickshire headquarters in Birmingham. It must be said that while every top ground has looked after Godfrey and myself extremely kindly and extremely well, it is only at Edgbaston where we could find ourselves without lunch. Knowing that we were left to our own devices, Bob Readican, an old pal and client, invited us to a small tennis and squash club just opposite the county ground. His guest that day was Douggie Hobbs, a carpet magnate in the Midlands and, as it so happened, another Ladbrokes client. Godfrey and I were happy to have some company – and something to eat! –

and we joined them there. It turned out to be a most delightful lunch . . . and a most profitable one. A television set was switched on, ostensibly for people to watch the cricket but they were in fact screening horse racing. Douggie asked me if he could possibly have a bet. I said "Of course" and he placed £500 on a horse that won, I think at 2-1. But by the end of that afternoon, Mr Hobbs, who had come to watch cricket, had stayed in front of the television and lost thousands!

After tea I inquired, "Is there anything else I can do for you, Douggie?" "No – I am only sorry I bumped into you," he answered. It was not said nastily; Douggie Hobbs was too much of a sportsman. It cannot be fun losing large sums, but the beauty of 'good' gamblers is that they have their winning days as well as their bad ones and like Douggie they cough up promptly and with a smile. Douggie did not pay for our lunch that day, but even had he done so I would not have been embarrassed or felt sorry about taking his money. Nor would he have expected such sympathy. He did not have to go on after that first winner; nobody was forcing him to have another bet and then another. He could just as easily have won £20,000 off me and we both knew that. As I have said before, there is no such thing as a 'cert' and bookmakers can win and lose as surprisingly and as fortuitously as each and every punter.

It is always a sentimental journey back to Nottingham because it was the ground at which – if you discount my small wager with Joe Hardstaff – I thought cricket betting began. I say 'I thought' because an article entitled 'Betting and Cricket' by 'The Man on the Spot' taken from an old publication called the *Sporting Mirror* came into my hands during The Oval Test against India in 1990. To my surprise it refers to betting odds on a cricket match being carried by newspapers way back in 1882 which only goes to prove, I guess, that there really is very little that is new in the world! Anyway, Ladbrokes always had a strong connection and friendly relations with Trent Bridge through our property division – indeed, we built and paid for their new scoreboard. When we asked the club chairman, Frank Gregory, if we could experiment with cricket betting at the ground he and his committee were happy to give us the go-ahead. Thus it was that we began our operation at Trent Bridge in 1971. What began as a toe-dipping exercise had become a cross-Channel swim before 1972.

I picked Godders up and we drove to Trent Bridge for our first appearance; a very wary pair of openers we were, too. But we were pleased enough with the business to decide that we should go into all the Test grounds. People looked horrified. "You will never get into Lord's, not in a hundred years," they said – but we did. I spoke with Jack Bailey, then secretary of the MCC, and with Donald Carr who was secretary to the Test and County Cricket Board and we actually moved in for the 1972 season. In all that time I think there have been only ten or twelve complaints (mainly from MCC members) claiming that noise from the tent was disturbing. Donald Carr investigated and found us 'Not Guilty'. I suspect there was more noise from the adjacent Bollinger tent!

For a decade, Godfrey and I drove all over the country enjoying the cricket and the people and finding that the experiment of 1971 was now an accepted part of the cricket scene: except at Old Trafford. There we were locked out because the chairman of Lancashire, Cedric Rhoades, was totally opposed to the idea. "There will be no betting at Old Trafford as long as I am here," he stated and nor was there until we made a breakthrough in the eighties. We had tried some of the county grounds, places like Hove, Chelmsford and Ilford but they were not viable and we had to drop them. But we did want Old Trafford and one day when I ran into Rhoades at Trent Bridge, I took the opportunity of a long chat with him. Notts were marvellous to me – they provided a room for us to discuss things privately, which we did for a couple of hours. I put our case, pointing out that we did not make people bet and did not wish to do so; nor did we tout for business – people had to come to us. We simply wanted to provide a proper service for those who did wish to bet. I added that the counties benefited, as Ladbrokes paid for the privilege of using their grounds by means of advertising fees. Cedric, a strong churchman, argued that he did not think the opportunity to bet should be so freely available but then seemed to open the door a little by saying, "If you can persuade the Committee to vote for it, then I am a democrat, I will not stand in your way." At this point he turned to leave, smiled and said: "But the Committee do what I tell them."

It was time for Godfrey to join the attack. He met the Treasurer of the Lancashire club and as a result of their joint efforts the Committee finally agreed, in 1986, to allow us in. It had been a long wait and when we were let in the facilities were never really good enough. It was indeed a pleasure, therefore, when in 1990 Paul Allott, the Lancashire and former England pace bowler, opened our new marquee directly behind the wicket at the bottom end of the ground. In 1991 we will also be opening a new marquee at Lord's, which will be the finest at any ground in the world and will no doubt encourage even more personalities to look in, perhaps to bet, perhaps to invite us for a glass of wine, or simply to pass the time of day. That is the beauty of cricket. Whereas soccer is over in ninety minutes, cricket goes on all day. People wander about, relaxing, reflecting and recalling other times, other matches, other players.

At The Oval, my little corner became the social centre of the place. Godfrey and I would stock up with wine (or at least we did until drink was no longer allowed in the Long Room) and many cricketers would stop for a glass. I can recall one day when half a dozen former captains of their country stopped off. Similarly at Lord's it is impossible to walk anywhere without bumping into someone you know. There is a particularly strong affinity between the racing world and cricket: first day of the Lord's Test is almost always the Thursday of Royal Ascot. By the Monday the racing fraternity have returned their hats whence they came and many wend their various ways to NW8.

157

Michael Stoute is a regular in the Members' enclosure at Lord's and so is the Queen's trainer, Ian Balding, as are several Members of Parliament (Nick Scott and John Carlisle can be found in the Bowlers' Bar), and many of Britain's business magnates. I remember walking to the bar under the Grandstand and seeing multi-millionaires Mick Jagger and Robert Sangster with Charles Benson drinking beer out of plastic mugs. Colin Cowdrey once sat me down with his Barclays Bank chairman, Sir Anthony Tuke, to discuss the morality of running a business in South Africa. In another box, to which I was almost certainly taken by Godfrey, I was introduced to the Archbishop of Canterbury. He did not go so far as to have a bet but he showed a deal of interest in the current odds on that particular match; I found him a most genial and amusing companion.

One of Godfrey's favourite men – probably because he had been an England tour manager and looked after Godfrey so well! – was Freddie Brown. A great captain before he became the manager, Freddie never failed to pop into our tent for a little bet and to boast about all his successes at his local betting shop; and Bryan Valentine was another who made any visit to Lord's twice the pleasure.

It was Valentine who introduced Colin Ingleby-Mackenzie to Brown Shipley. Colin was the superb captain of Hampshire who led them to their first championship in 1961. His ground rule was that the players should be in bed before breakfast and it is said that he once went out to toss with the opposing captain while still wearing his dinner jacket! That is Colin but, his shrewdness as a gambler apart, there is much more to him than meets the eye. He is a marvellous host be it at the racetrack, in his box at Lord's or his favourite spot in St James's – Greens – and with his hearty laugh and his ready humour, one always feels better for having spent an hour in his company. I have never left him and his delightful wife 'Storms' without feeling uplifted.

And then, to paraphrase that famous calypso, there were those two old pals of mine: Ken and Jim. What wonderful companions they were, Ken Barrington and Jim Laker. So very different, the chatty Berkshire boy with the instant laugh and the Yorkshireman, who never used three words if one would do, with the most wicked, dry sense of humour. Different, yet so very much alike: both great cricketers, and both men who just loved their little gamble. Kenny was the fun guy, Jim the serious one, quiet and studious. If I were to ask Jim whether he thought the pitch would last five days, he would become very thoughtful until you began to wonder if he intended to reply: then he would offer, "I think I would like to be bowling on it on Tuesday," as if to say "You can pick the bones out of that." Neither of them would bet in large amounts. Jim loved his £2 doubles and trebles and talking about yesterday's successes – you never heard much about yesterday's losses! He would stroll into the tent and, while I suspect his mind was pretty well made up, would walk up and down looking at the racing pages of the newspapers that we would pin up around the walls to see who was tipping what. Then he would lay his bets, chat for a while until he was due back on BBC Television (was there ever a more authoritative commentator?) and say, "Well, I must go and do some work now." As he was a bowler, so Jim was a punter: pretty shrewd. He certainly had more successes than losses and bookmakers did not make too much money out of J. C. Laker.

The £1 and £2 bets that Kenny struck – only on cricket, rarely on the horses – gave him immense enjoyment. He would ask the price of a certain eventuality and I would reply 3-1. "Three to one," he would echo, "but I can have 7-2 on it, can't I, Ron?" He was not such a regular as Jim, but that did not matter. I warmed to this almost-schoolboy baiting and realised that more than half his pleasure came from squeezing half a point over the odds out of me. I never failed to humour him – that was my bit of fun for the day. And somehow I always suspected that he would not have had a bet at all had he not been so accommodated. I was holidaying in the Canaries when I saw his name in a headline on the front page of the *Daily Telegraph*. Kenny was team manager to the England side that was playing in the Caribbean and at first I thought he must be playing because of injuries. I borrowed the paper and then learned that he had died from a heart attack at the terribly young age of fifty. I had to leave my wife and son Chris by the pool; I needed to be alone. I went back to the bedroom and cried my eyes out. I doubt if I was the only one. There must have been many grown men in a similar position when the news reached them, for he was a much-loved man. His father was a soldier and Kenny battled for his club (Surrey) and his country just like an old soldier. It is wonderful that there is a lasting memorial to him at The Oval – the Ken Barrington Centre. This £6 million indoor cricket school and sports centre beneath the fabulous new stand that has been erected at The Oval, is intended to serve all young sports people, boys and girls, with an emphasis on cricket, within the Surrey and London's Inner City region. For a man who came from a poor background and who began his cricket career as a groundsman who bowled leg-spinners at Reading cricket club, nothing could be more appropriate.

Memories of nights at the Dragonara Hotel in Leeds where the cricket folk normally used to stay for the Headingley Test match come crowding back even as I write about Ken and Jim. Often I would just sit and listen, not saying a word for an hour or more, as they talked about the game they loved. It was a fascinating experience just being a part of their fraternity for a short while, and I learned much about the game as nights turned into mornings and famous old players continued yarning or debating.

Len Hutton had flitted in and out of my life, beginning with those wondrous days at The Oval and ending so sadly just a few days before he died in the summer of 1990. I saw him three times during the last weeks of his life – once at his beloved Headingley where we sat on July 18 watching the one-day International and talked about the Indians. Len was entranced by the 'boy wonder', young

Tendulkar; he studied him closely as we sat watching through the committee-room window and though he seemed tired and drawn he became animated as he talked about the Indian. He told me that he thought Tendulkar would grow into one of the finest batsmen we would ever see. "Look at the way he moves his feet, Ron. It is all there, and he is only seventeen." I asked Len if he was travelling to Trent Bridge to see the second one-day game, and he smiled and said, "No. I need a couple of days' rest now." But he did make Godfrey's seventieth birthday party even though he was clearly not well, and that must have been his very last social get-together with the cricketers whose company he so enjoyed and who totally idolised him.

I have not missed a Test match now for almost a decade (and then my run was only broken because of a heart attack) and I do not think those early days at The Oval were equalled until the Test at Lord's against the Indians in August 1990. I was actually with Colonel John Stephenson, that lovely gentleman who is secretary of the MCC, in the MCC box on the day Kapil Dev hit his four sixes off four balls to save India from the follow-on and I had to break the track record running to the other end of the ground to the Ladbroke tent. My haste was very necessary. I change the odds at the end of every innings but when India saved the follow-on England were no longer such hot favourites to win. There might have been others beating a path to our tent to try and make a quick killing before we had changed the odds!

Even before Kapil had so turned that game with a flourish, Graham Gooch had looked for two days as though he might outscore Hutton. He finished with 333, of course, and those sunlit, run-laden July days led me to reflect upon my boyhood days across the river in Kennington. The Hobbs bat, sad to say, has long gone but the memories remain; cricket is nothing if not a game for reflection.

10

ELVIS, NESSIE AND THE ALIENS

There have to be limits in life and gambling should be no exception. Although we took many thousands of pounds, I shall regret until I go to my grave taking bets upon whether Elvis Presley was dead or alive. I am afraid I was rather caught on the hop when that salacious paper (you can hardly call it a newspaper) *Sunday Sport* first appeared on the news-stands. They ran a story that Elvis was still alive and the next morning punters were going into our betting shops and asking for a price on this 'debate'. I received several telephone calls from shop managers asking what odds they should offer and – expecting it to be all forgotten within twenty-four hours – foolishly suggested 1,000-1. I say foolishly not because the odds were wrong (Presley is dead: I know he is, you know he is and I could have offered a million to one) but because it meant that we would have to transfer those transactions from one year's books to the next, year after year (with the bet still running) causing administration problems that we could have done without.

It was a thoroughly tasteless exercise, I have to admit, and despite all the publicity one I wish I had never started. Once it had started, however, it was quite impossible to stop. Betting was so heavy that I was forced to halve the odds to 500-1, then cut them to 200-1 and finally bring them down to 100-1. Within a very short time indeed we had a £2.5 million liability – in other words, what we will pay out if Elvis actually does turn up rather than remain with his toes turned up.

I still do not know what possessed me that Monday morning: thoughtlessness or carelessness perhaps. Certainly it was not very clever of me. For all I knew (or know now, for that matter) it was *Sunday Sport* 'plants' who were hitting our betting shops and seeking odds merely to obtain publicity or to give some credence to their ludicrous 'story'. If that was so, then I fed them exactly what they desired. And yet, years earlier, I had stood by my moral standards when people wanted to bet on another macabre question: would Mae West prove to be a man or a woman when she died? I refused then on the grounds that (a) it was a quite appalling proposal and (b) we could never prove it either way. With that Presley betting I was as critical of myself on that Monday morning as I am today; it was the first time I began to think that if that was what our business was coming to, then it was nearing the time for me to get out.

At one end of the scale, it is like an insurance business. Life and death apart, however, just about anything goes in our business. I remember years ago Bob Manson, who then ran Holmwoods and Back and Manson which is now a part of the Brown Shipley group, sitting at Test matches and discussing the subtleties of his underwriting compared with my bookmaking. As we would agree, the differences are very few. If you go into a betting shop to bet on England winning a Test match or the World Cup, you are gambling just as people who insure something are also gambling. Sometimes in fact people may gamble for far bigger stakes by *not* insuring. If you fear a fire or a burglary then, if you are sensible, you insure against the possibility; if you wish to take a risk that nothing untoward will happen to your property, you can gamble by not insuring it. The major difference between betting and insuring is that with the former you wish to win and with the latter you do not!

You might be very surprised indeed to discover how many bets we strike each year against people having twins.

This has become an important part of our business and these days more and more insurance brokers, when asked to insure against the possibility, recommend that the parents-to-be contact us instead. The odds on having twins can vary from 33-1 downwards. We do have to make some pretty stringent checks, however. We inquire into family histories of twins, going back to great-grandparents and pay much more attention to the lady's side of the family, for this appears to be a more critical factor than twins on the father's side.

We seek a doctor's certificate of the Estimated Time of Arrival and we will not take bets after the first nine weeks. (It used to be twelve but all the sophisticated scans that are available these days mean people may be aware of their 'double trouble' by that stage!) And, naturally, we require a guarantee that the wife has not been on fertility drugs that can mean triplets or quads, never mind twins.

Such 'insurance' bets are nothing new; since we began political betting in 1963, we have gambled on almost anything and everything. Sometimes we have made money from them, sometimes not; but above, way above, the monetary gain, all these weird and wonderful bets have won us the most precious commodity of all: publicity. There was actually a classic example of us losing money and still making front-page headlines: we were 'the bookies who could not pay out' and the *Daily Express* actually led their page one with the story. This 'scandal' came about when John Player invited us to bet at their pre-Wimbledon tennis tournament in Nottingham in the seventies. Since that day I have learned that tennis is the one sport at which bookmakers will never, ever win; somehow, and specifically in the lesser tournaments, the players seem to know just who will win and who will lose (maybe my Chinaman is doing a little moonlighting!). I doubt if we have broken even on tennis betting since that first appearance – and then we were beginners, with a lot to learn. I was at the Headingley Test match, so I could not attend the tennis. To be honest, I did not expect much business, and instructed the staff not to take money with them. Any winners, I decreed, could be paid out of the day's takings. I was slightly surprised, therefore, to receive an SOS halfway through the day from Nottingham. It seemed that they were doing business, but they were losing and could not pay out. What should they do? Normally this would not have been a problem as I could always obtain money quickly enough in an emergency, but I saw this as a little PR opportunity.

"Tell all your customers that you simply cannot pay and that I am on my way down to sort out the crisis," I replied. As I drove down to Nottingham that is exactly what happened. People trying to collect their winnings were told that we had had a lot of winners and we could not pay out. Inevitably, the press sniffed out the story fairly quickly and my arrival merely heightened the drama. The tennis season means the 'silly season' in Fleet Street; they were greedy for anything. I was overwhelmed by reporters wanting to know what was wrong and what I was doing about it as soon as I reached the Nottingham courts. With my sternest of straight faces I told them that I was 'looking into it' and that no one should worry; I would ensure that all winners would ultimately be paid. The newspapers 'bit' as I knew they would and the *Daily Express* page one exposure alone made me feel that my long drive had been worthwhile. Their headline, in the biggest type they could use, said 'Tennis Bets Storm'. The *Daily Mail* recorded that 'Tennis betting breaks the bank', while the *Daily Mirror* reported, 'Tennis star bets break the bookies'. Even the brilliant American player Arthur Ashe joined the rumpus; he called for a ban on betting, which made yet more wonderful headlines! I have never been very fussed about betting on tennis but here was another important lesson — you can conjure up a story out of almost nothing.

That is why I was so impressed at the way William Hill took a spectacular leaf out of my book last summer (1990) with a wonderful story about the successor to the Archbishop of Canterbury. They reported that they had been swamped with money, including several bets of £1,000, on

Bishop Taylor of St Albans. They 'feared a leak from an insider' and were therefore suspending all betting on Bishop Taylor. Like an osprey homing in on a browsing trout for its breakfast, the media lapped it up; newspapers, radio and television all made mention of it – some made a meal of it. I know it was a dull period for betting, and to the practised eye, this was a brilliant effort to get the market moving. They had turned a flat market and a flat newsday into a very neat little promotion. I smiled to myself as I sat at home reading the papers and I felt just a teeny bit envious of their success! For it reminded me of Stanley Longstaff and myself at our very best.

These days, the other bookmaking firms have caught up with Ladbrokes in the PR business, but in those early days we were so far in front it was never a contest. We quickly became involved when even the smallest of things were happening. When Greta Anderson attempted to swim the channel both ways and needed money badly, she 'insured' herself by asking us to lay her £500 to £40 that she would complete the two-way swim. She did the first stage comfortably enough but she was forced to quit after battling nine hours to get home. It was a brave attempt and again we helped to engender newspaper publicity. When she rang to inquire how she paid the £40 she had lost, Cyril Stein told her, "Please do not worry. Send it to a charity of your choice." His view was that we already had our winnings – all the publicity Greta's swim had gained for us.

In much the same way, money was not the prime concern when we bet on the London-to-Sydney car marathon organised by the *Daily Express* in the sixties. This was a wonderful adventure, given immense promotion by the newspaper, of course; and happily, Ladbrokes received their fair share of it. Yet we still took £11,000 and showed a profit of 15 per cent, which was a splendid bonus and good business for that era. This was due in part to the fact that Roger Clark the favourite ran out of steam in Bombay

166

and in greater part to the adviser I called in, a former racing driver called Tony Ambrose.

The election in 1968 for the Oxford Professor of Poetry was hardly a contest likely to make big news, yet we opened a book and ensured that it reached a wider audience than, as in earlier years, simply *The Times*. When a Russian, Yevgeny Yevtushenko, entered the election we put him into the betting at 5-1 (and you can have 5-1 that I have spelled it correctly!). A lot of people bet upon him but the favourite was a Dr Edith Starkie; so much money was staked upon her that she remained odds-on for the whole week of our campaign.

About 30,000 Masters of Arts were enabled to vote – provided they turned up personally during the four hours the polling booth was open at Oxford. In fact, I think less than 1,000 actually did vote and they provided a splendidly romantic ending for us; the outsider, a writer called Roy Fuller romped home. When an odds-on favourite is beaten it is always poetry for us poor bookmakers!

Neil Armstrong proved that we can and do lose when he became the first man on the moon in July 1969 – although Ladbrokes lost nothing like the amount William Hill did. We had been offering 100-1 on man not stepping on to the moon within the decade, that decade being the sixties. If I say we were being generous with our price, then consider the William Hill dilemma: they were going 1,000-1. And, even though the space programme was moving at quite a pace, neither of us cut our odds at any stage. I suppose it was that those of us born in the twenties and thirties could not really grasp the likelihood of Armstrong taking one small step for himself and a giant step for mankind.

As children we had joked about the moon. Now Neil Armstrong was hitting a golf ball on it and Ladbrokes were paying out thousands to those who had believed it would be achieved before 1970 and had backed that belief with money. Just how much William Hill lost I do not know but obviously the majority of those who wished to have a bet would have done better with them because their odds were so much better. And the great irony was that while they were paying out the big money we scooped all the publicity; they got none!

A day or so after Armstrong took his 'small step' I was due to take my mother and father out to dinner when I received a sudden invitation to be a guest on the Eamonn Andrews Show to discuss our betting on the event. I initially refused because my father was an old man – he was to die in January 1972 – and I valued his coming out with me; dinner with him was the more important appointment. But the show's organisers upped my fee and promised that cars would be laid on to pick me up and that my parents and I would be at the restaurant together, so I agreed.

That meant I was to take part in my first television show before a live audience, so very different from the recorded programmes I was used to doing. I was terrified, but would not have wished to miss the experience. Mostly when you are being recorded there is time to amend things; even change your mind. Sitting there knowing that several million viewers are listening to your every first thought was an entirely different matter. I think 'daunting' is the word I would choose to describe it. My companions did not much help my state of mind, either. They were all stars; I was the 'unknown'. I did not even know Eamonn well, but he was a kindly, generous (we had a few whiskies, I can tell you) and understanding chat-show host. I had not previously met Roy Castle (as funny in private as he is on stage), that marvellous actress Honor Blackman and the eternal beauty, Eva Gabor, and Eamonn smoothed the way for me. Despite my stage fright, it was a splendid show; we each did our little bit for Eamonn and Ladbrokes received some superb exposure. That really was one of the great coups. By the time I met up with Mum and Dad in the Gran Sasso restaurant in Beckenham I was actually feeling sorry for William Hill. They had offered the big odds, had taken most of the bets and lost most of the money, and yet again we were getting all of the publicity.

It didn't seem very fair – yet was life ever meant to be fair?

When people ask which was my best or my favourite coup it is difficult to give a precise answer. I remember when in 1974 that soft-porn actress Linda Lovelace came to Britain to promote her film *Deep Throat* I was asked to organise her publicity and did so well – taking her to Royal Ascot and Lord's – that we had many wonderful picture shows and stories which included her photograph three days running on page one of the *Evening News*. And that was some publicity! She was a publicist's dream. With Ladbrokes I had so many coups, and they all did something for us – some more than others, of course, and some when we particularly needed a little boost. Certainly it would be difficult not to mention 'Nessiteras Rhombopteryx' and 'The Aliens'.

The world seems captivated by tales of the mystery of the deep and stories of 'Nessie', the Loch Ness monster, date back to the sixth century. Rumours of her existence attract half a million visitors to the loch, bringing some £25 million to the local community annually and accounting for about 2-3,000 jobs in the tourist industry. Generally in springtime, at least one person will claim to have seen the hump-backed monster. This inspires droves of tourists to flock to the Scottish Highlands and into the Ladbroke shop sited in the lovely little town of Inverness which nestles on the shores of Loch Ness. (I was stationed there for a very short while before moving into the War Office after I 'escaped' from Thetford.) It is mostly Americans who walk in – and it is not for the money they might win. They simply want the betting slip that they then carry home to show their friends. We were there, they can then claim, seeking 'Nessiteras Rhombopteryx', as Sir Peter Scott so cryptically called it.

It was 1977, I think, when we first began betting on the likelihood of her existence. Later that year an illogical amount of money suddenly started to pour in. Before we knew what was happening, we had a £180,000 liability and I was feverishly cutting the odds from 100-1 to 66-1, down to 50s, then 33-1 and then finally all the way down to 6-1 before sanity prevailed. There is no doubt that my job during that hectic spell was suddenly on the line. Joke or no, the rumour from the management floor was that if a monster was found, Ron Pollard wouldn't be! And Peter George, Managing Director of Ladbroke Racing but certainly not the bravest of gambling souls, came into my office to declare that the wealth of betting indicated to him that a monster was indeed to be found, "Otherwise, why all this money?"

The answer to that question lay in the spots where the betting was taking place: they were all university towns like Exeter, Bristol, Southampton, Reading, Manchester and Edinburgh. University students up and down the country were swamping us with their money because a research team from the Boston Academy of Applied Science who visited the loch during the summer of 1974 had now published a report together with what purported to be their 'photographic evidence' and this was printed first in a student magazine. Little did they realise that they were turning the bookmaking business inside out for a few days, and making me think that I was about to be fired.

I had been the victim of a mammoth hoax which wasn't terribly funny at the time. But if betting has to be fun, who was I to deny them such pleasure? And it went without saying, of course, that all the newspapers followed the story up, some seriously – quoting Sir Peter Scott and other naturalists on the fact that there were monsters in the deep – and some just a wee bit debunking. It was further superb promotion for Ladbrokes.

My belief about Nessie is a simple one. If there was ever only one monster, it would be long since dead: if there was more than one, the loch would be teeming with the little perishers. So bet on, bet on I say. If there are no springtime sightings ever, there will be no tourists; if there are no tourists there will be no betting and if there is no betting, a wonderful piece of Scottish mythology will die.

Thank goodness there are no monsters in outer space

(well, I am prepared to bet on that), only aliens. And those aliens, wherever they may be, have provided Ladbrokes with £30,000 a year for more than a decade and with perhaps more publicity, good publicity, than any other single activity in a century of bookmaking. In a way it ill behoves me, a Spiritualist, to debunk the Californian group *Unarius*. They purport to be Spiritualists also, although I have my doubts that their understanding and mine of that word and that religion is one and the same. Their leader, Ruth Norman, came into my life in 1977 when we were first asked by the Californians if we would take bets on the arrival of aliens on earth.

We had received some weird requests before, but this one staggered me. Finally, however, I agreed we would take their bets, at odds of 500-1 and down and that we would pay out in the event of aliens 'landing or crashing on earth, alive or dead' within one year of the bet being struck. This became an annual affair: each year, and always at the same time, their cash would arrive. I presumed that *Unarius* had a yearly gathering at which they were 'advised' to continue. Mrs Norman's husband, Ernest, had set up the group in 1954 and when he died she took over the leadership. Based in El Cajon, *Unarius* compiled their title from the first letters of the following: *UN*iversal *AR*ticulate *I*nterdimensional *U*nderstanding of *S*cience. Members are dedicated to 'helping man to move forward in his evolution'; to free mankind of 'mental frustrations to enjoy a peaceful life and to attain psychic liberation'. They claim to have spoken with people from fifty-two planets. I do not relate any of this in a derogatory sense at all – they genuinely believe that they have the peaceful solutions to world problems and can contribute to advances in medical science.

Crackpots? That is not for me to say, but I will tell you that Mrs Norman never struck me as being nuts. We never actually met, but we often spoke on the telephone and we had many a chat via a radio hook-up. I thought her a very nice lady – she claimed to be the reincarnation of Mona

Lisa – and when she learned that I was a Spiritualist she sent me some of her texts and books which were said to be spirit messages from former world leaders such as Sir Winston Churchill and Presidents such as Kennedy, Eisenhower, Woodrow Wilson and Calvin Coolidge. These messages had been taped (these were for sale) and then transcribed into book form (again, for sale).

This situation continued until just two or three years ago when our annual liability in the event of aliens putting their spacecraft down in Trafalgar Square or Manchester's Oldham Street had reached millions. But now Mrs Norman does not seem to have the bet herself. Money does still arrive, but from her associates and considerably less than it used to be.

Whether they are losing faith or simply running out of money I do not know. Nor would I complain – for a decade it really has been a PR man's dream. There has been continuing publicity and none of it needed to be contrived. I even promised that if Ladbrokes did have to pay out, one of those aliens would hand over our cheque. (I guess that picture would make a few page ones around the world!) Mrs Norman accepted this promise quite seriously. To her, aliens were a serious matter. She once told me how she had prepared a site in California for them to land on safely and I well recall her scorn when I asked when she was coming to Britain. I said that I would meet her at Heathrow and arrange for her to stay at one of our hotels. "Don't be silly," she said tartly. "When I arrive I shall be coming in one of their spacecraft." Well, that told me. But, as I say, she never appeared to be anything but sane; and as one of those prepared to lay odds against man stepping on to the moon and who was, in 1990, still offering 250-1 against a manned landing on Mars before the end of the century, who am I to say that Mrs Norman and her fellow-believers may not, one day, be proved right?

After all, Mrs Norman's friends are not exactly alone in the States. Polls have shown that 57 per cent of all Americans believe in Unidentified Flying Objects and 9 per cent claim to have seen one.

It has actually been reported that one body within America's secretive National Security Agency (called the Dundee Group because their leader once kept his pencils in a marmalade jar of that make, would you believe?) are quite convinced that UFOs have already landed.

However, 57 per cent of Americans, the analysts who spotted 'something out there', the Dundee Group and Mrs Norman and her friends can all have long odds that aliens, friendly or otherwise, will not land on earth in the next twelve months. It really is quite amazing how mention of aliens or UFOs sparks off the betting. So, too, do pictures of the notorious circles in wheat- or cornfields. The romantic like to think that they are left by visiting spacecraft in the dead of night. The more cynical suggest that they are most likely to have been created by naughty farmers or conman photographers for sale to newspapers.

One such newspaper photograph in 1989 led me to being asked to lay odds not only on aliens landing, but 'taking over our Government by the year 1992'. I decided that unless anyone considered Neil Kinnock an alien, no one else was likely to be taking over Parliament and I offered 5,000-1 against such a happening. The gentleman – a Briton, I might add – accepted the odds and laid us £500, so if a funny little one-eyed man with webbed feet and a scanner poking from the top of his green head is seen at the Despatch Box in Westminster, Ladbrokes will be paying him out £2.5 million – if we are around to pay, that is!

My favourite story of little green men came from Essex. Some practical jokers in Littley Green in 1989 thrashed out a circle in a cornfield; it was said that they wished to talk about 'Littley Green men'. And in 1981 Alison Hodgson, a pretty secretary from my old home town of Peckham, bet us a fiver at 5,000-1 that she "would be having tea with a Martian before the end of 1982". She thought life was tedious and wanted a bit of fun. I suspect an out-of-work thirty-two-year-old, Ken Stafford, was a little more serious when he bet us that he "would win the Open Golf Championship by 1990". He could just about crack 100 around his local public course but said that he was "fed up with the Americans winning all the time" and he felt that our chaps did not seem to have "the same bite and determination". Presumably he has now heard of Faldo and Lyle and our other Ryder Cup heroes! His fiver would have been better placed on the aliens.

There were so many of these weird and wonderful bets that I can hardly remember them all. It was not true that I took bets on whether Tom would ever eat Jerry, although I was asked for odds on Perry Mason losing a case, but even now I have to laugh whenever I think about the 'snow at Christmas' business. It is true that we did lay bets on whether there would be snow on Christmas Day and that if the London Weather Centre reported one single flake falling at noon, we would pay. Quite often our liability can be as much as £250,000. The weathermen pop out on to their roof to check and we have not had to pay once in the twenty years or more that we have been taking the bet. All that is fact – it is true. What were never true were stories that my Christmas dinner was ruined by my worrying about the weather changing or that I went without my turkey and Christmas pud so that I could stand on the weathermen's roof and check that they were not mistaking some piece of floating flotsam for a snowflake.

But we still do a roaring trade on dreams of a white Christmas. Our marketing department actually sells a sort of Christmas gift voucher for £5 and £10 just like you get in Boots except that ours are betting slips; if it snows, the recipients collect! Who knows, perhaps one year there really will be snow on Christmas Day, but I can assure you that it most certainly will not spoil my Christmas dinner.

However, when in 1978, a team of British balloonists were attempting to cross the Atlantic, and came to Ladbrokes for their 'insurance', we bet them £50,000 to £5,000 that they would not do it and their epic journey gave me a few sleepless nights and a nearly ruined holiday, I can tell you.

I was holidaying in Devon when they were due to finish the trip and I seemed to be spending all my time listening to radio reports of their progress. I was getting more and more anxious as they got closer and closer and they actually dropped into the sea only about 100 miles from our coastline. I had spent hours wondering how on earth I was going to be able to recoup some of that £50,000, so sure was I that they were going to make it. It was worse than getting sand in your sandwiches, but in the end it all ended well for us, if not the balloonists.

We had to drop betting on religious affairs for a time when shareholders complained, but that also had its good moments. Many years before Hill's PR coup referred to earlier, I remember making Donald Coggan favourite to become the next Archbishop of Canterbury. We took £30,000 on that and when he had been appointed he was asked – on television – when he first thought he might be the winner and he replied: "Have you ever heard of a firm called Ladbrokes?" implying that it had been good enough for him when we made him our favourite but denying that he had actually bet upon himself! The same sort of reasoning in reverse was given by a Cardinal when asked at what stage he realised he was not to be the next Pope. "When Ladbrokes amended my odds from 8-1 to 12-1," he smiled. My advisers on that occasion were the editors of religious newspapers and reporters on religious affairs; they were well chosen and did not let me down.

I suspected that those shareholders who complained at our betting on religious affairs had a point when I was asked for a price on whether a church hall might be turned into a pillar of salt. Apparently, a preacher had objected to the hall being rented by a group of homosexuals, insisting that it would become a block of salt. I received an envelope with £1 inside and a note asking me what the price was on such an occurrence. Betting on men from Mars was one thing; this was quite another. It was by far the daftest bet I had ever been asked to take and, despite fears that I might be turned into a pillar of salt for turning my back on it, I rejected the bet, returning the £1 with a little note of apology.

The one thing that I most regret never quite coming off was the Talduwa Planters' Club racing, although I did get us some splendid publicity in the *Daily Mail*. I ran into my old friend Ian Wooldridge and we naturally enough took time out for a lunch-time drink and chat. I chanced to mention that that very morning I had received an invitation to handle exclusive betting rights at this club in Sri Lanka. "What on earth is that?" questioned Ian. I showed him the letter saying, "It appears to be a race between thirty bloody great elephants." And, indeed, that is just what it was — a biannual affair, to celebrate the Tamil Harvest Festival.

Ian tried to involve me with America's most famous bookmaker, the Runyonesque Jimmy the Greek. "I would love to get the pair of you out there betting on these elephants," said Ian, "then we would find out who was the better man." As the Yanks have been ringing me to find out my odds on American elections for some years, I suspect they knew very well which one of us was the better man. None the less, it might have been good fun. As I have said often enough before, however, you cannot expect to win them all.

11

CASINOS: HOW THE BATTLE WAS LOST
BUT THE WAR WAS WON

The stakes were high when Ladbrokes and The Playboy
Club fought the 1979-81 War of the Casinos: £1,000
million. With oil-rich Arabs pouring into Britain, some of
them prepared to stake a million pounds a night at the
roulette wheel and the blackjack table, that was the incredible amount being wagered in the London clubs. It was,
you might have thought, enough, more than enough, for
everyone. But that mixture of greed, vanity and ego – a
Devil's brew if ever there was one – combined to ensure
that the war had no winners.

In the early seventies Ladbrokes acquired the licences for
several provincial gaming clubs (in Birmingham, Luton,
Leicester, Tees-side and Leeds) and two in the heart of
London's Mayfair, The Hertford in Hertford Street and
their 'flagship', The Ladbroke in Hill Street. While these
two were totally different, they were the finest clubs in the
whole of Britain. As befits a showpiece, The Ladbroke was
lavishly decorated and furnished; it had perhaps the best
restaurant in London – certainly it was my favourite – and
most importantly for the high-rollers who sought privacy
while they gambled, there was a suite of rooms on one of
the upper floors reached by a private lift and so secret that
very few people knew of its existence. It was in that suite,
with its white carpet and mirrored walls, that many
millions of pounds would change hands in the course of a

year, as the wealthiest and leading players in the world, men like Adnan Khashoggi, Crown Prince Fahad Ben Abdul Aziz, the mega-rich Arab sheikhs and members of the British aristocracy like the Lords Derby and Lucan, Bernard van Cutsem and members of the Hambros banking family, made London and The Ladbroke their particular playground.

Stories of their gambling exploits were legion; it did not seem to matter how much they won or lost – they always returned. And their tipping was generous in the extreme. There were a very large number of people who wished to be the cloakroom attendant at The Ladbroke, for he was reputed to take home more each year than Cyril Stein. Every time some players went to the toilet they would give the attendant a £100 tip. And the girl at the reception counter who looked after the coats was quite stunned at the gift she received from an Arab who had been a client for only three weeks. He told her one evening, "I am going home tomorrow so I have brought you a little present." That 'little' present was an £800 watch!

But that is how the big gamblers were – and I suppose, still are; money simply wasn't a matter of concern. There is, of course, a very real danger to all gamblers, big and small alike: when money is exchanged for gaming chips it no longer represents real money; it becomes 'Mickey Mouse' money and is treated as such, rather like spending millions of lira when holidaying in Italy! I am very lucky: I may be a punter when I think the odds are in my favour but I am strictly not a gambler. I have never once had a wager in any casino – not even when I have been 'advised' where to place my money. As far as I am concerned, playing the tables is not very different to playing fruit-machines in that nothing depends upon your own skill. I can never bring myself to put money into those infernal machines, pull a handle and trust to luck.

If money was of no concern to the high-rollers, it was suddenly no problem to Ladbrokes either; it was, quite literally, like confetti. We had so much of the stuff we hardly knew what to do with it. In all honesty, I think it was almost an embarrassment. Where turnover had been counted in the hundreds of thousands, it was now tens of millions; profits which had been tens of thousands were now millions, which made it all the more ludicrous for the casino bosses to go to war. Although the Ladbroke group profit had, by 1979, now grown to £50 million, of which around half (£24 million) had come from the casinos, Cyril Stein was not satisfied. Other establishments had big-money gamblers and that was something it seemed he could not tolerate. He wanted every penny that was available in London: he simply could not bear the thought of big losers going somewhere other than into the Ladbroke clubs. So he instituted a major marketing operation with a single, simple message to his marketing team: "Get as much business as you can."

In itself, that was the perfectly correct thing to do. In any other business you would get the Queen's Award for Industry (which indeed Cyril would win for the Hilton Hotels chain ten years later) for such initiative and enterprise, but in 1979 it led to him being pilloried and to Ladbrokes losing their casino empire.

While he did not specify precisely how that extra business should be obtained, he certainly had to know how customers could be lured from other clubs, because it was a normal part of our betting operation to try to 'steal' a rival's client when we knew he was a big spender. We would entertain wealthy gamblers, taking them on trips to see the Arc de Triomphe in Paris; we would tempt them with slightly better odds than were being offered by which-ever firm they were betting with; we would even pay hotel porters to 'point' would-be gamblers in our direction if ever they were asked where the best place was for a night's gambling. So when the Ladbroke marketing men started recording the registration numbers of the Mercedes cars, the Porsches and the Ferraris which were driven to or parked outside The Playboy and other gaming clubs, that too was just another, acceptable, part of the game. What was totally unacceptable, however, was the use of the police computer to trace the owners of those cars; this was illegal and was to bring about their downfall.

Gordon Irvine, then a Board director of Ladup, the casino division, was later to be charged with corruption offences in connection with the now infamous 'Operation Unit 6' which was somehow – a police officer was later acquitted of giving us information – to acquire the names that went with the cars and then to talk them into becoming Ladbroke clients. Those running other casinos, like Victor Lownes of The Playboy, did not appreciate their wealthy customers being poached one little bit. With their American parent company, The Playboy had easier and greater access to the rich men of the world than we had and Lownes wished to keep them at The Playboy.

First hint of any trouble came with little newspaper snippets towards the end of 1977 from unnamed sources and stories in the satirical magazine, *Private Eye*, suggesting that 'Ladbrokes may be in trouble' and that Ladbrokes were 'being investigated' by the Gaming Board. Most employees shrugged their shoulders; it was not their business. Nor did there seem any real alarm among the staff when things took a turn for the worse in 1978. Firstly, a well-known reporter, Stuart Kuttner, ran a big story on the front page of the London *Evening News* – based, I must say, on very few facts; and then our casino headquarters in a little London mews just off Park Lane were raided. The police took away masses of documents, and these were to form the basis of the charge that we were not fit and proper persons to run a casino when they objected to the renewal of our licences.

I would have to say here that while no one can argue that misuse of the police computer was criminally wrong, to contend that we were 'not fit and proper persons' was in my opinion ludicrous. We ran the best clubs, had the best food and the best staff. Unlike many clubs later there was never any suggestion that we did not own the most honest clubs in the world. Not one punter was ever cheated of a single penny and even the Chief Inspector of the Gaming Board, Mr Reginald Doak, told Knightsbridge Crown Court in November 1979 when we were appealing against the loss of our licences that the Ladbroke operation had "always been run fairly and honestly".

That would certainly not be the case outside Britain. I have, for instance, been in a casino in Europe where the manager, thinking that he was doing me a favour, would advise me to bet on a certain number at the roulette wheel. "Put your money on 22," he would say and while I never did, because I have yet to have my first bet in a casino, I would watch as 22 duly came up. For that spin, the wheel, obviously, was not quite straight. But certain casino operators do not have to resort to such trickery as fixing a wheel. I can tell you that there are three or four croupiers in the world who can spin the wheel and the ball so skilfully that they can actually dictate which number will win to the benefit of their employers. These men – all based in America, of course – are priceless. What is more, you would never even realise what was happening.

Such skulduggery never went on at Ladbroke casinos (and it may not be pure coincidence that for some years Arabs who used to bet in London went elsewhere when we were no longer involved). Yet our reputation counted for nothing when the police – strongly backed by Victor Lownes – opposed the renewal of our gaming licences. Lownes was always open and vocal in his opposition to Stein and to Ladbrokes. Like Cyril, he did not want a share of the mega-millions – he wanted all of it.

As the pressure mounted, so the Ladbroke shares started to slide (we had by this time climbed into the top 300 British companies) and I began to worry where it might all end. My personal view, then and now, was that Cyril Stein was more sinned against than sinner, having merely mounted a marketing drive for clients; when he discovered illegal methods had been used, he sacked those he considered responsible. And yet, I feared for Ladbrokes. No single individual was bigger than the company and I decided that I was the only one in the firm who was strong enough and a good enough friend to say to him: "Cyril, don't you think you should resign?" When I called him and put this argument to him, he flatly rejected any such move. "I have not even contemplated it. There is no reason for me to do so, Ron. I have done nothing wrong."

It began and ended there. Neither of us has mentioned that call since. I had only the best interests of the company at heart – Cyril would have known that; I would never really have wished to see an entrepreneur like him, a businessman of such immense expertise, leave the company. My idea would have been for him to return when the heat had gone from the situation, perhaps as president in the way Joe Coral became president of Corals. Cyril understood and has never held that telephone call against me. But not everyone had quite the same motives as me. There were others – City Editors on national newspapers among them – calling for his resignation. To them all, Cyril echoed his words to me: "Why should I? I have done nothing wrong." And at the company annual meeting after we had lost our licences, Cyril was caught smiling when one shareholder told him, "You have been a naughty boy." Shareholders know which side their bread is buttered on!

Behind the smiles, however, the Stein mind was working overtime. He wanted revenge on the man who set out to crush him: Victor Lownes.

Stein and Lownes were very different people. Cyril is an Orthodox Jew, generous to charities and shrewd enough in his business dealings to command total respect from London's 'Square Mile'. He was also the nephew of an on-course bookie and he had to fight as he clawed his way to the top. Cyril is nothing if not street-wise. Lownes in contrast had a hedonistic life-style, laced with Bunny Girls and high living; he was born with the proverbial 'silver spoon', grandson of a wealthy Chicago businessman.

Cyril set up an investigation into The Playboy operation and he did not mind what it cost; he got two former Playboy group employees to tell all they knew about any wrong-doings at their clubs. They knew enough to bring the Lownes house tumbling down quicker than any wall in Jericho. Their information was handed over to the police and was enough, when they gave evidence in court in October 1981, to have The Playboy licences taken away.

One revealed how large debts were 'written off' by the use of dud cheques and another how £2.5 million was spent annually on entertaining 'good' clients, and buying them presents like Cartier watches at £5,000 a time. And it was further said in court how Clement Freud, then a Liberal MP and a director of The Playboy, gambled at The Clermont, one of their clubs, thus contravening the Gaming Act which stipulated that directors should not bet on their own premises. Having gloried earlier in having a go at Ladbrokes and Cyril Stein, the newspapers were now revelling in lurid headlines about Freud and The Playboy.

Yes, it was a dirty business and Lownes had won the opening battle, but Stein had won the war. The evidence that Stein unveiled proved most effective. The Playboy lost its licences and Lownes left on his fifty-third birthday. Along the way, Freud resigned. Certainly there were no tears shed at Ladbrokes when the news broke. We did not go quite so far as to crack open the champagne but Cyril Stein wore the look of a well-satisfied man for a long, long time.

There was much to regret about the casino war. Everyone was a loser. Ironically, Ladbrokes who were the war's first victims, turned out to be the luckiest losers of all time. Without the luxury of The Ladbroke Club (which, sadly, was burned down in 1979– and The Hertford, and the general break-up of London as the gambling centre of the world, the high-rollers simply went away. They gambled elsewhere, which meant a great deal of foreign currency that had been coming into Britain was no longer doing so. The one thing which I regret above all, however – and I am sure Cyril does also – was the loss of Geoff Spreckley. Here was a dynamic young businessman; he had built up the Spar grocery chain and then been recruited by Ladbrokes to become Managing Director. He was not a racing man or a gambling man – if he went to the dogs he would bet in 10p pieces! But he was a businessman in Stein's own mould, hard-working and with an agile brain. It was, perhaps, natural that he should become the trouble-shooter (or, as it was more nicely put, the main board representative!) when the casino division first hit troubles. With the ultimate loss of the licences, Geoff became the fall guy, a scapegoat for others' misdeeds. The day he left – for a paltry £140,000 pay-off – was probably the worst in the whole history of the firm. Racing management has never been quite the same. He was the most forward-looking executive the group ever had and his 'demise' has been a great loss. He went off to run his own little bingo hall operation in Essex and I for one missed him very much indeed.

I was worried about the whole situation, and particularly the falling share price as my shares represented my savings. And yet, I am happy to record, I did not sell a single share throughout the whole affair which, as anyone who has followed the fortunes of Ladbrokes in recent years will be well aware, has been to my immense good fortune. There was no doubt, however, that many Ladbroke shareholders, a majority of Fleet Street's City Editors, and a large number of stockbrokers and analysts viewed the casino crisis as a disaster of Titanic proportions. In reality it was a blessing in disguise.

There is no reason to suppose that, in the passage of time, the big gamblers might not have become bored with London and found new places in which to lose their money. The loss of the casino licences actually ensured that the company is very much more firmly based now. Had we continued to run the casinos we might well have become over-dependent upon them. Now, Ladbrokes has diversified and as I will relate next, with its betting, property and hotels and outlets in Europe and America is one of Britain's leading and most successful companies. Truly a blessing in disguise.

12

CYRIL STEIN: NOT ALWAYS RIGHT, BUT . . .

In 1964, Ladbrokes was just about bust. As I related earlier, we had lost £2 million in two weeks on fixed-odds football, had been under orders 'not to lose' on our racing or the firm would go under and we had about fifty full-time employees. Today Ladbrokes is in the top thirty-five British companies, employs about 77,000 people in fifty countries around the world and with a turnover of £3.6 *billion* made a profit in 1989 of more than £300 million. That is what you call growth. While many have contributed to this amazing success story, one man stands alone as the visionary, the architect and the builder of this enormous empire: Cyril Stein.

In his twenties, Cyril – nephew of a bookmaker – ran his own credit betting office in London's West End. He quickly went out of business. He will even today question whether he was a bookmaker. He was – and obviously a singularly unsuccessful one. But as a management man, one who turned an old-fashioned company into one of the largest on the London Stock Exchange, one that continues to make profits even in times of recession, he stands alongside the finest Britain has ever produced, alongside the Lords King and Hanson and those knights Ernie Harrison and John Harvey-Jones.

He has succeeded against all the odds. When we lost our casino licences everyone had him for dead. I felt there was a case for his resignation and told him so; more importantly, so did many in the City. Ten years on from that time it was clear that had Cyril gone, the company might well have stagnated instead of becoming one of the nation's high-fliers. He is in the office at eight, or before, each morning that he is not flying the Atlantic (Concorde now allows him to do America in a day!). He is there long after everyone else has gone. He has a quality, that indefinable something, that makes him do the right thing at the right time despite whatever may be going against him. He knows what he wants. He sets out his aims and goes only for those targets. He can see the light 100 miles ahead and does not go off the road to the right or the left.

If he has a relaxation it is probably racing and gambling; he loves the sport and still bets in thousands. (Equally, his contribution to charities can be counted in many hundreds of thousands.) He actually played his part in the Six Day War in the sixties from one room in our Ganton House headquarters in Ganton Street and a dozen telephones: he raised millions for the Jewish cause in about thirty-six hectic hours and Cyril's powers of persuasion had to be heard to be believed. At one stage we all thought he would make his home in Israel (where forests are named after him and his wife Betty for their charitable work) when he retired, taking up politics, but I am not sure that will be the case now that his son Daniel is in America as an executive of the property division there and his only daughter, Marion, and the grandchildren are in England.

We used to have a saying in the office that 'Cyril may not always be right, but he is never wrong!' It was most apt, because Cyril never accepted he was wrong. When he had a bet on a horse that he felt was a sure-fire winner, and I accepted a large bet on the same animal from a client, he questioned my judgement. When the horse lost – and Cyril lost – it wasn't that I was right and he was wrong; it was that I was 'lucky'. I may have been lucky, Cyril may have been lucky, I don't know. What I do know is that over the past decade, the growth of Ladbrokes has been quite unbelievable and that it has been to the benefit of shareholders, of which I am one.

As I have mentioned, Ladbrokes were founded back at the turn of the century by Arthur Bendir, and became the bookmakers to the gentry. They virtually qualified for a Royal warrant, taking bets from Buckingham Palace on the direct line to the Old Burlington Street offices, but it was a firm that, when Cyril's uncle, Max Parker, bought it in 1956, was antiquated and almost Dickensian. If you were not in *Debrett*, you could not bet. When Edgar Wallace wrote a play, it was Ladbrokes who were always mentioned. And when the phone rang, the words "Good morning, your Grace" and "Thank you, your Grace" would often echo around the cubicles where clerks sat with quill pens. It was Cyril who decided to broaden the base and open it up to the public. He decided to advertise, leaving older employees and clients horrified, even though those first advertisements went only in *Tatler* and *Country Life*. He never saw himself and those who worked in the business as 'bookmakers'. He saw them as High Street retailers, 'the Marks and Spencer of betting'. Within a year of Parker buying Ladbrokes for £100,000 they knew that they were on the right road. Not only were changes being made but £105,000 outstanding at the purchase time had now been collected, so they had acquired the company for nothing!

I suspect that the company's foundations for the twenty-first century were even then being laid, but as we entered the eighties, with the loss of the casino cash behind us and a Thatcher Government bringing job losses and company closures that were beginning to affect us, the real strategy for the future was being developed. At this stage Cyril did not wish to see his name in the papers. He felt let down by a lot of newspapermen who had written things about him and the firm that he did not like. He even had a row with me about it. "What good has all that entertaining done us?" he grumbled, and did not (or would not) understand that while a lot of journalists had remained good friends and had been quite soft in what they had reported, the fact remained that each and every newspaper must, if it is to retain credibility, write things as they are or at least as they see them.

I have always believed in entertaining journalists, taking them to places like Brussels and Malta and Paris. But I never once asked a single one for a favour. They always had to write the truth as they saw it – even if the truth hurt or if they didn't always get it quite right – and despite Cyril's feelings, there were City journalists like Pat Lay and Norman Whetnall who, ably briefed by our own City PR man Trevor Bass, never wavered in their belief that Ladbrokes would become a major company and that Cyril Stein would be at the helm.

However low Cyril kept his profile, nevertheless the company was growing. In 1980 our profit on a turnover of £665 million was £32 million. In 1989 the profit before taxation was £302 million and turnover had grown to £3,695 million. And this growth was obtained in both good years and bad years for the nation. In the seventies, nearly all our profit came from gambling of one sort or another. It was not a firm base.

One major and lucky punter in a casino could actually have wiped out our entire annual profit in a night. Today, 50 per cent of our profit comes from the hotel division, 27 from racing, 13 from our Texas Homecare centres and 10 per cent from property, so Ladbrokes is even more firmly based for the nineties than it was for the eighties.

If further proof is required, Ladbrokes Property division built in 1990 a huge shopping centre at Perry Barr, just outside Birmingham. More than 80 per cent of the units were let even before we opened, and this at a time when the High Street was in disarray because of the high interest rates. At the start of the eighties we were 150th in the league of the best and biggest British companies. Ten years on we were 34th and set to climb higher. A major part of the diversification was the hotel chain. In 1987 we bought the Hilton group for £645 million and this may prove an even better deal than Cyril's Uncle Max pulled off in 1956, for by the time this book appears the hotels will probably have been revalued at something nearer to £3.5 billion. At one stage we thought Lord Hanson might win the battle for the Hiltons and he probably wishes now that he had!

The hotel division was to take off when John Jarvis joined us. Here was a man of immense flair, who over a decade stamped himself on the group as a supreme management man. I certainly saw him as Cyril's successor when he retired from the chairmanship and it was a major shock when John left Ladbrokes in 1990, wanting the challenge of having his own group of hotels bearing his name. I understand that need for a challenge and am certain he will do well; John is not one of those who live on the coat-tails of others. Nevertheless, he will be much missed at Ladbrokes.

The base for our mammoth hotel division had been set up about twenty years earlier when we built our three Dragonara hotels (named after the first one we owned, in Malta) in Bristol, Tees-side and Leeds. These were exciting times for me. Three executives were asked to take one hotel each under their wing – Cyril's cousin, David Green, had Bristol, William Doody, Tees-side and I accepted responsibility for Leeds. By the time we opened, I was betting at Headingley and my good relationship with the England cricket team ensured that for years they always stayed at the Dragonara in Leeds. My contacts with Yorkshire Television allowed me to arrange contracts for people to stay there that exist to this day.

I would spend two, sometimes three days a week in the city, meeting all the big businessmen there like Beric Watson of Waddingtons, convincing them that the Dragonara was the place for them. I suppose each of us put in a glowing report but my first one informed Cyril that my contacts were "100 per cent and would last". That was precisely how it turned out – the majority have stayed loyal to the Dragonara for twenty years. We were also years ahead of others when it came to ideas. In the early days we had an executive think tank, seeking ideas for marketing and promoting the hotels and building up weekend occupancy. Nearly twenty years on, I still have the memo that lists some fourteen of the ideas that we came up with – which included free meals, group interest weekends (birdwatching in Bristol was one thought!), camping weekends (children in tents, their parents in our hotels), champagne weekends at beer prices and a 'guaranteed weather' weekend, which promised a refund if it rained!

Yes, these were thrilling times and such a change from the day in 1962 when I first walked through the Ladbrokes front door. I remember still – how could one forget? – being greeted by Richard Kaye in the most gentlemanly way: "Morning, Pollard. Care for a sherry?" And this before eleven o'clock. When Cyril joined the firm, lunch was still served to the staff by dinner-jacketed waiters. It must have been a culture shock when he took the company by the scruff of its neck. But the changes he instituted were vital. Until then William Hill had been unchallenged. Now he had real competition and the impact on Ladbroke Racing turnover was remarkable. By 1967 it had grown to £39 million (with a profit figure of £426,000) and in 1989 it was £2,170 million, showing a profit of £91 million.

When a company operates on a nett profit of only 3 per cent as Ladbroke Racing does, it is vital that you are 100 per cent efficient at all times; if you are not, that profit can very quickly become a loss. No one is more bullish about Ladbrokes than I, but I do have the odd worry. When we were a small company, for example, two or three of us would sit down with Cyril and decide on a policy. I was a great one for abiding by that policy once we had settled on it. One of our decisions then was that we would never involve ourselves with any business that had goods on shelves. I was very, very surprised, therefore, to see Ladbrokes acquire Texas Homecare in 1986. If ever a business had to have a few million tied up on shelves, that was it. I suspect Cyril might, in his more reflective moments, perhaps have wished the old policy had been adhered to, particularly during 1989-91 when interest rates were so high and Government policy was to slow down consumer spending. While Texas makes profits, it does tie up a great deal of capital.

Similarly, I question the wisdom and the long-term viability of Ladbroke Racing spending £800,000 refurbishing a gigantic betting shop in the centre of Birmingham when we were building a major shopping centre at Perry Barr. Betting shops are connected with chimneys and with people; soon betting shops will be open for night racing and I wonder just how many people will be walking up and down Stephenson Street, Birmingham, in the evenings? It will obviously take a long time to recoup £800,000 and if I am right in my assumption that shopping will sooner or later be done at large centres on the edge of cities – like Perry Barr! – it may never be recouped. And as for giving Southampton University £50,000 to research 'Why People Bet' all I can say is that I have been giving everyone at Ladbrokes the answer to that for many years now, and they need to spend only the cost of this book, not many thousands, to discover the answer.

It is difficult to know quite what to do about matters like this. When you are semi-retired, and working as a consultant but not on a day-to-day basis in the office, you no longer feel a part of things or able to influence matters. Do you write and say "Dear Cyril, I do think you should keep an eye on . . ." or do you say nothing in case people think it sour grapes?

All I can say is that I love the company, and I have a vested interest in its well-being because I own more shares than some of the group directors; they are my pension and so any critical looks I may take will be in the best interests of both the firm and my good self!

Cyril Stein will understand that perfectly. Down the years we developed a unique bond of trust and loyalty. We were good friends – not close, because I don't think anyone outside his family could ever claim to be close to him. Because he moves through life so quickly he tends to pick up relationships, put them down and then pick them up again. He appears to be a little flippant in this regard, but he never means to be insincere. If you are not required at a certain time, that is it. He would want to know all that Tony Howard had to tell us about matters when it was election time, but then he would not think about Tony for four more years. That was not my way – I preferred to cultivate people and remain friends all down the line. But that is the way I am and that is the way Cyril is.

Such is our friendship, however, that I think he would give me anything if I asked for it – and equally, if he asked me for a favour I would find it impossible to refuse him. On the other hand, as Victor Lownes found out to his cost, Cyril made a very bad enemy. Furthermore, he used to get funny ideas about people. He would come and complain that there was too much noise. I would agree. He would say, "Sack that Paddy Brogan. He is always making a noise." I would reply that Paddy wasn't in that day and Cyril would retort: "Well, sack him tomorrow, then!" But of course he wouldn't be sacked. I don't think he ever liked being alone, either. He would often come into my room after a day's racing and chat about nothing at all. Then, perhaps around seven thirty, he would say, "Well, I must be off now. I am due at the theatre." He had just been killing time and needed a friend – who probably did not then get home until about nine o'clock!

Despite this involvement with the boss, it would be fair to say that I never really noticed all the management turbulence as the company expanded. I was on an island in the middle of an ocean but the waters never reached up to me. I had my own excitement, my own job, and at least one major frustration. This came when what I thought might bring us greater rewards than anything before in racing was scuppered by the Falklands War in 1982 after Argentina invaded our islands way down in the South Atlantic.

While I would not for one moment compare the loss of life to a loss of money, the Falklands cost us dearly. In the autumn of 1981, prior to the following year's World Cup in Spain, I had arranged to meet the President of Real Madrid to discuss whether we might be able to bet on the World Cup at their Bernabeau Stadium in Madrid. I should have guessed that things might go wrong: as Terry Southwell, my Marketing Director, and I flew into Spain, Iberia carried my luggage on to some still-unknown destination. But at the outset of our talks, there was no hint of trouble. Had we been Royalty the club President, Mr de Carlos, could not have received us more graciously. On the Saturday morning, sitting in the lounge of Madrid's top hotel, I saw Anthony Quinn, an actor whom I had admired for years. My conversation with him was interrupted by a telephone call from Mr de Carlos. He was sending a car and wished me to go immediately to his apartment to meet the whole board.

I was slightly taken aback, not expecting such a sudden turn of events, but I went and, without a note, presented our case for half an hour or so. When I had finished, I offered to leave but the President shook his head. They were, he said, very happy with my proposal and did not need any privacy to debate it. I was quite overjoyed when – with only one dissenting vote – the board agreed that Ladbrokes should set up betting areas around the stadium. I drove back to the ground with the President to decide on our sites and was amazed at what I saw. It really is a fabulous stadium, with huge dressing-rooms and a magnificent trophy room which surely cannot be bettered anywhere else in the world; it is longer than my garden and covered in silverware from wall to wall. Many of the ornate trophies were for Real's basketball successes and though most people in Britain know of them as a soccer team that had legendary triumphs during the days of Alfredo di Stefano, their No. 1 sport is basketball. Mr de Carlos invited Terry and me to be the club's guests at the Sunday match against their close rivals, Barcelona, and by the end I had begun to understand what made the game so popular. I really felt quite exhausted from sheer excitement.

Before flying home – after being presented with his

Number 7 shirt by Laurie Cunningham, the wonderful black player who quit English football to play for Real only to die in a car crash last year (1990) – I met their World Cup organiser, a Señor Saporta, and accepted his invitation to the World Cup draw in the December. There seemed only loose ends to be tied up and we would then be betting at, as distinct from on, the World Cup for the first time, with this merely the opening gambit for a deal that would see us open betting shops all along the Costas: del Sol, Blanca and Brava. Such was the potential there with the many thousands of British holidaymakers who flood those resorts each year, that I expected it to bring us in tens of millions of pounds. Unfortunately, the Argentinians invaded the Falklands, we sent our Task Force and the rest is history. Spain supported Argentina and Britain's victory in the war became defeat for my grand plan overnight. Our negotiations with the Real and Spanish authorities were not re-opened (the financial disappointment apart, they were very nice people and I was sorry not to meet them again) and as far as I know no further attempt has been made to this day. What is it they say about the best-laid plans? It was a pity, but I would not complain.

My principal role was to ensure first that the Ladbroke name was known and secondly that it was respected and I think I succeeded, nationally and internationally. But what a difference the attitude of individuals can make to the development of PR in a company. When I went to Cyril Stein and spoke of my desire to get the Ladbroke name on the front pages with political betting, rather than only on the sports pages, his reply was both immediate and positive. "Well, don't just stand there, Ron. Get on and do it." Twenty-five years later, with still the same aim of developing the Ladbroke name although now on a worldwide basis because of our planned expansion in the United States, our agents Shandwicks through their Tim Kaye had arranged for me to broadcast in the USA on radio stations and coast-to-coast television. As a matter of form, I sent Peter George, the chairman of Ladbroke Racing, a memorandum informing him of these arrangements and out of politeness asking for authority to travel.

Imagine my surprise when I received a terse refusal written on the top of my memorandum to him. "Paul's view is 'No', which I support. P.G." (Paul Silvergleid being one of our American employees). I was to have appeared on the Larry King Show, carried by 2,500 radio stations with an audience of up to 15 million people, and two days earlier, on May 4, 1988, I would have had an eleven-minute TV slot on the CBS Night Watch Show which claims a 10-15-million audience. I simply do not understand the decision to this day; it has never been explained to me. But I can assure you that at the time it was very demotivating to a PR Director of twenty-five years' standing who had spent that quarter of a century endeavouring to build the Ladbroke name, and I found it more than mystifying in 1990 when I learned that Ladbroke Racing directors were now accompanying prize-winners of a competition to America. How times change!

Despite that, my earlier success in betting upon American elections meant that Americans knew the name of only one bookmaker: Ladbrokes. As we are now operating in five American states (Michigan, California, Pennsylvania, Texas and Wyoming) this has been of enormous value to us. We own racetracks there for trotting, horse and dog racing, and have been overwhelmed by the response to our 'betting theatre'. We will ultimately have six of them off-track, where people can dine in style and comfort, watch racing on big satellite screens and bet, and we are handling 600,000 dollars a week at the one that has already opened. That is some business and it can only grow. Nearer home, there are now almost 2,000 betting shops in the UK with a further 1,055 in Belgium; the Racing Division, which now counts Vernons Pools among its possessions, came up with a £91 million profit last year. Reflecting the strategy of dealing only in prime sites, the million-square-foot Bay Colony Corporate Centre in Boston was 85 per cent let before it was finished – testimony again to a sound and growing property division.

Our 144 hotels in forty-seven countries throughout the world not only produced a profit of nearly £168 million but the Hilton International UK division won the Queen's Award for Export Achievement in 1990. Wherever you look in the annual report Ladbrokes is outstandingly successful. And it is my total belief that the best is yet to come.

13

HOW I MISS YOU, MISS WORLD

As I have already said, the Miss World Competition has given me some of the most amusing moments in my career. In my video cabinet at home there is a brief clip of a television show which investigated our betting operation on Miss World. I just love that tape, all ten minutes of it, for it catches me at a most revealing moment. In 1982 Michael Aspel and Danny Baker presented a very entertaining early evening programme called the Six O'Clock Show and I was to take part in their behind-the-scenes look at Miss World. They chose a good year, for in 1982 I had made up my mind quite early as to who I thought might win and had, indeed, already struck a few bets for myself on Miss Dominican Republic which, if she won, would bring me in £5,000.

In those days with Miss World, as in the early days of political betting, other bookmakers tended to follow me. I dictated the odds; what I offered, they offered, when I didn't bet, they did not bet.

I liked to sort the girls into four groups, A, B, C, and D. Into Group A would go maybe eight but no more than twelve names; out of them should come the winner. Once I had decided on the groups, I would concentrate only on those in Group A. The rest were all 33-1 or more. It was, therefore, imperative that I had a really close look at all the girls each year. But this year I had decided on a little subterfuge. Although I was confident enough that she could win, I offered Miss Dominican Republic at 16-1 and sure enough our rivals did likewise. So, spreading it around very gently, I had £300 on her to win £5,000, while at the same time warning my office staff to be very careful about what bets they took on her without reference to me. When someone asked if that wasn't rather unfair of me, I replied, "You've got to make a living, son," and so you have. All is fair in love, war and gambling.

Danny Baker duly interviewed me and I explained how important it was for me to have a sighting of the girls and how Julia and Eric Morley tried to make it more difficult for me with every passing year. Indeed, three years earlier, the *Daily Star* had carried a story, on their front page of all places, about Julia 'declaring war' on Ron Pollard, and in 1982 she was again condemning betting on her pride and joy, saying it was "dragging it into the cattle market" and that she was determined to stop me. Julia was already too late! I had, as the tape shows, been jogging with all the girls in Hyde Park, despite the attentions of their 'minders', beefy young bodyguards who were supposed to keep people like me at a distance. I actually bought a track suit and running shoes and looked like any other Hyde Park jogger as I joined their morning run.

And, as I have already revealed, I had disguised myself as a waiter at the Dorchester and managed to get another good look at the girls in their national costumes when they were guests at a Variety Club lunch. I have to admit that I did try to get in to the usual Sunday swimsuit parade which was held in the Great Room at the Grosvenor House Hotel, but failed.

Still, all was not lost: Monte Fresco, a superb *Daily Mail* photographer, one of several from that family who became high-class press photographers and also a very good friend of mine, became my 'eyes' for the day. He reported what he thought and nothing he said necessitated a change of mind. Miss Dominican Republic, Miss Finland and Miss Switzerland were my three against the field and would, I was pretty certain, dominate the 1982 Miss World competition. And this is precisely what I forecast to Danny Baker when he came to interview me before the judging was to begin. It was a fairly bold forecast, because I omitted Miss Trinidad and Tobago altogether, even though an awful lot of money had been pouring in on her over the previous seven days. She had been a 12-1 chance, but betting on two-legged fillies is no different to four-legged ones; such was the weight of money on her that I was forced to cut her to 5-4 favourite, the shortest price, I think, any contestant had been during my twenty-five years' involvement with Miss World.

Danny Baker is a lovely London lad, cheeky and with a very frank and open way of interviewing and reporting. He asked me a few questions and then wanted to know about my own betting. I admitted that "if the public is wrong in going for Miss Trinidad and Tobago and I am right" then I would be winning a "few bob". "A few thousand?" persisted Danny. "Well, all right," I told him, "yes, a few thousand."

With the Six O'Clock Show camera team in tow, Danny and I watched the contest on a television in the racing room at Ladbrokes' head office, having had a few drinks in the Boardroom first. Their film clip shows me dragging hard on a cigarette and with a rather large Scotch by my right hand, as it was announced, "And the runner-up is Miss Finland." I was poker-faced and simply nodded as Danny jibed, "It looks like it is weighed in for Miss Trinidad now, Ron," clearly expecting the winner to be the tall, dusky beauty from the Caribbean. That, of course, was his money talking – the 25p bet he had on the favourite. "And Miss World 1982 is . . ." and the announcer hesitated just long enough to add even more tension to the moment ". . . Miss Dominican Republic."

I fear that I rather lost leave of my normal dignity. The video shows me leaping to my feet, punching my fist into the air and shouting, "Hooray! You little cracker. What about that then, you cracker." Anyone who doubts it when I say that betting can put fun, excitement and entertainment into people's lives should take a look at my video and at my very real excitement at that moment. Ladbrokes had cleaned up (had Miss Trinidad and Tobago won, we would have paid out £500,000) and I had won £5,000. My excitement had little to do with that money. Certainly one would rather have £5,000 in the bank than lose £300, but as I explained in the first chapter of the book, it was my ego, its accelerator pedal flat on the floorboards, that was making me almost burst. I had been right; I had been bold enough to forecast on TV that I thought Miss Dominican Republic was the likely winner, not Miss Trinidad, and I had been right. What happened to Miss Switzerland I never found out, but I had predicted the one-two on Michael Aspel's show to maintain a pretty good record of tipping winners down the years.

Every time I savour that little tape – and I have to say that I never fail to enjoy it and smile at myself – I only regret that I have never been able to obtain a tape of the show I did with Frank Bough on BBC the year America's Marjorie Wallace was to win. The Miss World contest ensured that I was always on one major channel or the other and in 1973 Frank nobbled me first for his show, which went out live; in other words, it was not recorded and could not, therefore, be edited. At that time, Frank was known as TV's 'Mr Clean' (it was before he was forced to admit in 1988 that he had become involved in a "nightmare world I never knew existed" of drugs and sex parties which led to him disappearing from the screen for a while before reappearing on ITV as urbane and professional as ever), and having talked to me about this and that, then asked who was the favourite. I told him that Miss America was and Frank wished to know why. "Well, I fancy her," I replied.

Frank went scarlet and looked flustered: clearly embarrassed and more than a little angry, he virtually brought the interview to an end there and then. As we walked off the set he demanded: "Whatever made you say that?" "Say what?" I inquired, innocently. "How could you say on air that you fancied her?" he thundered. "Frank, I fancy her to win, that is a betting phrase." He was even more embarrassed. "Oh, goodness gracious. I think I totally misinterpreted you . . ." His voice tailed off and Frank is probably wondering to this day whether he did or didn't and I am still wondering why I never managed to obtain a copy of the show!

I suppose one of the mistakes the male public has made over Miss World down the years is that they do actually bet on the one they 'fancy' and that one, all too often, is the sexy one. But the sexiest girls never ever win the title and once I understood the way Julia and Eric briefed the judges, it became much easier for me to categorise the contestants and to select a possible winner. It must have been 1963 or 1964 when I first became involved and until we were unable to bet in 1989 when the event was moved to Hong Kong, I had a strike rate of better than one winner every two years. And even when I did not nominate the winner, there was a better than even chance that I could assess who was not going to win and that was sometimes just as important.

The late Nat Cohen was a big show-business name, a film producer and a man who liked his bet. I found him at the Dorchester talking with Eric Morley one November lunch-time when the Miss World circus had hit Park Lane. I joined them for a drink and received an immediate lecture on being 'very careful' how I bet on that year's contest. Nat clearly wished me to ask "Why?" so I did. "You are going to find it very difficult to make a book this year," he said triumphantly. "I have already seen the winner. She is an absolute knock-out, something very special and very beautiful. She is the only one." Nat was in love, totally captivated, and I sniffed a little business ahead. "Who are we talking about?" I asked. "Miss Venezuela," he replied, repeating, "she is a knock-out." I said that I had better go and have a look at this gorgeous girl and Nat told me to hurry back because he wanted a price on her.

He was right – Miss Venezuela was absolutely stunning;

a real sex-bomb. But I knew straightaway that, devastatingly beautiful as she was, she would not win. So I went back to the bar and in answer to Cohen's searching gaze, I said, "Nat, you can have 12-1." Over another drink he took £1,000 to £80 that Miss Venezuela would win and offered the opinion that I was "stark raving mad". "Well, would you like it again, then?" I teased. Yes, Nat would like it again ... and again ... and again until he had placed £400 on Miss Venezuela to win him £5,000. Needless to say, Ladbrokes collected. The sexy ones never win!

The money we would take on Miss World varied wildly. In the early days it was a novelty and betting was quite huge. The television audience was never less than 10 million and often as high as 15 million. All the fellows who thought they were good judges of the female form would have a bet on their 'fancy' before they went home to the wife to watch it on the box. And the newspapers were marvellous, with big pictures of the best lookers and a line-up of all the 'runners', with my prices prominently mentioned. So we would always take £150,000 and sometimes as much as £250,000, which in those far-off days was quite a lot of money.

The most beautiful girl who ever competed, my Miss World of the Century, if you like, would have to be Eva Ruber-Staier, who represented Austria in 1969. She was a fabulous, fabulous lady, so lovely to look at, yet also with the most tremendous personality (my goodness, I am beginning to sound like Nat Cohen!).

Of the many thousands who contested this title down the years the one I felt most sorry for, the one who had the roughest deal, was the blonde Anne Marie Sikorsky, Miss Belgium, in 1974. I first saw her in a line-up of the seventy or so contenders in the Dorchester. They were paraded in alphabetical order and I was there to look at them all professionally. But I no sooner got past Miss Belgium than my eyes just went back to her. No matter how hard I tried, I could not get to the end of the line, my eyes simply scanned back to Anne Marie. She was quite beautiful, by far the outstanding girl in the room.

I was closely involved with the *Sunday Express* at that time, and they took a picture of us together which was ultimately published in the paper and I was promptly thrown out. I forecast that she could not lose. What followed, amazed me. I was never going to pick one that did not make the last fifteen. Anne Marie did not make that final number and she was devastated. I still can't believe it.

The following morning, I tried to contact her at the hotel to tell her how sorry I was that she had not been successful. I was told that she had left much earlier than expected for a flight home to Belgium. I guess she was as disillusioned as I was. I do not know what went on in the judges' minds that night, but no one could blame this beautiful girl for escaping from a nightmare as soon as she was able. It certainly did not surprise me to learn, twelve months later, that she had walked out of the beauty queen and modelling business and settled down to a married life. If Eva was the loveliest to win the title, Anne Marie was by far the loveliest never to do so.

There were pitfalls the size of elephant traps for these young women, who were suddenly handed fame and had not been brought up to handle it. A couple of them had brief, on-off affairs with the Manchester United footballer, George Best, who, in the seventies, was the biggest sporting star in Britain and had girls climbing drainpipes to windows at hotels where the team stayed to try to romance him. Mary Stavin, a ravishing Swede, was one of those who fell for the dark and sexy footballer (she ditched her steady boyfriend and George left his wife Angie for her, but it was an ill-fated affair, with Mary complaining that he took other girls to their bed). Mary allied her good looks to an enormous sense of responsibility. She was the 1977 winner and in her year of office she raised the quite staggering sum of £6 million for charity. The darling boy from Belfast also had a whirlwind affair with Marji Wallace, but her fame came from being the first Miss World to be

dethroned. Only twenty years old, Marji – Miss America
– took the crown in 1973, but reigned for only 104 days
before Julia Morley sacked her.

Marji flew home to Indianapolis without Julia's permission and the Miss World organiser did not like that one
little bit: "She knew she had commitments when she won
the title; you could say her private life got in the way of
her work." That jet-set private life was in fact very public.
She had affairs with Best, with Tom Jones and later a
much-photographed liaison with Jimmy Connors, the
tennis player. But perhaps the one true love of her life was
Peter Revson, a motor-racing driver (and heir to the Revlon
perfume company) who was to die in an horrific crash
shortly after Marji was sacked. She took a near-fatal drug
overdose but a six-year marriage to a multi-millionaire in
1978 and becoming a born-again Christian finally eased
the pain of Revson's death for another who found being
Miss World too much to handle.

For Helen Morgan, one year later, a reign of 104 days
would have seemed a lifetime. She lasted only ninety-six
hours. Helen had never hidden the fact that she was an
unmarried mother, but no sooner had she won than the
wife of a man who claimed to be the father of her son
threatened a divorce action. This was later dropped – but
too late to save the twenty-two-year-old model from Barry
a great deal of heartache. Those circumstances today
would not cause much of a ripple, but there was an
extremely hypocritical morality then. Helen was very
honest about it all: "Yes, I have a baby boy. No, I am not
married. And no, I am not ashamed." Although the Morleys always denied it, Helen claimed that they put "enormous pressure" on her to resign "on moral grounds –
although I was probably the most moral girl of the lot".
She did quit, "to protect my baby, to protect my mother-
hood and to protect my privacy; this was all more important than the title". But for three years Helen had "the
worst time of my life", and I was delighted when in 1982
she was finally married. She is still as happy today, a

mother of two living in Surrey, as she looked that day in Chelsea Register Office.

Mind you, there were also pitfalls for those who only stood and bet on Miss World. I always had a special connection with Miss Malta because as I have already said Ladbrokes were involved in the hotel business in that country. We had first bought the Dragonara in Valletta, a fine hotel with a splendid casino. We then purchased the Grand Hotel Verdala, in Rabat, with its beautiful marble entrance hall and reception area, and as a result we were linked with the promotion of the Miss Malta contest.

A marvellous couple called George and Margaret Deggie ran this, through their G.M. Production company and the way they looked after me, or any visiting head office executives from London, did wonders for the ego. If I landed there with a few racing journalists, for example, the red carpet was laid from the tarmac to the aircraft before the engines had ceased to whine. Jonathan Powell of the *Sunday Express* talks about that red carpet treatment still! A lot of so-called public relations experts in Britain could learn a great deal from these two. One year they asked me to crown Miss Malta, which I found to be a far more interesting task than being a judge. You were introduced to all the girls, fêted, photographed, given the best seat in the house with anything you wished to drink; and that was it. All you had to do was smile, kiss the lucky young lady, and put the crown on top of her head: no judging, no decision taking, no explaining in the lift to some half-drunk and very irate person why his or her daughter hadn't won! Yes, I did enjoy that and it also gave me one of life's beautiful ironies: I had met a Miss World contestant, and had a really good look at her, long before Julia Morley had!

Another year, it was my responsibility to escort Malta's representative in the Miss World contest to the Ladbroke hotels and casinos up and down Britain and on this occasion I was due to drive her to Birmingham. I duly picked Miss Malta up at her hotel and found her to be a rather raunchy and sexy young lady. Before we were half-way up the motorway, she had all but seduced me. I can only say that it was the most exciting journey that I would ever take to Birmingham and such was my state when I reached that city that I drove the wrong way up a one-way street and almost into the arms of a police motor-cyclist coming the other way.

Rather flushed and very embarrassed, I apologised. "I am so sorry, officer. You see, I am a stranger here. I am just bringing Miss Malta to see your city." Miss Malta did not fail me. She gave him the sort of look that she had been giving me for the past hour and asked if he would like her autograph. By the time she had finished leering at him, had asked if he had ever been to Malta, and to look her up if ever he did, I was forgotten. I escaped with a "Please be very careful in future, sir" and Miss Malta and I went on to the Ladbroke Casino while he, no doubt, went off to the police canteen to embellish his little run-in with a Miss World contestant.

It was a little like driving the wrong way up a one-way street when it came to dealing with the Glamorous Grand-mother competition. Whatever success I had with Miss World, I could not repeat it with the grannies; I never once picked the winner. It was a competition promoted by Butlins and all the half-decent PR people had by now caught on to the fact that if they wanted a little extra spice and some publicity for their competitions they needed me to quote prices on them.

I was a little choosy about which ones I did get involved with for, while I wanted publicity for Ladbrokes, it had to be the right publicity. So, we would only bet on those getting TV exposure, like Miss Central TV, Miss Thames TV and the Glamorous Grandmother competition. This last was never an easy task. I organised photographs of the twenty finalists to be sent to me but this was not terribly satisfactory: there is nothing like seeing the girls in the flesh, as it were. There is an old racing expression about believing what your eyes tell you, but that didn't mean what you saw on a photograph. Then there was the age-range: some grannies were an eye-catching thirty-four and others were a slightly more mature sixty-eight. So where Miss World was, again in racing terms, a 'Stakes' the Glamorous Grans were in a 'Handicap'. All I can say is that I was singularly unsuccessful, which only goes to show that you should never bet on handicaps.

When we had realised from our political betting that the public was game to have a go at anything, the Miss World Competition was our first venture into the unknown. It was a spectacular success in every way. We actually staged a Miss Ladbroke Competition, which Eva Ruber-Staier judged on one occasion, but we could not bet on this because the public had no access to the contestants.

There was criticism along the way, of course; not much, but enough to make us examine our consciences. I was quite clear where I stood – I saw nothing wrong at all in betting on pretty ladies any more than I did in betting on politics or who might be the next Archbishop of Canterbury. (An Editor of the *Church Times* once had a bet on who would be the next Archbishop, I may tell you!) My method of categorising the girls into four sections was not in any way sexist – as I have said, the sexy ones were never going to win. I would have done exactly the same had we – Heaven forbid! – ever decided to bet on Mister World. But Michelle Donnelly, Miss UK in 1981, protested at our "sickening" betting on Miss World. She said she "was not a racehorse" and advised us, much as Julia Morley often did, to go away and stick to horse racing. It would be fair to say that a handful of our female staff at Ladbrokes agreed with such complaints but in the main I think most sided with my argument that it was simply "a fun bet" which added interest to the competition for millions.

Certainly I am sorry that it is no longer what it used to be. It has been a good friend and I miss it. When Thames and the BBC felt that it had run its course and they did not wish to show it live – bowing to the 'cattle market' protests perhaps? – the Morleys decided to take it abroad. Hong

Kong staged it in 1989 and although it was back in Britain at the London Palladium in 1990 it was somehow not the same. It was recorded and televised late at night and the usual publicity was missing. Perhaps Mrs Morley may be reflecting that all the promotion betting won for the event was, after all, worth more than she had recognised.

I look forward to the day when Miss World returns to its former glory and is seen live on a major network; and now that the Morleys wholly own once more the competition, having bought it back at a cost of £800,000 a share of the rights from Owen Oyston's Trans World Communications, which he acquired in 1988, who knows? Perhaps one day soon that will happen and I will once again be betting on it.

14

LOOKING BACK TO THE FUTURE

Many people imagine that a life spent in the bookmaking business is a life spent in racing, but I hope I have shown in this book that I have been lucky enough to experience a great deal more of the world in the pursuit of my business. However, racing remains the staple of bookmaking and it seems appropriate that I should end by looking back at the racing business and thinking to its future.

Racing must be the only business in the world where the poor subsidise the rich. This is not a joke. As far back as 1978 the Royal Commission into Racing said that the sport should not be addicted to subsidy, but nothing has changed since that date. Bookmakers are currently paying around £36 million into the Levy, the majority of which goes in prize-money. In essence this means that the man in the street with his 50p doubles and a 50p treble each day, is contributing to the well-being of the sheikhs and the other big owners. Do not get me wrong: I am not against the Arabs – I believe that they have been very good indeed for British racing and I do not know where the industry would be without them. Actually, you have only to look at how many trainers stay in business, thanks to the horses the sheikhs place with them, for the answer to that one. None the less, it is the wealthier owners who normally pick up the big races and it is to the big races that much of the Levy goes. It is long past time that the words in the Royal

Commission Report were heeded: addiction to subsidy must be cured.

If I were to continue that theme I would have to add that governments should not become addicted to the tax from betting, either. Their take as of 1990 was £420 million from a near £5 billion business, yet they do nothing for racing and put virtually nothing back into sport. If anything, that is worse than the situation with the Levy – at least that money goes back into racing – and is a national disgrace. If there were to be a change of government I am quite sure that this position would be altered radically and quickly.

Yet, while there has to be criticism of what has happened and what is still happening in certain instances, what I must say with passion and with gratitude is that it has been a great life; a splendid half century as *Wisden* might put it. And what changes there have been – from starting stalls to photo-finish cameras, from morning dogs to evening horse racing.

When I began in racing fifty years ago, the dogs only ever ran in the afternoons and the evenings; horses only ran in the afternoon and where there was a bookie there was a jockey. It has been a complete turnaround. If it were suggested today that a jockey was in league with a bookmaker it would be page one news for weeks. It is amazing in an industry where so many millions are going round and round that there is so little corruption. Even though there is not enough money in the world to make me harm a horse (or any other animal, for that matter) that would not necessarily be true of every person in racing or who deals with them in sports like show jumping. As I was putting the finishing touches to this book there was a nasty story that two horses which ran at Doncaster, Bravefoot and Norwich, had been 'got at'.

It has to be said that while there was clearly something wrong at Doncaster, horses can be funny animals. Down the seasons hot favourites have lost and outsiders have won to the consternation of many and to large cries of "Fix".

If an owner or a trainer tells a bookmaker that his horse "isn't off today" that does not imply it has been doped; it may still be short of its peak, and, like Sebastian Coe or Peter Elliott, being prepared for one particular big race. I well remember seeing Henry Cecil at Newmarket and, inquiring after his runner in the next race, being told, "It has shown me nothing at home, Ron." I said nothing to anyone, but watched as the horse drifted in the market from 8-1 to 12-1 and then romped home! I saw Henry in the winner's enclosure and he smiled and said, "They do make fools of you, don't they?" Indeed they do and if horses ran true to their form every time they ran that would be an end to our business; if three out of three first or second favourites won instead of two out of three, then you really would have to put up with a Tote monopoly! I am not saying that horses have not been stopped over the years – I am sure they have. But I never knew of any such wrong-doing; had I known of anyone at any stage doing anything to a horse, I would have been on the nearest phone to the police.

Horses were normally doped (which could mean giving them a bucket of water just before race-time, of course) to stop them from winning; my understanding from a veterinary surgeon some years ago was that there is no substance that can make a dog or a horse run faster than its best. In other words, if a dog's best is 32.77 seconds no drug will make it go faster than that. It must be said, however, that between 1960 and 1990 there was only one certain case of doping or skulduggery and that was Pinturischio in 1961. Even though it is true to say that one person was sent to jail for his part in the incident, no one has ever known who the 'paymaster' was – although I have always had my suspicions. However, there is a vast difference between suspicion and proof, as a libel court would no doubt point out were I to print that belief. As in the Doncaster cases, the 1961 affair had to involve a person who was sure to make money as a result of a horse not winning. Nobbling the favourite and then backing the second does not necessarily help a punter – the second favourite may not win, as was the case in both races at Doncaster. Therefore it has to be a bookmaker.

The difference between Pinturischio and the two instances thirty years on was that the first was favourite for the Derby and the subject of a lot of ante-post money. He was 'got at' and did not even run in the race, which as far as I am concerned meant that it had to be a bookmaker with an ante-post liability – in other words one who stood to lose a lot of money if the horse won – that was involved; who else could make anything?

There were several other allegations down the years, most notably I suppose Playschool, Gold Cup favourite at Cheltenham in 1987, and Gorytus before the 1982 Derby. Yet nothing was ever proved and in the Gorytus case each and every test, exhaustive tests backed by all the aids scientists can command, was negative. From time to time every industry will come across a bad apple; mine is no exception. If those two horses at Doncaster were doped, then the whole racing industry led by the bookmakers would say unequivocally that the culprit or culprits should be found, they should be brought before the courts and they should receive the full penalty of the law. Such people cannot be allowed to tarnish a multi-million-pound industry or to destroy all the integrity and respect we have earned in these past thirty years.

Of course, when jockeys are paid millions of pounds each year, the thought of them becoming involved in such jiggery-pokery today is laughable. Nor would the major bookmakers be involved; they are part of huge conglomerates these days and the risk simply would not be worth it.

The smaller men make a good living honestly, but there is the odd small bookmaker I know who is happy to make £1,000 on a good day and it would be naïve not to accept that at least one such man is gullible enough to do the 'dirty' work for those who intend to stop a horse; he would be quite happy to take all the bets he could lay at slightly better odds on the one he knew could not win and before passing on the day's profit take out £2,000 for himself. I saw the Doncaster race on television and when someone like John McCririck tells a nationwide TV audience that he would not back Bravefoot "because the market stinks" there has, quite clearly, to be something wrong.

Whatever happened at Doncaster, and at the time of writing I certainly do not know any more than I read in the newspapers and I do not know the outcome, it is imperative for the sport I love to ensure that such things cannot happen. You had the race gangs in the thirties, gangs of East End thugs with violence their first and last argument which thankfully I was too young to be involved with. Yet I was locked in a cupboard with a lot of money, out of the way of the police, and I knew of the police connivance with bookmakers. But then, that was in an age when all betting except on credit was illegal; when a man in Stoke would post a bet to Glasgow, where the law was different, only for it to be reposted to London. In this environment was it any wonder that crooks flourished?

It was only in the fifties that the campaign was mounted for betting and gaming to be made legal and for the laws applicable to the rich man to apply equally to the poor. All the forward thinking and the forward-looking movements have been made by bookmakers during these past thirty years. Stories of heavy arguments and disputes about the Levy, and about us taking them to the Home Secretary might make good reading but the fact is that it was the bookmakers who in 1958, three years before the Betting and Gaming Act with the Levy decision came in, proposed a voluntary contribution from their turnover or their profits – and I would stress that word voluntary.

In bringing in the Betting and Gaming Act, the government was very brave. It was a major step forward to agree that there should be betting shops in the High Street, and no one knew quite what to expect.

In the early days the restrictions were pretty terrible. There could be no loitering – you had to be in and out – and the shops were basically designed to make you wish you were out rather than in them. What a change there is today. Now tea and coffee can be served; you can walk upon carpets rather than linoleum; because punter and bookmaker alike have been good boys, there are also television sets installed for the customers to watch. There have been no problems, no fights, no other troubles, so the Government has decided that the bookmaker has passed his 'apprenticeship'.

Betting shops have not been a licence to print money and indeed since their numbers reached 14,500 in the seventies they have been cut back by the law of supply and demand to less than 10,000, which seems to be the number that is sustainable. Despite the fact that the profit on betting is no more than 3 per cent, and sometimes a lot less than that, a lot of people who ought to know better have condemned bookmakers for diversifying and using 'racing money' to do so. That is total nonsense. The money that has accrued through Ladbrokes' betting shops has merely served to increase our betting-shop empire. When companies like ours are seen to be running a business properly and able to handle money competently, they will always find people willing to lend them money. That is what we have done: borrowed for other enterprises on the strength of our proven ability as good businessmen.

Despite the fact that we pay our government taxes and our Levy money, VAT (which unlike other businesses we cannot reclaim), and Corporation tax, whenever more money is required in racing the old parrot-cry goes up, "Get it from the bookies." We are not, of course, the bottomless pit that some seem to think, but when £50 million was required for research and development at the time that Bob Green formed Satellite Information Services (and what a debt the sport owes to this former managing director of Mecca Racing who is now trying to transform the racing scene in America) we and the other major bookmakers came up with the cash that has established SIS as a vital part of the racing game. In truth, the only way we can improve our business is by increasing our turnover, which is why big companies have tended to eat up the smaller ones until 38 per cent of all betting shops are now in the hands of Ladbrokes and William Hill.

Because, some years ago, I thought I knew a reasonable amount about bookmaking, I had my own small business for three or four years, but I soon discovered how hard it was for the small man to make it pay. In fairness, of course, I was faced with the additional problem that my work with Ladbrokes meant that I was unable to run the shop myself and I therefore had to have a manager. There are still a large number of small bookmakers throughout Britain, mostly one-man businesses. Properly run, which means the owner running it himself like the corner shop grocer or local shoe repairer, they make a profit. I was trying to make a living for the manager as well as a little something for myself and that simply wasn't on. In the end I was very happy to sell out to Ladbrokes.

I am and always have been a supporter of the smaller man: the bookie in Little Sodbury. I recognise all the difficulties and I do hope they survive because there is a place for them. If you go back to the roots of betting, in the streets, it was always the local bookie who was the benefactor. If Mrs Brown down the road was ill, you could bet that the bunch of grapes that arrived for her were from the bookie. He knew old Jack, probably everything there was to know about him and he always had time for a word or two with him. The local bookie was probably a mason or in the Rotary and while he didn't give the sort of terms that you would get today, restricting pay-outs to perhaps a maximum of 33-1, when compassion was needed he was there. I was on holiday in Keswick in the autumn of 1990 and spotted a small bookmaker's shop. There was no name over the door – he did not need it because everyone would have known him. So, long may the small man be there, because it will be a sad day and a bad day for racing if the big bookmaker becomes too big.

I know what the next argument will be – who is to say what is too big? Well, quite rightly it is the purpose of the

Monopolies Act to solve that in the public interest, but my view is that we are about there now; if you take in Corals the big three have over 50 per cent and I cannot accept that this should be allowed to grow.

Some people worry, I know, that betting shops are an open invitation to the weak to go in and get themselves into trouble. I disagree: the great thing about betting shops is that you have to have money in your pocket. If they were giving credit in the way the big banks attempt to give you credit, that would be totally wrong. Banks can lead people and particularly youngsters to despair by encouraging them to take up too much credit, which has not only been horrendous for the people themselves but bad for the country, having led in my opinion to many of the economic ills of the 1980s.

Having said that, there are two factors about which I am deeply worried. One concerns the Amusement With Prizes machines and the other is evening opening of betting shops.

There will, I feel certain, be a clamour for the AWP machines to be allowed in shops. The law must not be changed to allow that; these must never become part of the fixtures and fittings of a betting office because if they are, everyone loses – as I shall explain. Bingo (and let me make it clear that I am in favour of bingo because I think it has done a lot of social good) is the classic example. Seventy-five per cent of those playing are women over forty-five years of age. At bingo halls they allow AWP machines. As a result, 30 per cent of the ladies who go intending to play bingo never do; they have lost their money in the machines before the bingo has begun. That, I fear, is what would happen if the machines were allowed in betting offices: punters would spend their betting money for the day in the machines, whose owners pay no tax and no Levy. Can that be right?

Legislation is long overdue to ensure that amusement arcades are licensed in the way betting offices have to be and that action can be taken against unscrupulous people who allow, and indeed encourage, young people to play these wretched machines. The argument I am about to make over illegal betting and opening hours applies equally to the money lost in AWP machines.

The change that Parliament simply cannot refuse to make regards the opening hours of betting shops. They must be allowed to open in the evening when there is night racing. At the moment they can open as early as they like but have to close by 6.30 p.m. It is totally illogical that the places licensed for taking bets on racing have to be shut while 10 per cent of all fixtures are being staged. We know that there is a problem with illegal betting, which admittedly is stronger in some areas than others. (It is bad in Sheffield, and I know of one street in North London where every other shop is an illegal betting office.) Those who poo-poo whenever this matter is brought up should think more clearly about the problem because everyone loses where there is illegal betting – the Government loses its tax, the Levy which gives support to the racing industry is less, the licensed bookmaker loses, justice as I have suggested earlier can lose, and there is every chance of the punter losing, because if he walks back to claim say £1,000 winnings there is a likelihood that he may not be paid. BOLA must make it a priority to fight for shops to be open whenever racing takes place which would of course mean on Sundays if and when racing on the Sabbath is allowed.

There has been a myth that I am opposed to Sunday racing, which has grown I suppose because I have always pointed out the disadvantages rather than extolled the virtues of it. I most certainly am not against it – I take the view that everyone should be allowed to do what they like with their leisure time provided it does not interfere with anyone else. But it is absolutely *vital* that if Sunday racing ever does come about in this country then betting shops must be allowed to open.

This has always been a major concern of mine and three or four years ago I chanced to meet David Mellor in the House of Commons when he was a Home Office Minister.

We discussed the matter and he said, "Well, Ron, we might have to suck it and see," by which he meant that we would have to experiment with Sunday racing but without betting shops. I told him fiercely: "David, you cannot suck it and see. You will destroy all that I and others have been doing for twenty-five years. You will open the door to illegal betting; if a man has an illegal bet on Sunday, where does he bet on Monday and Tuesday? If you suck it and see, I assure you that you will simply destroy the tax structure." I do believe that those words were heeded, that the attitude has changed and that we will not get Sunday racing without betting shops being open. At least, I hope so! In every other respect I am quite ambivalent about Sunday racing: while I am not opposed to it I would not do anything to bring it about. From a betting point of view it will be very, very difficult. Many of the staff are part-timers and mostly women. I do not wish this to sound in any way sexist, but we have to accept the reality of life and Sunday lunch is an established family tradition. I would not wish to do anything that caused strife or damage to family life because that is the most precious thing we can ever possess. A husband may be happy to stay at home with the kids on a Saturday but may not be quite so happy to do so on a Sunday, even if there were only eight or ten involved each year.

Nor would there be any money in it for bookmakers, as the expense of opening on the seventh day would be horrendous. You always have to pay for asking people to work on Sundays and this would apply to everyone involved – turnstile and security men, trainers and their lads, caterers, car-park attendants and all the others who work so that others can play. There would be a big temptation to transfer many of the big races to a Sunday and it is imperative that this is not allowed to happen. Racing needs more money, new money in addition to what is already there and it would be the height of folly to move existing races to a Sunday.

There have been overtures – which I hope will be scuppered – about moving the Derby to a Saturday. Lord Wyatt of the Tote says that we are stupid to have such a showpiece on a Wednesday, but when I discussed this with Tim Neligan of United Racecourses who run the Derby, it was clear that there was much Lord Wyatt had not thought through. It would be questionable, for example, whether it would be right to race the Derby on grass that had been raced on for three or four days, particularly if there had been wet weather. No! The traditional races should be left where they are and new sponsors found and new races instituted for Sundays.

While I do not think it right to make people work on a Sunday if they do not wish to do so for family, social or religious reasons, there is one particular body that I would feel desperately sorry for: the stable lads. They work terribly hard mostly for a wage that is less than the average. To call them lads is to lead some people to look upon them as seventeen- and eighteen-year-olds. Not so: they can be fifty-five, having vast experience and having given immense loyalty to their stable. Dedication and devotion are understatements when it comes to the lads and their horses. One does not begrudge Pat Eddery his £6 million a year, nor any of the other top jocks their rich pickings. But it is the lad who makes it possible for them to ride their winners – the men who ride them out and care for them every day. A big race jockey might give a horse a fast trial one morning, but it is the stable lad who does the hard work every morning. Indeed, some jockeys have quite often never seen the horse before they are lifted into the saddle. So I trust that as racing expands, as I believe it will in the 1990s, with more and more people going racing, the lads get a better deal. Their living accommodation has been much improved – sometimes thanks to charity; such men should not have to rely on charity. A living wage and decent conditions should be a right.

The public are also entitled to expect a better deal as we approach a new century. While there are some splendid tracks, with superb facilities for corporate entertainment, there are a lot that could do with considerable improvement. Not all of Levy loans should go towards building these posh new stands with their entertainment facilities for big business; the man in the street should be looked after too.

Most people are getting more leisure time and we must ensure that when a man watches racing on television at home and decides that it might make a good afternoon out, one to which he could take the family, the facilities are good enough and he is looked after well enough to make him say, "Well, I think we'll do that again." He most certainly must not feel that he has been ripped off.

It is a vast industry, with 1,100 fixtures, 7,000 races and 70,000 runners and it requires a great deal of administering. As I have said before, I think that the Jockey Club now does a very good job but no one in the sport can afford to relax. Television (BBC and Channel 4) does racing proud with a total of 350 hours' coverage in 1989, more than any other sport. It is a sobering thought that on Arc de Triomphe weekend in October 1990, Channel 4 screened more races than American viewers see on their major networks in a twelve-month period. I know that not everyone thinks such TV exposure is good for the sport, arguing that some prefer to watch from the comfort of their armchair rather than go. I do not accept that argument at all; I believe that it encourages people to think about going racing and it most certainly encourages people to bet, which has to be good if you have the welfare of racing at heart.

In September 1990, in the Pam Spooner column of the *Racing Post*, Peter George, the chairman of Ladbroke Racing, is quoted as saying: "One of the major factors bringing new people into the market has been the growth of sports betting." Readers of this book will know that this cannot be true, as I was first to offer odds on all the sports twenty years ago. No: there are two reasons why more people are coming into the market-place and they are undoubtedly the changes in the law since 1986, which allowed more comfort to be provided, and the arrival of SIS and communication technology. There is an ever-increasing demand from the public for improved standards of comfort and it is to the credit of major bookmakers that once they were legally able to do so they provided them. Incidentally, while there has been pressure for special areas inside betting shops for the large cash punter, I am not sure these people would go along with the idea. If anyone thinks about it, they would quickly realise that the heavy punter would be too easily identified by would-be villains.

Those who still seek a Tote monopoly in this country are doomed to disappointment. There is absolutely no chance. After sixty-five years of existence, the Tote is responsible for less than 4 per cent of the betting turnover. Proof, if it were needed, that the vast majority of the betting public totally rejects the system. The Jockey Club was, I know, hoping for a new Tote chairman when Margaret Thatcher hurried through Lord Wyatt's reappointment for another two years shortly before she was forced to resign as Prime Minister in 1990. The Chief Executive, Christopher Haines, has been quoted as saying that if he ran the Tote he could "raise its profits to £18 million". The fact is, however, that he doesn't run it, Lord Wyatt still does and for every £1 placed with them, £25 is laid with bookmakers and their profit is small by comparison with the leading bookmakers. You will not find too many at the Levy Board, the SIS or among those seeking sponsorship demanding a Tote monopoly. That group between them in 1990 will have taken £50 million from bookmakers and during the same period the bookmakers collectively will have made a net profit of around £130 million from horse racing, before Corporation tax. On top of that, racing will have lost another £350 million – the money the Chancellor of the Exchequer will have taken without giving a penny back to racing.

I suspect, however, that this may change. I believe that the days of the Horserace Betting Levy Board in its present form are numbered. What is required in this country is a general sports levy which could be financed by the Chancellor of the Exchequer putting aside 25 per cent of the betting duty – i.e. 2p in the pound – for this purpose. A Sports Levy Board would have to be constituted and members appointed by the government of the day. This would produce £100 million a year for the benefit of sport – all sport. Just think what that could provide in the future in the way of facilities and coaching for all our young people. We would be setting an example to the rest of the world and I am sure that, in the course of time, our youth, be they star material or just kids who wish to play sport, would be fitter and better equipped for their daily lives.

When Labour wins an election, what I am suggesting will surely come to pass and I would hope at that time to be given the chance to play my part. Indeed, I would be delighted if I were to be asked to fulfil any role that would benefit the sport and the business to which I have devoted my life. I felt honoured by John McCririck's campaign in the *Racing Post* in which he called upon Christopher Haines, Chief Executive of the Jockey Club, to "get Ron Pollard into the portals of Portman Square". McCririck had nominated me to be the first bookmaking member of the Jockey Club a year before and now called again "for the street-wise, ex-Ladbrokes odds-maker extraordinaire" to be made a member of the Jockey Club. There has never been one and I can see no valid reason why such a chamber should not include a bookmaker and that was certainly the view of the writer and commentator who penned these quite heart-warming words: "Here we have a litmus test of Haines' clout. If he can get Pollard elected and utilised that will demonstrate political muscle even though a year has been wasted since he was first urged to bring in the canny, highly regarded betting guru."

They were nice words and I appreciated them. The racing industry cannot be immune from recession, and this is not the time for people to be running it down. As I have said, I would be quite happy to play my part in any way. Whatever the future holds, however, I am content to watch the sport I love continuing to flourish. As I notch up my half century in racing it is a very different game from when I first joined: straighter, more vibrant and wonderfully buoyant. It can only run on from here.

NED SHERRIN

Loose nEds

From lunching with Peter Ustinov to speculative thoughts on the Royal Christmas, the opening night of *Miss Saigon*, a discourse on avocados and an awe-inspiring Bette Davis, *Loose nEds* is a sparkling assembly of conversations and confidences, reviews and revelations, speculation and shared experiences – all drawn from the pen of one of our sharpest and wittiest contemporary observers.

Whatever his chosen subject, Ned Sherrin approaches it in the characteristically effortless and individual style that has won an avid weekly following for his regular newspaper column and widely-acclaimed BBC Radio 4 series, *Loose Ends*.

'Ned Sherrin has a Johnsonian grasp of many matters . . . Yet at heart he is a puckish Boswell.' *Jack Tinker, Daily Mail*

HODDER AND STOUGHTON PAPERBACKS

RICHARD PITMAN AND JOE McNALLY

WARNED OFF

Eddie Malloy, former champion jockey, is down and very nearly out. Falsely accused of involvement in a horse-doping ring, he has served a five-year ban from his beloved turf and the chances of re-employment are slim indeed.

Then Eddie discovers a murder victim on a wintry Newmarket Heath and the racing authorities offer him a chance to redeem his reputation and possibly revive his career by helping solve the crime, which seems certain to be linked to the man who framed him five years before.

Though suspicious of the authorities' real motives, Eddie accepts and sets off in pursuit of his first lead. And before long, Eddie is caught up in a savage spiral of violence, drugs, blackmail, greed and double-cross which makes the tough world of steeplechasing he knew so well look tame in comparison.

Smouldering with suspense, full of the atmospheric evocation of the racing game, crackling with sharp dialogue and brilliantly observed characters, WARNED OFF marks the debut of a formidable writing partnership.

RICHARD PITMAN, former top jumps jockey, is now a racing columnist with the *Sunday Express* and is known to millions as a BBC TV racing broadcaster.

JOE McNALLY works for Satellite Information Services, the world's largest commercial broadcaster of live horseracing.

HODDER AND STOUGHTON HARDBACK FICTION

ALSO AVAILABLE FROM
HODDER AND STOUGHTON PAPERBACKS